PLATO IN RENAISSANCE ENGLAND

ARCHIVES INTERNATIONALES D'HISTOIRE DES IDÉES

INTERNATIONAL ARCHIVES OF THE HISTORY OF IDEAS

141

SEARS JAYNE

PLATO IN RENAISSANCE ENGLAND

PLATO IN RENAISSANCE ENGLAND

SEARS JAYNE

Brown University, Providence, U.S.A

KLUWER ACADEMIC PUBLISHERS

DORDRECHT / BOSTON / LONDON

Library of Congress Cataloging-in-Publication Data

Jayne, Sears Reynolds, 1920-
    Plato in Renaissance England / by Sears Jayne.
        p.   cm. -- (Archives internationales d'histoire des idées =
    International archives of the history of ideas ; 141)
    Includes bibliographical references and index.
    ISBN 0-7923-3060-9 (hard : alk. paper)
    1. Plato--Influence.   2. Renaissance--England.   3. England-
    -Intellectual life.   I. Title.   II. Series: Archives
    internationales d'histoire des idées ; 141.
    B395.J37   1995
    141'.2'0942--dc20   94-29929

ISBN 0-7923-3060-9

Published by Kluwer Academic Publishers,
P.O. Box 17, 3300 AA Dordrecht, The Netherlands.

Kluwer Academic Publishers incorporates
the publishing programmes of
D. Reidel, Martinus Nijhoff, Dr W. Junk and MTP Press.

Sold and distributed in the U.S.A. and Canada
by Kluwer Academic Publishers,
101 Philip Drive, Norwell, MA 02061, U.S.A.

In all other countries, sold and distributed
by Kluwer Academic Publishers Group,
P.O. Box 322, 3300 AH Dordrecht, The Netherlands.

Printed on acid-free paper

Printed in the Netherlands

CONTENTS

ACKNOWLEDGEMENTS

Permission has been given by the following publishers to quote books under their copyright. I am pleased to acknowledge these permissions with thanks:

Cambridge University Press:
John Purvis, *Tudor Parish Documents of the Diocese of York.*

Council of the Early English Text Society:
ES 47 *Wars of Alexander,* ed. W. W. Skeat.
ES 69 John Lydgate, *The Assembly of Gods,* ed. O. L. Triggs.
ES 76 George Ashby, *Dicta et opiniones diversorum philosophorum,* ed. M. Bateson.
OS 211 *Dicts or Sayings of the Philosophers,* ed. C. Bühler.

Cranbrook Educational Community:
Dicts or Sayings of the Philosophers, ed. W. Caxton.

University of Toronto Press:
Court of Sapience, ed. E. Ruth Harvey.

EPISTLE DEDICATORIE

To the three no less vertuous than faire
Graces of Leagrave
the Lady Lynn, the Lady Emily, and the Lady Elizabeth

Many and sundrie are the giftes and presents which are sent between friend and friends, of value according to the habilities of the sender. Some present giftes of great worth, as plate, jewels, and such like; others meaner things. Myself, finding mine own estate but of a weak kind, am bold, instead of such giftes, only to bestow part of my brain's fruite upon your ladyships, praying you to vouchsafe it your acceptance as Alexander did a cup of cold water offered unto him of a simple husbandman.

As it hath ever been my study to please thee, so now I would that this last of my endeavors in this kind should find such generous entertainment at large as, though it do thee no honour, yet it shall do thee no dishonour. But I rather pray than hope that he that turneth these pages may know thee, that in the pleasure of that knowledge he may vouchsafe a more kinder reception to the defaults of mine owne. As thus: but these his infortunate failures as an author may be the more aptly forgotten by remembraunce of his far fairer fortunes as a father.

And thus with my most humble and hartie prayers to the Almighty for your ladyships' long life and prosperitie, I end this December, 1994.

S. J.

TO THE GENERAL READER

In Renaissance England it was thought seemly, when sending a new book out into the world, to provide it with two letters of introduction: one for the reader to whom the book was dedicated, and another for readers in general. In accordance with that custom, I have dedicated this book with a letter to our three daughters, (my letter is modelled on one by Richard West in *The Court of Conscience*, 1607). My Letter "To the General Reader", however, can follow Renaissance custom only imperfectly, for this book is not addressed to readers in general; it is addressed only to my colleagues in the field of Renaissance English literature.

For almost a hundred years students of English literature have been taught in graduate school that during the Renaissance the English people had to depend for their conception of Plato upon the writings of Marsilio Ficino, and since Ficino was a Neoplatonist, the best way to refer to the English conception of Plato during that period is to speak of it as being "Neoplatonic". This theory appears to have originated in 1903 in an American doctoral dissertation entitled *Platonism in English Poetry of the Sixteenth and Seventeenth Centuries* by John Smith Harrison (Harrison, 1903 ed., Preface pp. vii–viii).

The idea that English Platonism was actually Neoplatonism has survived at least five subsequent books on the subject (Schroeder, 1920; Schirmer, 1924; Cassirer, 1932; Dannenberg, 1932; and Baldwin, 1994), and is in fact still being taught in graduate schools today. (A typical handbook statement of the doctrine is that by Isabel Rivers, 1979, pp. 35–39.) As a result, students of Renaissance English literature now almost universally regard the term "Neoplatonic" as a more accurate and sophisticated substitute for the term "Platonic". To cite only a few examples the term "Neoplatonic" has been applied to:
Breton (Reed, 1923, p. 532)
Spenser (Casady, 1941, title)
Reynolds (Kinney, 1972, p. 2)
Donne (Mauch, 1977, title)
Jonson (Summers and Pebworth, 1979, pp. 178–181)
Shakespeare (Roe, 1994, title)

For all its ubiquity, however, this practice has now outlived its usefulness. One major count against it is that historians of Philosophy no longer regard Ficino as a Neoplatonist. The distinction between "old" and "new" Platonists is at least as old as Diogenes Laertius. Laertius used it to distinguish among three schools of Platonists: the original Academy founded by Plato (Hicks ed., 1972, Book 3, ch. 9); a "Middle Academy" established by Arcesilaus (Hicks ed., 1972), Book 4, ch. 28) and a New Academy, founded by Lacydes (Hicks ed., 1972, Book 4, ch. 59). Cicero modified Laertius' usage slightly, employing the term "New Academy" for the Academy of Arcesilaus (*De academicis* I.iv, Rackham ed., pp. 422–429). But the term "Neoplatonic" was not used in any language to refer to the Alexandrian school of Plotinus and his followers until the eighteenth century, when Leibnitz (1646–1716) used it in Latin in that sense. The earliest English version of the term was "neo-platonician", which appeared in *Fraser's Magazine* in 1831 (vol. 4, p. 54). Leibnitz's distinction became standard usage among historians of philosophy, and remained so throughout the nineteenth century. It is found in Jowett, Zeller, Ritter, Taylor, and Hermann, and it was these authors whom Harrison had in mind in speaking of "latter-day criticism".

But Leibnitz's distinction was based on a conception of Plato that was colored by the preferences of his age. In Leibnitz's view Plato's philosophy was primarily a system of ethics, based on reason. Accordingly, Leibnitz regarded as authentic works of Plato only those dialogues such as the *Republic, Symposium* and *Phaedo*, that deal with ethical rationalism. Works of Plato that appear to wander away from ethical rationalism Leibnitz tended to regard as *obiter dicta* or even *spuria*. Having defined Platonism in this special way, Leibnitz and his admirers were then able to make a sharp distinction between Platonism and the thought of Plotinus, which they described as a mystical monism quite unlike anything that Plato himself could have conceived. In order to emphasize the difference between Plotinus' oriental mysticism, and Plato's Hellenic rationalism, they called Plotinus' thought "Neoplatonism".

This distinction between Platonism and Neoplatonism, which was so clear for Leibnitz, has become steadily more and more blurred for modern scholars. Modern scholarship has restored a number of epistles and dialogues to the canon of Plato's works; it has taken a much more objective view of such troublesome dialogues as the *Timaeus* and *Parmenides*; and it has examined much more carefully the testimony of Plato's own contemporaries and that of his immediate successors, and the work of Plotinus and his pupils. The effect of all this work has been that modern historians of Philosophy no longer use the term "Neoplatonism" in the loose sense in which it was once accepted (see Tigerstedt, *The Decline and Fall of the Neoplatonic Interpretation of Plato*, 1974). Most historians now prefer to use more general terms, such as "Platonism" (Kristeller, 1968), "the Platonic Tradition" (Klibansky, 1981), or "the return of Plato" (Garin, 1986). In any case, they regard it as anachronistic to apply the eighteenth-century term "Neoplatonic" to Ficino, or to any other Renaissance writer. Since modern historians of Philosophy (such as Copenhaver and Schmitt, 1992, pp. 127–195) no longer regard the term "Neoplatonism" as an accurate name for the Renaissance stage of the Platonic tradition, I suggest that it would perhaps be prudent for students of English literature to avoid bandying about the term "Neoplatonic" as loosely as they now do.

There is, however, also a second reason for abandoning the practice of automatically labelling all Renaissance English references to Platonic theories as "Neoplatonism". That reason is that at no time during the Renaissance were the English people ever limited, as the myth suggests, to a single conception of Plato; rather, they knew about Plato from many different sources, and entertained several different conceptions of his work. To reduce their many views of Plato to the single basket-term "Neoplatonism" is to fly in the face of the known history of Plato's reputation in England. That history was not known in the time of John Smith Harrison, but it is today, as I hope to show in this book.

For the last forty years I have been attempting to collect allusions to Plato by name in writings by all English authors from 55 B.C. to 1603. (My discussion of the Medieval part of this material can be found in Jayne, 1991 and 1993, pp. 16–243.) My definition of "writings by English authors" has embraced writings in Anglo-Norman and Latin as well as in English, and I have tried to cover completely, in all three of those languages, the genres of poetry, drama, prose fiction, biographies, dialogues, satires, essays, dictionaries, encyclopedias, commonplace-books, library catalogues, booksellers' records, translations, and prose tracts in History, Literary Criticism, Philosophy, Ethics, Politics, and Psychology. I have read only selectively in the genres of sermons, letters, university curricula and exercises, biblical commentaries, ephemera such as ballads and news-sheets, and prose tracts in the fields of Alchemy, Astrology, Geography, Law, Magic, Mathematics, Medicine, Theology, and Travel.

Although I will never be able to read everything ever written by an English author during my designated period, I have now collected enough evidence (gathered in 8 typescript volumes; see Jayne, 1991, 1993) to be able to say with confidence that throughout that long period there were always at least two different conceptions of Plato in current use in England. In part, such a conclusion was to be expected, for in western cultures there has always been some difference between professional and amateur approaches to any subject. In modern times, for example, there have always been two schools of thought in England about Shakespeare: on the one hand there is the view that he was the author of many great plays, and on the other there is the amateur view that he was only the son of a butcher in Stratford-on-Avon, the plays attributed to him having been written by someone of higher social rank, such as the Earl of Oxford, or Sir Francis Bacon. In the case of Plato, the tendency to read him in different ways has been reinforced by the deliberate ambiguity of his method: he used the dialogue form, and liked to state his ideas in the form of myths. Still another complication in Plato's case was the fact that until 1423 almost none of his works were available in England for anyone to read.

Throughout the Middle Ages the controlling factor regarding Plato's reputation in England was the fact that almost no actual text of any of Plato's works was available. Until 1111 A.D. there was no copy of any work of Plato in England in any language. Between 1111 and 1340 only part of one dialogue, the *Timaeus,* was available. About 1340 one more dialogue became available: the *Phaedo.* Those two dialogues, both in Latin translation, are the only works of Plato that we can place certainly in England before 1423, when "the Platonic Renaissance" began. In the absence of actual texts of Plato's works, medieval Englishmen based their knowledge of Plato on two different kinds of material: 1. accounts of Plato given by other authors, such as Cicero, Augustine, Jerome, Apuleius, Boethius, Seneca, Aulus Gellius, Valerius Maximus, and Isidore of Seville; and 2. inauthentic works which they attributed to Plato in the absence of authentic ones. For various historical reasons, these inauthentic works tended to be works in the fields of Medicine and the pseudo-sciences (Alchemy, Astrology, and Fortune-telling). Thus the medieval Englishman's conception of Plato was a vague mixture of information about Plato the historical philosopher, derived from the secondary sources, and a mythical Plato who was thought to have been a physician-magician-scientist, derived from the supposititious works. On the whole, the more learned of medieval Englishmen (chiefly monks, friars, and secular clerics) tended to give more credence to the notion that Plato was a philosopher, while laymen tended to think of Plato as a physician, but the two conceptions are found thoroughly mixed up in writers of both types, whether learned or lay. Thus Adelard of Bath (c. 1090–1160), a layman, regarded Plato mainly as the author of the *Timaeus*; while the Archbishop of Canterbury, Thomas Bradwardine (c. 1290–1349) thought that Plato had written a work called *Plato's Calf.*

During the Renaissance the English acquired two more conceptions of Plato. I believe that these two Renaissance conceptions evolved from the two different stages of the revival of Plato in Italy. But the view that the Italian revival of Plato occurred in two separate stages is by no means universally held. The most recent authority on the subject, James Hankins, regards the Plato revival in Italy as a single, coherent process, which is best described city by city. I respect Professor Hankins' opinion, and, as will be apparent, I have drawn heavily on his work, but I think that even his own evidence tends to confirm the interpretation that he explicitly rejects, namely Eugenio Garin's view that the Italian revival took place in two separate stages (Garin, 1969, pp. 261–363, especially pp. 269–285; for Hankins' criticism of Garin's view see Hankins, 1990, vol. 1, pp. 15–17).

One of the considerations on which Garin based his interpretation was the striking fact that the first translations of Plato that were written in Italy occurred in two bursts. The two episodes overlapped slightly in chronology, but as Garin pointed out, they had different origins, and the translators involved had different interests. The first group of translations appeared at scattered intervals between 1402 and 1456; during that period there were three attempts to translated the complete *Works* of Plato, but only 21 translations of 14 individual works actually reached completion (see Table 1, p. 12). All of the projects in this first group of translations derived in some way from the influence of the first important teacher of Greek in Italy, Manuel Chrysoloras, who first arrived in the country in 1390.

The second episode of translating Plato began about 1446 and ran to 1476 (see pp. 67 and 81 below). During this period 12 more projects were undertaken. Eleven of these were merely translations of individual works, but the twelfth was another effort to render the complete *Works*. Fortunately, this time, the people who set this elusive goal for themselves had the resources to see it through; they were the Medici banking family of Florence. The Medici family first undertook the massive project in 1458; ten years later, when the family was in its third generation, they finally brought it to completion. The Medici project, and all eleven of the other translation-projects in this second "episode", as I have called it, derived from the influence of a second visiting Greek scholar, Gemisthus Pletho, who had arrived in Italy in 1439, nearly fifty years after the arrival of Chrysoloras.

Like the evidence concerning translations, the facts of the revival of Plato in England tend to support Garin's thesis that there were two different revivals of Plato in Italy, but I shall not leave it to Garin to make the case. In order to show exactly how English knowledge of Plato developed, I shall give my own account of each of the two Italian revivals. I shall discuss the Chrysoloras revival first; then, after I have shown the effects of that revival in England, I shall return to Italy and discuss the Pletho revival, which affected England much more gradually (I have given a fuller account of the revival of Plato on the continent elsewhere; see Jayne, 1993, pp. 1778–2086).

There is one further aspect of my account of the English revival that requires some explanation. When the two Italian revivals of Plato migrated from Italy to France, they became associated respectively with two different groups in French society: the Chrysoloras revival became associated with the schools, whereas the Pletho revival became associated with ducal and royal courts. This French distinction between a "school" conception of Plato and a "court" conception carried over to England as well, and I shall therefore use those terms throughout my account of the English revival. Described in those terms the English revival may be summarized as follows:

1. An early wave of enthusiasm for the school Plato (1423–1485).
2. A long period of stagnation when knowledge about both the school Plato and the court Plato gradually increased, but in the face of general hostility (1485–1603).
3. A late wave of feverish enthusiasm for the court Plato, in two different arenas: at court, where there was a fad of Platonic love; and at the universities, where scholars were turning to Platonic Theology in an effort to hold back the tide of Cartesian

rationalism and Hobbesian materialism (1603–1700).

In this book I will deal only with the first two of these phases. (The third has already been studied in some detail by other scholars; see my Epilogue.) Although I have arranged my material in chronological order, as a history, I should emphasize that it is not a history of Plato's influence, but only of his reputation. Only a historian of Philosophy is qualified to write a history of Plato's influence in this period. All that I am qualified to do is to give a responsible account of one part of the evidence that a historian of Philosophy will some day have to use in writing about Plato's influence. My book is merely a history of allusions to Plato in England during the 180 years between 1423 and 1603.

This book was written in four main stints. The first was the year 1954–1955, when I worked in the libraries of London, Oxford, and Cambridge. The second was the year 1962–1963, when I worked in the libraries of Florence. The third was the year 1976–1977, when I worked at the British Library and the Warburg Institute. The fourth was the years 1982–1994, when I worked in the libraries of Harvard University. At various times I have received generous support for this project from the Guggenheim Foundation, the Fulbright Program, Villa I Tatti, and the American Council of Learned Societies, as well as from the several universities with which I have been associated. Thanks to these libraries and other institutions, I have enjoyed ideal opportunities for consulting the manuscripts and rare printed books relevant to this project. For those opportunities I am of course profoundly grateful; they have constituted the undergirding structure of my entire scholarly career. Among the many libraries upon which I have drawn, I am most indebted by far to the British Library, and I hope that all of the members of its departments of printed books and manuscripts who have helped me, wherever they may now be, will regard this book as their personal note of thanks.

Many individual scholars have responded to my requests for help on particular subjects; I have tried to acknowledge their contributions at the appropriate points in the book, and I extend to them all my warmest gratitude. In this last and longest of my scholarly projects, as in all of the previous ones, the moving spirit has been Mae Jayne. Without her indulgence and help I would never have attempted it at all. After so many years of editing and retyping, she will be relieved to come, not just once more, but finally, to the happy words, "THE END".

LIST OF TABLES

ABBREVIATIONS

AHDLM	*Archives d'histoire doctrinale et littéraire médiévale*
AHR	*American Historical Review*
ANTS	Anglo-Norman Text Society
BGPM	*Beiträge zur Geschichte der Philosophie des Mittelalters*
BHR	*Bibliothèque d'Humanisme et Renaissance*
BHS	*Bulletin of Hispanic Studies*
BL	British Library
BLR	*Bodleian Library Record*
BN	Bibliothèque Nationale, Paris
Bohn	Bohn series of translations
BQR	*Bodleian Quarterly Record*
CAS	Cambridge Antiquarian Society
CC	Corpus Christianorum
CL	*Comparative Literature*
CSEL	Corpus Scriptorum Ecclesiasticorum Latinorum
DAI	*Dissertation Abstracts*
DBI	*Dictionario biografico italiano*
DHI	*Dictionary of the History of Ideas*
DNB	*Dictionary of National Biography*
DSB	*Dictionary of Scientific Biography*
EETS	Early English Text Society (os=original series; es=extra series; ss=suppl. series)
EHR	*English Historical Review*
ELR	*English Literary Renaissance*
HD	Harvard University Library
HLQ	*Huntington Library Quarterly*
IMU	*Italia medioevale e umanistica*
ISJR	*Iowa State Journal of Research*
JCL	*Journal of Comparative Literature*
JHI	*Journal of the History of Ideas*
JMRS	*Journal of Medieval and Renaissance Studies*

JWCI	*Journal of the Warburg and Courtauld Institutes*
LOEB	Loeb Series of classical authors
ME	Middle English
MLJ	*Modern Language Journal*
MLN	*Modern Language Notes*
MLQ	*Modern Language Quarterly*
MLR	*Modern Language Review*
MP	*Modern Philology*
N&Q	*Notes and Queries*
NNBW	*Nieuw Nederlandsch Biografisch Woordenboek*
OF	Old French
OHI	*Opera hactenus inedita* (see Roger Bacon in Bibl.)
OHS	Oxford Historical Society
PBSA	*Papers of the Bibliographical Society of America*
PG	*Patrologia Graeca*
PL	*Patrologia Latina*
PMLA	*Publications of the Modern Language Assoc. of America*
PQ	*Philological Quarterly*
RES	*Review of English Studies*
RN	*Renaissance News*
Rolls	Rerum britannicarum medii aevi scriptores
RPL	*Res publica litterarum*
RQ	*Renaissance Quarterly*
S.C.	South Carolina
SCN	*Seventeenth Century News*
Scolar	Scolar series of reprints
SEL	*Studies in English Literature*
SP	*Studies in Philology*
SRen	*Studies in the Renaissance*
STC	*Short Title Catalogue* (see Pantzer in Bibl.)
TAPA	*Transactions of the American Philosophical Association*
TCBS	*Transactions of the Cambridge Bibliographical Society*
Teubner	Teubner series of classical texts (Leipzig)
TLAS	*Transactions of the Leicestershire Antiquarian Society*
TRHS	*Transactions of the Royal Historical Society*
Wing	Donald Wing, *Short Title Catalogue of Books Printed in England 1640–1800.*

PART I

THE PRE-TUDOR PHASE (1423–1485)

CHAPTER 1

THE CHRYSOLORAS REVIVAL OF PLATO IN ITALY (1350–1456)

Throughout the Middle Ages the Roman Church had effectively suppressed efforts to translate Plato into any western language. In France, for example, the Church encouraged the translation into Latin of the complete works of the Greek Father Dionysius Areopagite, but when Abaelard showed an interest in Plato, he was ruthlessly silenced (Jayne, 1991, pp. 466–490). As late as 1350 the only dialogues of Plato that had been translated into any western language were the *Timaeus*, translated in Spain by Calcidius about 385, and the *Phaedo* and *Meno*, translated in Sicily by Henricus Aristippus between 1154 and 1156. Thus when Petrarch, impressed by the praise of Plato that he found in the works of Augustine, tried to acquire copies of Plato's works, he was at first able to find only a Calcidius *Timaeus* (Petrarch's copy is now Paris, BN lat. 6280) and an Aristippus *Phaedo* (Petrarch's copy is now Paris, BN lat. 6567A) (Nolhac, 1954; Trinkaus, 1979).

About 1350 Petrarch had an opportunity to buy a manuscript of Plato in Greek; although he could not read Greek, Petrarch thought it important to own some Plato in Greek, and he bought the manuscript (it is now Paris, BN grec. 1807). This manuscript is a ninth century text containing the following works:

Canonical		Spurious
Clitophon	*Minos*	*Definitions*
Republic	*Laws*	*Confabulations*
Timaeus	*Epinomis*	*Demodocus*
Critias	*Letters*	*Eryxias*
		Axiochus

(Nolhac, vol. 2, 1954 p. 313; see also Trinkaus, 1979, pp. 11–15).

Petrarch himself thought that his manuscript contained 16 dialogues (*De ignorantia*. ed. Capelli, 1906, p. 76), but as the list above shows, the actual total was only 13. In 1360 Petrarch's friend Boccaccio, in Florence, wrote to Petrarch in Milan, asking to borrow his Plato manuscript in order to make a start toward getting Plato translated into Latin. Like Petrarch, Boccaccio did not read Greek; the translator whom he planned to use was a visiting Greek named Leonzio Pilato whom he had hired out of his own pocket to teach Greek and to translate Homer. (Pertusi, 1964; Ricci, 1952). Petrarch approved of the project but not of the man, and accordingly replied to Boccaccio as follows:

> You have asked me to send you the manuscript of Plato that I rescued from the fire at my house in France. I admire your enthusiasm, and I promise you that you may use the manuscript yourself at my home whenever you want to; that is the least I can do to encourage you in your noble project. But do be careful. Your idea of bringing face to face the two greatest princes of Greek civilization could easily turn out disastrously. The shoulders of a mere mortal may not be able to bear the weight of two divine geniuses at the same time.
>
> (Letter #25; *Lettere*, ed. Fracassetti, 1892 vol. 5, p. 205; tr. mine)

The fire to which Petrarch refers in this letter destroyed his small house at Vaucluse, near Avignon in France, in 1354 (Bishop, 1963, p.333). By the phrase "your noble project" Petrarch means Boccaccio's ambition of translating some part of Plato into Latin. By "mere mortal" Petrarch means Pilato, whom he did not think competent to translate either Homer or Plato, let alone both at the same time.

Petrarch died in 1374, and Boccaccio in 1375, but the torch of their ambition for improving classical studies in Italy was not dropped; rather it was picked up by a new champion, Coluccio Salutati (1331–1406). Salutati was a wealthy Florentine businessman who was elected Chancellor of the Republic in the same year that Boccaccio died (1375). Salutati admired Plato greatly, and evidently felt some responsibility for carrying on to the new generation the revival of classical learning that Petrarch had espoused (Oliver, 1939). Salutati carried out this self-imposed mission in several different ways, including the holding of meetings of writers and scholars in his own home (Ullman, 1963; Witt, 1983). What he did for the reputation of Plato in particular went far beyond anything that either Petrarch or Boccaccio had ever done: he persuaded Leonardo Bruni to undertake the project of translating the complete works of Plato (Bruni, *Epist.* 1.8, Mehus ed., 1741, vol. 1. pp. 15–17; Oliver, 1940).

Salutati's first opportunity for promoting Greek studies in Florence occurred in 1389, when the Ottoman Turks opened a military campaign aimed at the capture of Constantinople, the seat of the Greek Emperor, Manuel Paleologus. In response to this threat the Emperor sent Giovanni Chrysoloras (d. 1415) to Venice to feel out the possibilities for soliciting support in the West for his struggle against the Turks (Thomson, 1966). Chrysoloras spent the year 1390–1391 in Venice, using as a cover for his diplomatic mission the teaching of the Greek language. During that year one of his pupils was a Florentine named Roberto Rossi. When Rossi returned to Florence, he urged Salutati to try to hire Chrysoloras to teach Greek in Florence (Calecas, *Corresp.* ed. Loenertz, 1950 p. 64; see Weiss, 1958, p. 351 and Hankins, 1984, p. 149). For a time Salutati did nothing about this recommendation, but he was evidently already thinking about Plato; in May, 1393 he wrote to the Dominican monastery at Volterra requesting (unsuccessfully) a copy of the Aristippus *Phaedo* (Salutati *Epist.*, 1965 vol. 2, p. 444; Weiss in *Misc. Cessi*, 1958 vol. 1., p. 354).

In 1395 the Turks made another bold advance, setting up a naval blockade of Constantinople. At this point Salutati decided that it was time to act on Rossi's advice, and he sent to Constantinople as his personal envoy Jacopo Angelis, with a threefold mission:

1. Deliver to Chrysoloras a personal letter from Salutati inviting him to come to Florence to teach Greek; the letter to Chrysoloras is *Epist.* III, pp. 119–125.
2. Find manuscripts of the Greek texts of Plato, Plutarch, and Homer (*Epist.* III, p. 131).
3. Learn some Greek (Weiss, 1958, p. 352; 1955, vol. 2, pp. 803–827).

Angelis was not successful in his quest for a manuscript of Plato, but he did open negotiations with Chrysoloras. Within a few months (1396) the Florentine City Council had authorized funds and issued a formal offer to Chrysoloras (Cammelli, vol. 1. p. 34). By early 1397 Chrysoloras had arrived in Florence and opened a school for the teaching of Greek. Chrysoloras' method of teaching Greek involved extensive use of texts from Plato. Once the student had memorized the necessary declensions and conjugations, and was able to cope with a literary text, Chrysoloras gave him short passages from works such as Plutarch's *Moralia* and Plato's *Republic*. (Grafton and Jardine, 1986, p. 102). Thus Chrysoloras' course in the Greek language inevitably attracted new readers to Plato. We see examples of this effect in Florence in Leonardo Bruni and Ambrogio Traversari, and in Pavia in Uberto Decembrio and P. C. Decembrio (on Chrysoloras in Florence see Weiss, 1977, pp. 227–254).

An important part of Chrysoloras' teaching, and of the ethos of the Greek revival in general, was the belief that serious students of Greek should go to Constantinople for their training. Since the other teachers in Constantinople, like Chrysoloras, usually used Plato as a teaching text, the experience of studying in Constantinople inevitably involved learning something about Plato. It is thus no accident that six of the most active Italian students of Plato, Guarino da Verona, Rinuccio of Arezzo, Cencio de' Rustici, Antonio Cassarino, Francesco Filelfo, and Giovanni Aurispa, all received their training in Greek in Constantinople, as a result of the gospel spread by Chrysoloras and other Greek emigrés in Italy.

One consequence of the presence in Italy of Greek visitors such as Chrysoloras was that they fanned to a white heat the acquisitive instincts of the Italian aristocracy. As the Turks closed in on Constantinople, the wealthy lords of Italy, both secular and clerical, developed a passion for buying Greek manuscripts and sculptures while there was still time. The Greeks themselves adroitly promoted this Italian passion for Greek antiquities through high-pressure salesmanship. For example, in 1438 the Greek Emperor himself paid a visit to Florence, where some of the most covetous of the Italian collectors lived. Although the purpose of his visit was osten-

sibly to attend the Council of Florence, he carried in his baggage, like a good sales-
man, copies of several Greek manuscripts with which to whet the appetites of poten-
tial Italian customers. Among the manuscripts that he displayed were complete texts
of Aristotle, Plutarch, and Plato (Mercati, *Traversariana*, 1939 pp. 24–28; on
Traversari see Ricci, 1952 and Stinger, 1977). The book-buying mania part of the
Greek revival in Italy had important consequences for Plato. In Florence alone it
resulted in copies of various works of Plato being added to the collections of Niccolò
Niccoli (Sabbadini, *Scoperte*, 1964, p. 52), Roberto Rossi (Calderini, 1913, p. 359),
Amerigo Benci (Sicherl, 1962), Palla Strozzi (Bisticci, *Vita*, ed. 1938, p. 294;
Mazzatinti, vol. 2, 1886–1888, pp. 549–661) and Cosimo de' Medici (Pintor, 1960;
Piccolomini, 1875, pp. 106–112). Copies of Plato were also acquired in Milan by the
Bishop of Milan, Francesco Pizolpasso (Paredi, 1961), in Ferrara by Guarino da
Verona (Omont, 1892, pp. 79ff), in Venice by Francesco Filelfo (Calderini, 1913 pp.
356–363), in Urbino by Duke Federigo (Guasti, 1863, pp. 130–154), and in Rome
by Pope Nicholas V (Müntz, c. 1887; see also Bolgar, 1963, pp. 483–485). One of
the most famous cases of the importation of Greek books is that of the Syracusan
teacher of Greek, Giovanni Aurispa (c. 1376–1459) (see Bigi, *DBI;*: Sabbadini,
Scoperte, 1967 ed., pp. 46–47). Aurispa made two trips to Constantinople (1413–1414
and 1421–1423), on both trips he made it a point to buy up Greek books. During his
second visit, when he went as an emissary of the Gonzaga family in Mantua, he
acquired so many Greek manuscripts (238) that he could not afford to ship them all
home; eventually the Medici lent him the money to pay the freight for them from
Constantinople to Venice. This shipment alone contained two copies of the works of
Plato in Greek (Stinger, 1977, p. 36). One of these copies was defective in that it
lacked the *Laws, Republic*, and *Letters*, but Aurispa had no trouble selling that copy
two years later to the Mantuan teacher Vittorino da Feltre (1378–1446) (Traversari,
Epist. VIII.49, Mehus ed., 1741, vol. 2, col. 418).

   The most important single consequence for Plato of Chrysoloras' activities in
Italy was the production of 21 new translations of Plato's dialogues. This process
was begun by Chrysoloras himself. In 1400 Chrysoloras was lured away from Florence to Pavia by the prince of a rival city-state, Giangaleazzo Visconti, Duke of
Milan. Chrysoloras taught at Pavia for only two years but, while he was there, he
produced the first Renaissance translation of a dialogue of Plato, a Latin version of
the *Republic*. Since Chrysoloras was not fluent enough in Latin to take on such a big
project without help, he employed one of his students, Uberto Decembrio, to assist
him. (The exact part that each of the two men played in the translation is a matter of
current debate; see Hankins, 1984, pp. 61–64). Chrysoloras' translation has been
said to have been only recreational, a casual exercise on his part (Hankins, 1984, p.
60), but the fact that Chrysoloras had to have help with it (not to mention its magni-
tude) shows that the project was far from mere recreation: Chrysoloras was obviously ordered to make the translation by his employer. Giangaleazzo Visconti. It

seems likely, as Hankins has conjectured (1984, pp. 64–67), that Galeazzo wanted the dialogue because he had heard that it buttressed his insistence on retaining the monarchical form of government in Milan, as opposed to the republican form preferred in Florence.

In 1401 Uberto Decembrio informed Salutati that Chrysoloras was translating the *Republic* for Giangaleazzo (Novati, 1908). Salutati must surely have been annoyed by Giangaleazzo's triumph in squeezing out of Chrysoloras a translation of the entire *Republic*, while Salutati himself had nothing to show for the three years of his own patronage of Chrysoloras in Florence. Salutati had already tried unsuccessfully to acquire copies of the two Latin dialogues of Plato that Petrarch had owned, the *Timaeus* and the *Phaedo*, but he now (1402) tried again, ordering copies of both dialogues to be transcribed from copies lent to him for the purpose by Giovanni Conversano, of Ravenna (Salutati, *Epist.* vol. 3, 1965, p. 515; Salutati's copies are now in Vatican MS lat. 2063; Hankins, 1984, p. 35). The *Timaeus* and *Phaedo* were apparently the only dialogues of Plato that Salutati ever owned. He quotes both in his treatise *De fato et fortuna* (1396): *Timaeus* 28A in Bianca ed., 1985, p. 151 and *Phaedo* 58A-C in Bianca ed. p. 72. In the *De fato* he also cites *Alcibiades I* (Bianca ed. 1985, p. 205).

In his letters Salutati refers to the *Timaeus,* the *Phaedrus*, the *Republic* and to "Plato's Epigrams" (Salutati, *Epist.*, 1985, vol. 4, p. 682). Salutati also made some effort to consult secondary sources about Plato, as is shown by his acquisition of a copy of the essays on Plato by Apuleius (now Florence, Laurenziana MS 76,36; Weiss, 1958, vol. 1, p. 355).

Shortly after Chrysoloras finished the *Republic* translation for Giangaleazzo, late in 1402, Salutati ordered Bruni to make a translation of the *Phaedo* for him, using a Greek text lent to Salutati by his friend Palla Strozzi (Vespasiano da Bisticci, *Vite.*, 1938 ed., p. 294; Oliver, 1940, p. 319; Hankins, 1984, pp. 51–52) and a Latin trot in the form of Salutati's own copy of the Aristippus *Phaedo*. From Pavia Chrysoloras went to Verona, where he stayed only a few months (1403–1404), but his visit there was to have special importance for England because it was in Verona that Chrysoloras met one of his most talented students, Guarino da Verona. As we shall see, Guarino later enjoyed a particular vogue among English students (see p. 15 below).

From Verona Chrysoloras went to Rome, then Paris. In 1409, as I shall explain below (p. 13), Chrysoloras paid a visit to England at the invitation of the Archbishop of Canterbury, Thomas Arundel. Finally, and of more direct consequence for the reputation of Plato, in 1439 the son of Chrysoloras' collaborator on the *Republic* translation, Pier Candido Decembrio, produced a new translation of the *Republic*, commissioned by an English prince, Humfrey, Duke of Gloucester. (On P. C. Decembrio see Borsa, 1904). Since Humfrey failed to pay for the work after he received it, Pier Candido was naturally discouraged from undertaking further work in that line, but he owned a manuscript containing the *Laches* and *Lysis* (now Wroclaw

University MS Akc 60/49; Kristeller, 1966, p. 542, n. 27; see Hankins, 1984, p. 104), and in 1456 translated the *Lysis* for a friend named Ottaviano degli Ubaldini, in appreciation for a kindness done him by Ubaldini in 1449 (Zaccaria, 1956, pp. 54–55; Hankins, 1984, p. 104). Pier Candido owned copies that he himself had made of Bruni's second *Crito* and Cencio's *Axiochus* (Hankins, 1984, p. 105) and also knew well both the *Letters* and the *Republic* (see references in undated letters noted by Hankins, 1984, p. 105, now Florence, Riccardiana MS 827, fols. 24ʳ and 84ʳ - 84ᵛ). From England Chrysoloras returned to Rome, and from there went home to Constantinople, where he died in 1415.

Let us now return to Bruni in Florence, carrying out Salutati's assignment of translating the *Phaedo*. Before Bruni was able to finish the translation, he left Florence in order to accept a position with the papal Curia in Rome. While in Rome he formulated a project for translating the complete *Works* of Plato. First, he finished his *Phaedo* translation, and dedicated it to Pope Innocent VII, with a preface entitled "General Introduction to All the works of Plato", in which he says:

> If I ever finish translating all of the works of Plato into Latin, as I plan to do, my dear Niccoli, you will see that everything you have ever read before is insignificant by comparison with the majesty of this man. His style is incomparably elegant, he elevates mere arguing into dialectic, his insights are subtle. . .
>
> (*Epist.* I.8: Mehus ed., 1741, vol. 1, pp. 15–17; tr. mine; cf. Hankins, 1987, p. 260).

Behind these allusions to a project for translating the whole of Plato may lie the fact that Bruni's immediate superior, the papal secretary, Tomasso Parentucelli, had been pressing the Pope (Innocent VII) to subsidize a papal project for translating the works of several major Greek writers. (On Parentucelli see Giorgi, 1742). When Parentucelli himself became Pope (as Nicholas V), he gave this project high priority. Among many other Greek works that he commissioned to be translated, in 1450 he ordered George of Trebizond to translate Plato's *Laws* and *Epinomis*.

The exact relation between Bruni's projected Plato and Nicholas' translation-project is not known, but evidently Plato and Homer both figured in Nicholas' plans, for in 1453, when Constantinople fell, Enea Silvio Piccolomini (who later became Pope himself, as Pius II) told Nicholas that the fall of Constantinople would be tantamount to a second death for both Homer and Plato in Italy. (Vansteenberghe, 1963, p. 228).

Whatever Bruni's ambitions may have been for translating the *Works* of Plato, he actually completed only a very small part of the project. As soon as he had finished the *Phaedo* (1404), Bruni made a rough translation of the *Crito*, which was in the same manuscript (Berti ed. of Bruni's *Crito*, 1983, pp. 27, 163), and then went on to the *Gorgias*. He picked this dialogue, he said, because he thought it "useful for confirming the faith":

On moral matters Plato's teachings are so sound and beautiful that whenever I read his works I imagine myself hearing Peter and Paul handing down the rules for virtuous life.

(Pref. to *Gorgias*. ed. Bertalot, *Studien*, 1975, vol. 2, pp. 267–270; tr. mine).

Bruni had no copy of the Greek text of the *Gorgias*, and had to write to his friend Niccolò Niccoli (who had been a fellow student of his under Chrysoloras) to find him one. (Bruni, *Epist*. I.10, dated 1405). Bruni did not get around to finishing the *Gorgias* until 1409. (Bruni, *Epist*. III.13 and III.19). During the course of the next three years Bruni toyed with one other dialogue, the *Apology*, but by 1412 he was having misgivings about the entire project. Not only are many of Plato's theories, such as transmigration and the common use of women, plainly outrageous, but Plato's whole method is downright dangerous: Plato relies mainly on dialogue and myth, and his cavalier disregard for logic is such that no one but a very experienced reader should attempt the difficult task of sorting out the authorial from the fictional, the figurative from the literal in Plato's dialogues. (*Life of Aristotle*: ed. Baron, 1969, p. 45).

In 1413, however, Bruni's Plato project was suddenly breathed back to life when the Pope convened a Council of the Church at Constance. Bruni was to attend in the papal train, and decided to take with him to show around several copies of his small Plato collection: the four dialogues *Phaedo*, *Gorgias*, *Apology* and *Crito* (Hankins, 1984, p. 34, lists copies that circulated at the Council). The Council of Constance had been convened in the first place in order to settle the problem of the papal schism. Unfortunately for Bruni, the Pope who was his employer, John XXIII, was deposed by the Council in favor of Martin V. In 1415, therefore, Bruni had to leave Constance and return to Florence, where he went into a premature (though temporary) retirement.

For six years after returning to Florence, Bruni appears to have done nothing at all with his Plato-project. Then, beginning in 1424, and continuing for three years, he worked on his Plato-translation with renewed energy. It may be that the spark that set off his new enthusiasm was the arrival in Italy of the new manuscript of the complete works of Plato that Aurispa had brought back from Constantinople (Traversari, *Epistol*. VIII.5, Mehus ed., 1968, vol. 2, col. 361). In any case, between 1424 and 1427 Bruni rewrote completely both of the last two translations that he had made so half-heartedly in Rome, the *Apology* and *Crito* (Berti ed. of Bruni's *Crito*, 1983, p. 91). In 1424, he also started a translation of the *Phaedrus*; but he could not stomach the passages about homosexuality, and in the end expurgated about a third of dialogue (see Hankins, 1984, p. 42; Pref. to *Phaedrus*, ed. by Giovanni da Schio in *Sulla vita . . . di Antonio Loschi*, 1858, pp. 168–170; also ed. by Baron in *Humanistische. . . Schriften*, 1969, pp. 125–127; and by Hankins in 1984, pp. 325–327). Bruni next turned to the safer (and more relevant politically) *Letters*, and sometime between 1425 and 1427 translated all thirteen of them, dedicating them to a prominent of Florentine politico, Cosimo de' Medici (*Epist*. VII.1, Mehus ed.,

1741, vol. 2, pp. 70–76; for discussion of the circumstances see Hankins, 1984, pp. 43–45; see also Baron's attempt to date the *Letters* to 1411 in *Crisis*, 1966, p. 554).

In 1427, however, Bruni lost all leisure for translating anything, for he was elected Chancellor of the Republic. This spelled an end, as he then thought, to his dabblings in Plato, and he closed the book on his collection of translations, having attempted only six works: *Phaedo*, *Gorgias*, *Apology*, *Crito*, *Phaedrus*, and *Letters*.

For eight years the burdens of his office prevented Bruni from doing anything further with Plato. Then in 1435, learning that Cosimo de' Medici was interested in Plato, Bruni translated for him, as a gift, one speech from Plato's *Symposium* (the speech of Alcibiades, 215a–222a; for the dedication to Cosimo see Bruni *Epist*. VII.1, ed., Mehus, 1741, II. pp. 70–76; for date see Luiso, 1980, p. 126, and Hankins, 1984, p. 51). The *Symposium* fragment was the last attempt Bruni ever made to translate any part of Plato. In 1441, a friend, Niccolò da Ceva, asked him to translate another dialogue for him, but Bruni refused point blank. Ceva's request was in any case unreasonable (the dialogue that he requested was the *Republic*), but Bruni gives another reason for turning him down:

> There are many doctrines in this work that are abhorrent to Christian principles; for Plato's own good it would be better to suppress the work, not make it even more accessible.
>
> (*Epist*. IX.4; ed., Mehus, 1741, II. p. 148; tr. mine)

The doctrines in the *Republic* that Bruni calls "abhorrent" are those having to do with the common use of women. (My account of Bruni's work on Plato is based throughout on Hankins, 1984, pp. 24–56.)

At the time Bruni wrote this letter he was already seventy-two years old; three years later (1444) he died, having shown no further interest in Plato. Bruni was succeeded as Chancellor of Florence by Poggio Bracciolini (1380–1459) who did not share Bruni's enthusiasm for Plato. Bracciolini's tenure as Chancellor was brief; attacks on Florence from Milan soon forced the Florentines to turn for protection to the Medici family, the first of whom assumed office in 1434.

In the meantime however, the visit of Chrysoloras had produced another Plato enthusiast. Following the Chrysoloras line, a Genoese school-teacher, Antonio Cassarino (d.1447) had gone to Constantinople to study, and between 1434 and 1437 had been inspired by a teacher there, John Eugenicus, to undertake a translation of the works of Plato (on Eugenicus see Mercati, 1937). Eugenicus set Cassarino to work translating the Plato-section of Diogenes Laertius and the *Introduction to Plato* of Albinus, by way of preparation. Eugenicus took Cassarino's ambition seriously enough to give him, before he left Constantinople, a manuscript containing the complete *Works* of Plato (according to Le Grand, 1885–1906, p. 140; Hankins identifies this MS as now Cesena, Bibl, Malatestiana MS D 28.4; Hankins, 1984, pp. 107–117). Unfortunately, Cassarino's project was even more ill-fated than Bruni's. Cassarino returned to Italy in 1438, but was unable to find work in Venice, and moved on in

1439 to a place as a school-teacher in Genoa. Once provided with a regular income, Cassarino resumed work on his Plato project, and in the first year (1440) managed to translate two short dialogues, the *Axiochus* and the *Eryxias* (both now Vat. MS lat. 3349). Cassarino turned next to the *Republic*; he translated the entire dialogue in draft form, and was in the process of polishing his translation when he was suddenly killed (1447) (on Cassarino see Resta, 1959 and DBI, vol. 21; and Hankins, 1990, pp. 154–160, 427–428).

The next Italian who contemplated translating the whole of Plato's works into Latin was a Venetian school-teacher named Francesco Filelfo (c. 1398–1481). Filelfo, too, had studied in Constantinople, and it was there that he acquired his first Platonic text, a copy of the *Letters*, in 1427. By 1436 he had begun the work of translation, with a version of the *Euthyphro* and three of the *Letters*. Filelfo's intentions regarding his Plato project were evidently serious, but he had extraordinarily bad luck in trying to find Greek texts to work from. He did manage to find a copy of the *Timaeus*, and of a few other dialogues, but he suffered a series of disappointing frustrations in his efforts to buy or borrow texts: first, in 1450, when he tried to acquire the copy of the complete Plato that had been owned by Cassarino; again in 1456, when he tried to get a copy of the *Laws* from the Greek emigré Andronicus Callistos; and finally in 1463, when he tried to get a copy of the complete Plato from Cardinal Orsini in Rome. By 1463, Ficino had begun his translation of the complete Plato, and Filelfo abandoned his project altogether (Calderini, 1913, pp. 356–363).

To summarize, the effect of Chrysoloras' teaching in Italy was that wealthy Italians began to import copies of texts of Plato in Greek, and to sponsor translations of some of those works into Latin. Among those who attempted translations of Plato, at least three men projected translating the complete *Works*. The first of these, Leonardo Bruni (d. 1444) translated five complete dialogues (*Phaedo*, *Gorgias*, *Apology*, *Crito* and *Letters*) and parts of two others (*Phaedrus* and *Symposium*) before abandoning the efforts (Hankins, 1984, pp. 24–25, 29–53). The second, Antonio Cassarino (d. 1447) completed only three dialogues (*Axiochus*, *Eryxias* and *Republic*) (Hankins, 1984, pp. 107–117). The third, Francesco Filelfo (d. 1481) completed only one dialogue (*Euthyphro*) and three of the *Letters* (Calderini, 1913, pp. 356–363).

Although none of the three scholars who contemplated translating the complete *Works* of Plato completed the project, Chrysoloras influenced others as well to attempt translations. A total of 21 translation of 14 different works of Plato may be said to have resulted from Chrysoloras' visit. Because these early translators worked independently, and tended to be interested in the same dialogues, they wasted a great deal of effort in needless duplication: there were three different translations of the *Republic*, three of the *Axiochus*, two of the *Euthyphro*, and two the *Gorgias*. On the other hand, the translators also managed to produce new Latin translations of the lives of Plato by Diogenes Laertius and Albinus, and Guarino da Verona wrote a new life of Plato. The catalogue of all of this new material by and about Plato that resulted from the Turkish threat to Constantinople and the consequent visit of Chrysoloras reads as follows:

Table 1. Works of the Chrysoloras Revival

A. Latin Translations of Plato		
1402	*Republic*	Chrysoloras and U. Decembrio
1405	*Phaedo*	Bruni
1409	*Gorgias*	Bruni
1409–12	*Apology*	Bruni
1423	*Crito*	Rinuccio (cribbed from Bruni)
1424	*Apology, Crito* (2nd Version)	Bruni
	Phaedrus	Bruni
1425–27	*Letters*	Rinuccio
1431	*Axiochus*	Rinuccio
1435	*Symposium* (part)	Bruni
1436	*Euthyphro, 3 Letters*	Filelfo
1437	*Axiochus, De virtute*	Cencio
1438	*Euthyphro*	Rinuccio
c. 1438	*Halcyon*	Dati (student of Filelfo)
1439	*Republic*	P. C. Decembrio
1440	*Eryxias, Axiochus*	Cassarino
1447	*Republic*	Cassarino
1456	*Lysis*	P. C. Decembrio

B. Works about Plato		
1433	Diogenes Laertius (entire)	Traversari
1437	Diogenes Laertius (Plato only)	Cassarino
1437	Albinus (*Isagague*)	Cassarino
1438	Life of Plato	Guarino

CHAPTER 2

THE CHRYSOLORAS REVIVAL IN ENGLAND

Just at the time the Chrysoloras revival of Plato was taking place in Italy, the English people were turning away from France and toward Italy, partly because of the Hundred Years War (1337–1435) and partly because of the return of the papacy to Rome in 1378, which resulted in schism and the calling of the Council of Constance in 1413. It was mainly through contacts made at the Council of Constance that the English first became aware of the Chrysoloras revival of Plato in Italy. Most of the events of the English interchange with Italy during the fifteenth century have been described and documented by Roberto Weiss (1967). I will limit my own discussion to the new information about Plato that was conveyed during this period; I will discuss first the English visitors to Italy, and then the foreign visitors to England.

The revival of Plato in pre-Tudor England was almost entirely the work of members of the aristocracy, the lords of the realm, both temporal and spiritual, but above all, men of great wealth. They went to the continent for various reasons: some on Church business, some merely to acquire possessions, and toward the end of the period, some in order to improve their education. Let us look at some examples.

In 1398 Archbishop Thomas Arundel visited Florence. He went there merely as a tourist, on his way back to England from a trip on Church business to Rome. In Florence he happened to be entertained by the Chancellor of Florence, Coluccio Salutati. By chance Salutati was basking in the triumph of having, only a few months before, brought Giovanni Chrysoloras to Florence and opened the city's first official school for the teaching of Greek. Arundel must have heard a great deal about Chrysoloras during that visit, and probably also met him, for after Arundel returned to England, he corresponded with Salutati for the next four years (1399–1403), and in 1409 invited Chrysoloras to visit England, which he promptly did. Though the announced purpose of Chrysoloras' visit was to look for manuscripts of Origen, and he was in the country only a short time, he visited both London and Salisbury, and in both places would certainly have taken the occasion to brag about the teaching of Greek in Italy, and about the two new Latin translations of Plato that had recently been completed there: a *Republic* that he had himself done for the Duke of Milan, and a *Phaedo* that Bruni had done for Pope Innocent VII. (Bruni completed his translation of the *Gorgias* in November, 1409, while Chrysoloras was still in England.)

It would not have been lost on the English dignitaries whom Chrysoloras met during his visit that it was becoming the fashion among Italian princes, clerical as well as secular, to own translations of Plato. One of the Bishops whom Chrysoloras would have met at Salisbury was Henry Beaufort (c. 1377–1447), the Bishop of nearby Winchester. Four years after Chrysoloras' visit, Bishop Beaufort had an opportunity to meet in person one of the Plato-translators whom Chrysoloras had mentioned, namely Leonardo Bruni. The occasion was the Council of Constance, to which Beaufort was a delegate. As we have seen, at that Council Bruni was showing around copies of four dialogues of Plato that he had by then translated: the *Phaedo*, *Gorgias*, *Apology*, and *Crito*. Delegates to the Council would also have heard about Giangaleazzo Visconti's commissioning of a translation of Plato's *Republic*, from Chrysoloras and Uberto Decembrio. Thus a visiting English prince at the Council of Constance in 1418 might well have received the impression that if he wished to be in vogue, he should be trying to acquire a translation of one of Plato's dialogues.

As it turned out, Beaufort concentrated his attention at the Council of Constance not on Bruni, but on another student of Chrysoloras from the Florence school: Poggio Bracciolini (c. 1380–1459). Beaufort was sufficiently impressed with Bracciolini to invite him to come to England at Beaufort's expense. When the Council was over, in 1418, Bracciolini was able to take Beaufort up on his offer, and went to England for two years. (He left in 1420 because of the plague.) During Bracciolini's stay he, too, like Chrysoloras, would have given his English hosts first-hand reports of the current achievements in the study of Plato among Italian students of Chrysoloras. Even after his return to Italy, Bracciolini continued to correspond with his English friends, including Richard Petworth, who succeeded Beaufort as Bishop of Winchester, and Nicholas Bildeston (on Beaufort see Weiss, 1967; on Bracciolini see Walser, 1914).

The cases of Arundel and Beaufort that I have cited are only two examples of visits to the continent by Englishmen on extraneous business that resulted in new knowledge about Plato being brought into England. Other such visits were the visits of Netter to the Council of Constance in 1414, Whethamstede to the Council of Pavia in 1423, and Zenone to the Council of Basle in 1437, as emissary of Humfrey, Duke of Gloucester.

Much of the new English interest in Plato was merely a matter of a desire on the part of rich lords to own books. In this the English were only imitating a model that had been set them by Italian princes such as Niccolò Niccoli (Gordon, 1974) and Pope Nicholas V (Giorgi, 1742; Pastor, 1910: Muntz, 1887). The translators of the Chrysoloras phase had learned that translations of dialogues of Plato, like newly dug up Greek statues, could be peddled in Italy as status symbols to the wealthy Italian princes of their time, and this aspect of the Plato revival in Italy was carried over to England as well.

When a man like Beaufort, who had come to the continent in the first instance on Church business, came back and regaled his episcopal colleagues in England with stories of the good life as practiced by clerics in high places in Italy, it was not long before other wealthy English clerics went to Italy themselves to share in the plunder. A good example of this acquisitional kind of motivation was John Tiptoft, the Earl of Worcester (c. 1427–1470) (Mitchell, 1938; Weiss, 1936, 1957). Tiptoft's interests were entirely worldly, and he made no known contribution to the revival of Plato, but his own wealth and exploits were sufficiently notorious that he contributed importantly to the custom of travel to Italy among the nobility.

As time went on, English travellers tended to undertake the Italian journey for other reasons as well, some for their own personal education. The centers that most attracted English students during this period were Rome, Florence, Ferrara, and Padua (see Mitchell, 1936, 1937, 1952). The latter two places were strongholds of Aristoteleanism, but there were Platonists at Rome, and of course at Florence.

The most popular of the Italian centers was Ferrara. The great teacher Guarino da Verona attracted to Ferrara a remarkable series of English students:

1444 William Grey
1447 Robert Flemming
1456 John Free
1459 John Tiptoft
1459 John Gunthorpe

Of these men, two, William Grey and John Gunthorpe, took back to England with them several copies of dialogues of Plato. Among the other English academics who visited Italian centers for the purpose of education we should notice also Selling, Grocyn, Linacre, and Chaundler.

William Selling (d. 1494) had attended the lectures of Chalcondylas and Poliziano in Florence and hence presumably knew something about Plato. Selling returned from Italy in 1470 to found the first formal course in Greek in England, at Oxford. In 1472 at Oxford an unknown scribe named Thomas S – possibly the same Thomas of England whom Bruni says in a letter that he had befriended in Florence (*Epist*. Mehus ed., 1741, II. 18, vol. 1, p. 55) – owned a *Phaedo*, in Bruni's translation, and a copy of the *Life of Plato* by Guarino (Hunt, 1970, p. 33).

In 1475 William Grocyn (1446?–1519) and Thomas Linacre (c. 1460–1524) were both in Florence, studying with the Platonist Chalcondylas, who taught in Florence from 1475 to 1491, and whose eloquence a contemporary Florentine compared to that of Plato:

You will think that you are listening to Plato himself.
(Cammelli, 1941–1954, vol. 2, p. 82; tr. mine).

This commonplace was to be applied to Colet by Erasmus a few years later.

In 1479 Thomas Chaundler, Warden of New College, and later Chancellor of the University of Oxford, made his obligatory tour of Italy. He did not himself take an active part in the Plato revival, but he was sufficiently aware of current fashion to mention Plato in his correspondence. In one letter he quotes an apocryphal saying of

Plato (Bekynton *Correspondence*, Rolls ed., 1872, vol. 2, p. 316); in another he mentions Plato's *Apology* (Cambridge, Trinity College, MS 881, fol. 10ᵛ); and in a third he mentions Plato's *Republic* (See Bridges, 1949).

A second channel by which information about Plato came into England was through visits to England by continental scholars. We have already seen two examples of such visits: the case of Chrysoloras, who was sponsored by Archbishop Arundel, and the case of Bracciolini, who was sponsored by Bishop Beaufort. A foreign visitor of another kind was an Italian cleric named Piero del Monte. From 1435 to 1439 del Monte served as Papal Collector in England. During this period he became a close friend of Abbot Whethamstede of St. Albans, and also of Whethamstede's friend Duke Humfrey. Duke Humfrey asked del Monte to help him acquire some classical manuscripts, and del Monte accordingly wrote to Guarino da Verona and also to Traversari, asking them to send materials to Duke Humfrey (on Guarino see Sabbadini, 1964; Omont, 1892; on Traversari see Sottili, 1966). Del Monte also supplied some texts to Whethamstede, and to an Oxford student named Andrew Holes (Weiss, 1945; Bennett, 1944).

Still another visitor was an Italian scholar, Milo da Carrara, who was hired in 1447 by a wealthy London doctor, Thomas Francis, to make a copy of Bruni's translation of the *Phaedo* for him (Biagiarelli, 1978, pp. 237–239; the manuscript of this copy survives in Florence, Riccardiana MS 952).

The most interesting of the foreign visitors were four Greek refugees who came to London in 1455. In 1453 Constantinople had fallen to the Turks, and numerous Greek scholars had fled to the West as refugees. The Royal Council in England at the time included four men who had taken a special interest in cultivating the new interest in Greek studies: William Grey; William Waynfleet (Bishop of Winchester and founder of Magdalen College, Oxford); John Tiptoft, Earl of Worcester; and Andrew Holes, In 1455 the King's Council appropriated funds to support four of the Greek refugees in England, and directed George Neville, Bishop of Exeter, to make the arrangements. Accordingly Neville brought from Italy to London four Greek scholars: Demetrios Paleologos, Joannes Argyropoulos, Manuel Chrysoloras, and Emanuel of Constantinople (Gray, 1929; note especially p. 86, where Gray distinguishes this Chrysoloras from the one who died in 1415). Unfortunately, just as the refugees were arriving in England, the Wars of the Roses broke out (at the Battle of St. Albans, in 1455). The refugees' noble sponsors became preoccupied with the war, and as a consequence three of the four Greek scholars immediately returned to Italy. Only the fourth, Emanuel of Constantinople, stayed on, and he only in the personal employ of Neville.

By 1465 Neville had become Archbishop of York. In that year one of his Bishops, John Sherwood, Bishop of Durham, made a trip to Italy; knowing of his Archbishop's interest in Plato, Sherwood brought back as a gift for Neville a collection of manuscripts that included the *Life of Plato* by Guarino da Verona. Neville later gave this manuscript to Corpus Christ College, Oxford. (It is now Oxford,Corpus Christ College MS 84; on Sherwood see Allen, 1910). Neville evidently retained his interest in Plato, for in 1468 he commissioned Emanuel to make copies for him of the Greek texts of the *Timaeus* and the *Letters*. The *Timaeus* manuscript Neville later gave to Durham Cathedral. (It is now Durham University MS D&C C.IV.2; the *Letters* are now Leiden University MS Voss, gr. 56; on this episode see Gray, 1929).

On the basis of what we have seen so far, it would be fair to say that the main force behind the revival of Plato in England during the period 1423–1485 was English wealth. if English lords, both temporal and spiritual, had not been so rich, they would not have been able to travel as they did, to buy books as they did, and to commission translations and support scholars as they did. In short, the Plato revival was the product of conspicuous affluence in England. But to understand the financial foundation of the Plato revival in England is not to see how the revival worked. It worked through chains of acquaintance and gift-giving. We have seen some examples of such chains already, but the most important of the chains we have now to follow. This chain, which turned out to be the main line of the entire process by which the new Plato came to England during the period 1423–1483 was a chain that began with John Whethamstede and ran through Duke Humfrey and William Grey to John Doget.

The first of the English travellers to Italy who is known to have brought back new dialogues of Plato to England was John Whethamstede (c. 1400–1465). Whethamstede was a Benedictine monk, the Abbot of the monastery at St. Albans. In 1423–1424 Whethamstede went to Italy, ostensibly to attend the Council of Pavia, but actually to see for himself the classical revival that was taking place there, and to buy books for the library that he intended to build for his monastery (On Whethamstede see Hodge, 1933; Hurnard, 1936; Mulligan, 1974). During a visit to Florence Whethamstede met Leonardo Bruni, who happened to be working at the time on his translation of the *Phaedrus*, and his revised versions of the *Apology* and *Crito*. Whethamstede was so much impressed with Bruni that when he returned to England he urged Humfrey Duke of Gloucester (1391–1447) to employ Bruni as his personal secretary. Humfrey promptly offered Bruni the post, but Bruni declined Humfrey's offer. That rejection did not chill Whethamstede's admiration for Bruni: he began to quote from Bruni in his own writings (he was the first Englishman to do so) and even included a biography of Bruni in his series of lives of famous men. Thanks to Whethamstede's enthusiastic advertising, Bruni's works subsequently became well known in England. Copies of his works were acquired by William Grey, John Gunthorpe, Richard Bole, Robert Flemming, John Sherwood (Bishop of Durham), and John Doget, of King's College, Cambridge. In addition, some of Bruni's letters were collected in a formulary associated with Thomas Bekynton (d. 1465) (Now London, BL MS Cotton Tiberius B. VI. i). And in 1479 at Oxford was published an edition of Bruni's Latin translation of Aristotle's *Nicomachean Ethics* (STC 752; on

Bruni's reputation in England see Judd, 1961; Weiss, 1967, pp. 71–77).

One of the aspects of Bruni's work that interested Whethamstede was his knowledge of Plato. Whethamstede was apparently not able to get a copy of any of Bruni's own translations, but he did bring back from Italy to Duke Humfrey as a gift, copies of three dialogues of Plato in Latin: the *Phaedo* and *Meno* in the old medieval translations by Aristippus, and the *Timaeus* of Calcidius, with the commentary by Guillaume de Conches (These manuscripts still survive, in Oxford, Corpus Christi MS 243).

In singling out Duke Humfrey to take a lead in bringing the Italian classical revival to England, Whethamstede was motivated partly by friendship; Humfrey often visited him at St. Albans (Leland, *Commentarii de scriptoribus Britannicis*, 1709 ed., vol. 1, p. 437). Duke Humfrey was the uncle and Protector of the young King, Henry VI, and a man of enormous influence. One way to appreciate how much Whethamstede's selection of Humfrey meant is to contrast Humfrey's influence with that of a lesser contemporary who learned of the Italian classical revival about the same time. In 1432, a colleague of Bruni, Ambrogio Traversari, who had been one of the original group of students of Chrysoloras, completed a Latin translation of the most important ancient secondary work on Plato, the *Lives and Opinions of the philosophers*, by Diogenes Laertius. (An earlier Latin version of this work had already been available to Walter Burley in England.) Traversari's version became known in England almost immediately (1433) to a man named William of Worcester, who mentions it in London BL MS Cotton Julius VII. fols. 67^v–68^r, (see also Corpus Christi College, Cambridge, MS 210, p. 279 and Balliol College, Oxford MS 124, fol. 242). But William of Worcester was interested in that work only because he was busy working on a translation of the medieval *Dicts or Sayings of the Philosophers* (see EETS: os 211); his face was turned to the past. If the revival of Plato in England had had to depend upon William of Worcester, it would never have happened at all. Fortunately, it was Duke Humfrey, not Worcester, whom Whethamstede enlisted in the cause of importing Italian classicism.

An important part of the strategy that Whethamstede urged upon Duke Humfrey for bringing the Italian classical revival to England was to import new books, especially Latin translations of the Greek classics. At first Duke Humfrey tried to achieve this objective by commissioning the Papal Collector in London, Piero del Monte, to buy books for Humfrey during his regular return trips to Italy. But in 1437, when a Church Council was convened at Basle, Humfrey tried another tack. Humfrey was not himself a churchman, of course, but his nephew, King Henry VI, was sending an official representative to the Council, and Humfrey arranged with that representative to do some book-hunting for him on the side. The representative in question was an Italian, Zenone da Castiglione, who happened also to be Bishop of Bayeux. In the course of the deliberations of the Council, Zenone made it a point to meet Francesco Pizolpasso, the Bishop of Milan, who was a personal friend of two of the major translators of Plato of the time: Pier Candido Decembrio, of Milan, and Leonardo Bruni, of Florence. Pizolpasso himself knew something about Plato (he owned copies of the *Apology*, *Crito*, *Epistolae*, and *Axiochus*; (Fubini, 1966; Paredi, 1961), and he urged Zenone to go on to Italy from Basle when the Council was over, and meet both Decembrio and Bruni in person.

As it turned out, the entire Council was moved to Italy, first to Ferrara, and then to Florence, and Zenone was thus able to meet both Decembrio and Bruni without neglecting his Council business. Early in 1439 Zenone was able to arrange for Duke Humfrey to open a correspondence with Bruni and Pier Candido Decembrio (1399–1477), the son of Uberto, about a new translation of Plato's *Republic*. The fact that Humfrey was interested in the *Republic* shows that he had heard that Plato was useful for statesmen to read (Borsa, 1904). Later in 1439, Pier Candido sent Humfrey a sample passage (Book V) of his new translation, indicating that he was prepared to dedicate the whole *Republic* to Humfrey if Humfrey would finance the remainder of the translation. Humfrey vaguely agreed to do so. The completed translation was sent to him in two additional installments: the first five books in 1441, and the rest in 1444. Unfortunately Humfrey never paid Decembrio a penny for his work (for more detailed accounts of the entire transaction see in addition to Borsa, 1904; Craster, 1915; Fubini, 1966; Newman, 1905; Vickers, 1907; and Zaccaria, 1959; and the more recent accounts of Hunt, 1970; Sammut, 1980; and Hankins, 1990, vol. 1).

The only one of Plato's dialogues that Humfrey is thought to have read in any detail was the *Phaedo*. But his enthusiasm for owning works of Plato obviously influenced other English patrons and scholars. Among Duke Humfrey's admirers and imitators in the pursuit of Italian classicism the most important for Plato was the Oxford scholar, William Grey (d. 1498). Grey had been a student at Oxford in 1439, when Duke Humfrey gave his first dialogues of Plato to the University Library, and Grey was inspired by that gift to want to make similar benefactions himself. Three years later, in 1442, before Grey had been to Italy himself, he arranged to import and give to his college (Balliol) a copy of the *Axiochus* (then thought to be by Plato), in the Latin translation of Cencio de' Rustici (Appendix 1, #5). This copy was later copied in turn by at least three other people:

1. In 1447 by Henry Cranebrook, a Benedictine monk, then a student at Canterbury College, Oxford (Appendix 1, #8);
2. In 1451 by John Manyngham, then a student at Oxford (Appendix 1, #12; on Manyngham see O'Sullivan, 1962;)
3. About 1459 by Reginald Boulers, then a student at Oxford, but later Bishop of Hartford (Appendix 1, #18).

By making his gift of the *Axiochus* to Oxford, Grey accidentally established the *Axiochus* as the best known work of "Plato" in England. Between 1451 and 1578 there were more copies of the *Axiochus* in England than of any actual dialogue of Plato, except the *Timaeus*.

Grey was one of the first English travellers who was a serious scholar. In 1444 he went to Italy to study, and did not return to England for seven years (1444–1451). He began his studies with Guarino da Verona in Ferrara, but later also studied for extended periods in both Florence and Rome. During his stay in Rome he is reported to have met Cardinal Bessarion. There is no evidence that Grey's acquaintance with the greatest Plato scholar on the continent had any influence on the course of the Plato revival in England, and I know of no other connection between the pre-Tudor revival and the "Roman" revival involving Bessarion and Trebizond.

Grey's study with Guarino on the other hand, proved trend-setting. As we have seen, Grey was followed at Ferrara in 1447 by Robert Flemming, in 1456 by John Free (R. Mitchell, 1955), and in 1459 by John Tiptoft and John Gunthorpe. The tradition might have gone on even longer had Guarino not died in 1460. Gunthorpe returned to England to become chaplain to Edward IV, and later Dean of Wells,but in 1473 he made a return trip to Italy and brought back, among other books, four dialogues of Plato:

Axiochus (Cencio translation)
Apology (Bruni translation; 2nd version)
Crito (Bruni translation; 2nd version)
Timaeus (Calcidius translation)
(See Appendix 1. #19, #22)

Grey's visit of 1444–1451 was only the first of his sojourns in Italy. After a brief return to England in 1451, he went back to Italy and stayed for two more years. During the total of nine years that Grey spent in Italy he acquired a number of books relating to Plato, including the following:

Table 2. Grey's Platonic acquisitions

Work	Translator	Present Balliol MS No.
Axiochus	Rinuccio Aretino	131, fols. 20ʳ–30ᵛ
Euthyphro	Rinuccio Aretino	131, fols. 31ʳ–37ʳ
Crito	Rinuccio Aretino	lost from 131 (Mynors, 1963, p.110)
Axiochus	Cencio de' Rustici	315, fols. 62ᵛ–67ʳ
Republic	P. C. Decembrio	lost (Leland, 1774; Mynors, 1963, p.387)
Epistles	Bruni	lost (Leland, 1774; Mynors, 1963, p. 387)
Bruni's preface to *Phaedo*		125, fols. 217ᵛ–218ʳ
Proclus, *Elements of Theol.* Moerbeke tr.		113, 224B

(based on Mynors, *Catalogue of Balliol MSS*)

All of these books Grey left to his college at Oxford. Duke Humfrey like-wise had intended that his books stay at Oxford, in the magnificent library that he built to house them. But by the time of his death, in 1447, Humfrey had fallen into disgrace: he died in prison under charge of treason. The crown confiscated his property, and many of his books somehow found their way to the recently founded (1441) King's College at Cambridge (Munby, 1951). Among these was a copy of Bruni's translation of the *Phaedo*. Eventually this book caught the eye of one of the Fellows of King's, John Doget (d. 1501), who wrote a commentary on it.

In the same year that Doget wrote his commentary on the *Phaedo* (1473) a new college was founded at Doget's university: St. Catherine's. The foundation library of St. Catherine's included a copy of the new translation of Plato's *Republic* by P. C. Decembrio (Corrie, 1846). Thus the chain of interest in Plato that had begun with Whethamstede's 1423 discovery of the Chrysoloras revival of Plato in italy, went on, through the efforts of Duke Humfrey, William Grey, and Doget, to spread to Oxford and Cambridge. The centrality of the Whethamstede-Humfrey-Grey line to the pre-Tudor revival of Plato in England can be seen clearly by listing the 8 new dialogues of Plato that came into England during the period 1423–1483:

Table 3. Importation of Dialogues of Plato

Date	Work	Translator	First Importer
1423	*Meno*	Aristippus (1156)	Whethamstede
1440	*Republic*	P. C. Decembrio (1439)	Duke Humfrey
1442	*Axiochus*	Cencio (1437)	William Grey
1453	*Euthyphro*	Rinuccio (1423)	William Grey
1453	*Crito*	Rinuccio (1423)	William Grey
1468	*Letters*	Greek Text	George Neville
1473	*Apology*	Bruni (1423)	John Gunthorpe
1483	*Phaedrus*	Bruni (1424)	Unknown

Thus, beginning with an ordinary tourist-visit to Florence by the Archbishop of Canterbury in 1398, a brisk two-way traffic developed between England and Italy, and from 1423 onwards that traffic involved close English attention to several major figures of the Chrysoloras revival of Plato in Italy, resulting in the importation of eight new dialogues of Plato. After the long neglect of Plato in England during the Middle Ages, this sudden interest in Plato between 1423 and 1483 certainly suggests that if any period of English history is to be identified as the period of "the revival of Plato" in England, it is this period. But the mere arrival in the island of copies of several of Plato's works did not at once change the way Englishmen thought about Plato, and the "revival" proved largely abortive, as I will now try to show, first from the evidence of manuscripts and then from the evidence of printed books.

CHAPTER 3

THE RELAPSE INTO MEDIEVALISM

A. The Manuscripts

The continued dominance of the medieval conception of Plato in England before 1485 is apparent even in the bare statistics regarding copies of Plato's works. Most of the new dialogues of Plato that were brought in between 1423 and 1483 were given by their owners to libraries at Oxford; libraries elsewhere continued to own only the Calcidius *Timaeus*. Indeed, one of the dialogues that Whethamstede himself brought back from Italy in 1423 was a copy of the Calcidius *Timaeus* (Appendix 1, #1); that copy continued to be recorded in the catalogues of St. Albans. The *Timaeus* likewise continued to appear in other institutional libraries as well:

1448 St. Albans   #10
1451 Oxford   #11
1465 Wells   #19
1468 Durham   #20
1482 Leicester Abbey   #26–29
(numbers refer to Appendix 1)

More importantly, almost everything that English writers had to say about Plato during the period 1423–1483 remained basically medieval. This can be seen even in the two works that show the most impact of the new knowledge about Plato that was arriving from Italy. The first of these works is an essay about Plato written by the first importer of new dialogues of Plato, John Whethamstede.

Whethamstede was by profession an administrator, with very orderly habits of mind. He habitually took careful notes on everything that he read, and systematically distributed those notes among five notebooks, which he called *Granarium*, *Manipularium*, *Pabularium*, *Palearium*, and *Propinarium*. Whethamstede's notes about Plato went into the notebook called *Granarium*, where they are organized into a short discursive biography.

The part of the *Granarium* in which Whethamstede's life of Plato appears is in effect an alphabetical dictionary of moral philosophy; the entries are arranged in a single alphabet that disconcertingly includes the names of persons as well as of moral abstractions: thus there is an entry for *Abstinence* as well as one for *Aristotle*. The entry for Plato has never been edited or translated in print, and I shall therefore translate it in its entirety:

The Philosopher Plato. He was the expert who said that a state would be best off either when its kings were wise men or its wise men were its rulers. According to some authorities Plato was a man of humble birth and lived a very simple life until he was fully grown. But other more trustworthy authorities say that he was a man of very noble origin, born of a famous man named Aristides and a well known woman named Perictione. In any case he was drawn or directed to literary studies by his father and became so devoted to the great field of Philosophy that his ideas came to dominate those of all other philosophers both before and after him; he reigns on the throne of wisdom, as it were.

Although his teacher Socrates was the first to change the course of Philosophy in the direction of improving and reforming human conduct, Plato himself was the first to divide Philosophy into three fields: Ethics, Physical Science, and Logic. Plato was also the first to discuss Politics, and he wrote several excellent short books on that subject.

He was a very subtle student of other subjects as well, including Theology. For example, his works include a very clear statement of the doctrine of the Trinity: he says that God is a cause in three ways: first, He is an efficient cause by virtue of His power; second, He is a formal cause by virtue of His wisdom; and third, He is a final cause by virtue of His goodness. It was only because of God's goodness that He made every creature participate in His goodness to the extent that its nature is capable of that happy condition.

Plato's writings contain almost the whole of the first sentence of the gospel of St. John, from "In the beginning was the word" to "The light shone in the darkness, and the darkness understood it not." Moreover, Plato's *Timaeus* includes almost the whole of the first sentence of Genesis: "In the beginning God created heaven and earth, and the earth was without form and void, and darkness lay over the earth."

According to some authorities the reason why Plato knew more than other philosophers did about the creation of the world was that he once left Greece to travel in Egypt, and while he was there heard the prophet Jeremiah preaching, and it was from Jeremiah's words and writings that he learned what he later put into his own writings about this exalted subject. According to some other authorities however, Plato did not learn anything from Jeremiah, either in person or from his writings, because Jeremiah had died a hundred years before Plato's birth, and Plato had left Egypt more than sixty years before the Egyptian King Ptolemy had the writings of Jeremiah translated from Hebrew into Greek. Thus it can no longer be supposed that Plato could have heard Jeremiah in person or have had Jeremiah's writings in his hands. Therefore the things that Plato says about the Creation must be ascribed to the fact that God must have wanted to inspire him to say them.

But according to a third school of thought, even though Plato did not hear Jeremiah preach, and Jeremiah's books had not yet been translated from Hebrew into Greek, it was nevertheless from Jeremiah's writings that Plato learned what he says in his own works about the Creation and the Trinity. For, according to this view, Plato was a man of such extraordinary talents that when he went to Egypt, he learned both the Egyptian and the Hebrew language there, and it was in that way that he came to learn about the Creation and the Trinity.

In any case he was extraordinarily learned in Philosophy. But he is also said to have been endowed with the gift of clear and eloquent speech. He was so eloquent that Aristotle himself, who was an orator of great talent, was no match for Plato in the art of eloquence. Dion the Syracusan was Plato's teacher in speech, and Plato learned a great deal from him, not only about eloquence, but also about Theology.

In the field of Ethics Plato was also more distinguished than any other philosopher. He had such a calm and temperate disposition that once when a slave incurred his wrath, through some serious misdemeanour, Plato was not willing to punish him himself, and ordered his disciple Speusippus to do it, lest his own anger lead him to impose a disproportionate punishment on the man. In language too he was a man of such quiet moderation that on one occasion when Xenocrates, one of his disciples, had been saying many critical things about him, Plato put up with the tirade patiently, and when someone mentioned it to him later, merely said, "Perhaps Xenocrates said those things about me because they seemed to him to apply to himself."

He was a man of such maturity and modesty that he used to say that there were five things for which he gave thanks to Mother Nature: first, that he was a man rather than an animal; second, that he was a man rather than a woman; third, that he was a Greek and not a barbarian; fourth, that he was an Athenian and not something else; and fifth, that he was born in the life-time of Socrates.

Plato lived a virtuous life, and because he regarded virtue as the chief end of human life, he became renowned for his virtue.

(BL MS Cotton Tiberius D.V., fols. 138ᵛ–140ʳ; tr. mine).

Whethamstede's sources for this life of Plato he identifies as follows:

Valerius Maximus, *Memorable Words and Deeds*, Book IV, chapter 1, and Book III, chapter 7

Lactantius, *The Institution of Theology*, Book III, chapter 19

Jerome, *Against Jovinianus*, Book II, chapter 4

Augustine, *City of God*, Book VIII, chapter 10

John of Salisbury, *Courtly Trivia* (i.e. *Policraticus*), Book VII, chapter 5, and Book VIII, chapter 8

Apuleius, *De dogmate Platonis* and *De deo Socratis*

These sources are all pre-Renaissance, but we know that Whethamstede was following the developments in Florence at the time, for in his entry on Socrates , Whethamstede says:

The famous philosopher Socrates, about whom Coluccio (Salutati) the Chancellor of Florence, in his *On Fate and Fortune* Book II, chapter 8, writes as follows: If Christ had not come to teach us the meaning of true bliss and glory, certainly Socrates would have been the chief of all our martyrs for all future time. He was a man so completely devoted to virtue that both Seneca and Isidore call him the inventor of Ethics, and he is said to have been the first to have turned Philosophy in the direction of improving and reforming human behaviour.

(London, BL MS Cotton Tiberius D.V., fols. 159^r–160^r; tr. mine).

The other sources, however, that Whethamstede cites for Socrates are all pre-Renaissance:

Firmicus Maternus, *Mathesis*, I.2

Seneca, *Epistolae*, 74

Valerius Maximus, III. 8, and VI. 4

Aulus Gellius, *Noctes atticae* X

Isidore, *Etymologiae* II

Jerome, *Adversus Jovinianum* I

John of Salisbury, *Policraticus*, V.10

Walter Burley. *De vita et moribus philosophorum*.

Whethamstede owned a copy of the medieval florilegium *Dicts or Sayings of the Philosophers* (now London, Lambeth Place MS 265), and mentions Plato briefly in one of his letters (the *Annals of St. Albans* I. 143), but only to say that Plato was as wise as Solomon. Thus, although Whethamstede had been to Italy, and obviously knew something about the revival of Plato that was going on there, his own knowledge of Plato was still almost entirely medieval. And the same may be said of most of the other "collectors of Plato" of Whethamstede's generation: they went to Italy, and brought back works of Plato, but only to own them, not to read them.

The other major piece of English writing that shows some awareness of the Plato revival in Italy is the *Commentary on the Phaedo* written by John Doget in 1473. Doget (d. 1501) was a Fellow of King's College, Cambridge. (He later became Provost of the College; on his life see Hurnard, 1936; Weiss, 1967, pp. 164–167; and Emden, 1963.)

As a young student Doget had been one of the witnesses for Cambridge University at the trial of Reginald Pecock in 1457 (Patrouch, 1970). Several years after the trial, Doget had gone to Italy to study. He had spent altogether five years in Italy, as a student at Padua and Bologna (1464–1469). It was not until 1473, some years after his return from Italy, that he happened to notice in his college library the Bruni *Phaedo*, and undertook to write a Latin commentary on the dialogue. One might suppose, from the fact that Doget twice quotes in this commentary (fols. 32^v and 74^r) from Ficino's Latin translation of the Hermetic *Pimander* (published in 1471) that Doget's interest in Plato was a product of the Medici phase of the Plato revival in

Italy. It was actually the Chrysoloras phase, however, that was responsible for Doget's commentary. Doget himself makes a special point of the fact that it is Bruni's translation of the *Phaedo* that he is using, and in other ways as well his work shows that it derives from the Chrysoloras-Whethamstede line. Doget repeats the allegory of Cerberus as the Devil from Salutati's *De laboribus Herculis*, a copy of which Whethamstede owned, and Doget also quotes from Decembrio's translation of Plato's *Republic*, which Doget's college owned. But Doget did not write his commentary on the *Phaedo* primarily in order to praise Plato; his primary aim was to repudiate the rationalism of the Lollards and to show the importance of accepting on faith what the Church said, without asking embarrassing questions. Appropriately he dedicated his commentary to his uncle, the Archbishop of Canterbury, Thomas Bourchier (c. 1404–1460). Doget's *Commentary on the Phaedo* survives in London, BL MS Add. 10,344; its preliminaries have been published by Hankins, 1990, pp. 497–502. Doget's commentary is too long to print here in full; I shall therefore only summarize it, and quote a few short passages in translation.

Doget uses the commentary form as it had traditionally been used, from the ninth century onwards, as a vehicle for his own ideas. In this case his ideas have to do with the Christian account of the immortality of the soul. He handles the commentary technique as if he were commenting on the Bible; the quotations from the text of Plato are in red, and his own comments are in black. He ordinarily comments on a whole sentence at a time, and he ostentatiously adduces analogues from pagan writers as well as from Christian ones. Thus, on fol. 10^v., in approving Socrates' statement that death should be treated calmly, he quotes Horace and Cicero as well as Augustine.

Doget begins by establishing the orthodoxy of his point of view:

> The works of the philosophers seem to me a mixture of statements, some wrong, and some right. For example, on the subject of the soul Plato certainly says many things that are doctrinally sound. Therefore when I recently had access to Plato's famous work on the immortality of the soul, I thought it would be useful to devote some of my leisure to it, and by means of a commentary, point out and emphasize those of his statements that are doctrinally sound, and to refute or reject those that are not. I do not wish to be thought arrogant in doing this; although philosophy has its uses, I of course mean only to assert my own faith . . . but if anyone thinks I am wrong to do this, he may wish to read the books of many other Catholics such as Jerome and Augustine, who fill their books with the opinions of philosophers and the poems of poets. Even Paul himself quotes a poet (Epimenides) in his letter to Titus. And I think that if people had not considered Plato's work about the immortality of the soul of some value, they would not have translated it into Latin . . .
>
> (fols. 5^r–6^r; tr. mine).

Doget then goes on to discuss various attitudes toward death, praising Socrates' urging of a calm attitude, and criticizing those who advocate suicide. He then takes up the Socratic view that the wise man hopes for death, saying that what one actually ought to do is to submit to divine providence. He criticizes the secularism of Socrates' position, pointing out that the love of wisdom is no substitute for the love of God. The pagans tended to admire Mars, Mercury, Jupiter, and Saturn, but these gods were all killers, and the ancients were guilty of pride in thinking themselves wise when they did not know the true God. By contrast with the view of Socrates, the attitude of the true Christian when he faces death is shown in the cases of St. Catherine and St. Laurence. Such Christian strength of soul as theirs surpasses any rational philosophical view of death.

Doget concedes that there are some truths to be found in Plato. For example, in the *Phaedo* Plato commends the virtue of humility, and in the *Republic* Plato describes the "eye of the soul" (Doget, 1473, fols. 29^v–30^r, using the Decembrio translation of the *Republic*; the relevant passage in the *Republic* is VII. 518C).

On fol. 31^v Doget begins a long discussion of the theory of metempsychosis. In this section he criticizes Plato and Pythagoras for having believed that souls transmigrate into the bodies of animals. Hermes in the *Pimander* (fol. 32^r) and Porphyry are closer to the truth on this issue: they do not believe that human souls can become animals, but they do deny that sinners can go to heaven. It appears that in theological matters Plato followed Orpheus, Aglophemus, and Philolaus, who were his teachers, but what these authors actually believed is difficult to determine because their works have been lost.

We really do not need to try to refute the ancients, for we have the advantage of the Scriptures, but it is not enough to say that human souls did not go to heaven until Christ expiated human sin, nor does God treat all sins equally: He treats each one on its own merits. Catholic doctrine believes in eternal damnation and Limbo. The classical myth of the killing of Cerberus by Heracles is an allegory of the conquest of death, just as Christ conquered death through the Resurrection.

Commenting on Socrates' reference in the *Phaedo* to "the old opinion of transmigration", Doget says that Christians believe in the Last Judgment and the Resurrection of the flesh, and must therefore reject both the Pythagorean view that the human soul transmigrates into animals and the Platonic view that the soul is caught in an endless cycle of recurring incarnations. Plato's view cannot be correct, for Job says, "In my flesh I shall see God". But Plato probably knew about the Last Judgment and may be referring to it allegorically when he speaks of souls being released from the cycle of recurrence in the wonderful year.

The argument for immortality that Socrates draws from the nature of opposites may be true, but the fact is that God makes souls every day, and he can make them go into or out of bodies as he pleases, at any time. As for the argument that memory shows that the soul must have existed previously, Doget points out that this argument occurs not only in the *Phaedo*, but also in the *Timaeus* and the *Meno*, but Christians must nevertheless repudiate the doctrine of pre-existence.

Having disposed of the problem of the soul's existence before this life, Doget then turns (fol. 40^r) to the problem of the soul's existence after this life. He accepts Socrates' argument that the soul is superior to the body (fol. 43^r) because it is simple, unchanging, undivided, and immobile, divine, and immortal. He then (fols. 44^v–46^r) takes up the argument that the soul, in order to be true to itself, must shun all things of the body altogether (e.g. food, drink, and sex). The standard medieval argument, from Augustine, on this issue was that we must accept the flesh as well as the spirit because both will be involved at the Resurrection. Doget is not content to follow Augustine on this point. Rather, he says that Plato is right: we should reject the body and the visible world in general; we should seek to ascend to the invisible world (fol. 48^r).

Then, inexplicably, Doget reverts to the problem of metempsychosis again (fols. 48^r–49^v). He explains that this idea is an absurd aberration on Plato's part since man was made in the image of God and cannot possibly be transformed into an animal. Plato obviously believed in this doctrine since he mentions it again in the *Republic*, in the passage about the death of Pamphilus. But Porphyry as well as Augustine and Hermes in the *Pimander* all refute this doctrine (fols. 54^v–57^r).

Doget then turns to an issue on which Plato is more in accord with Christian doctrine (fol. 59^v), the unity of God. Plato, by some marvelous instinct, is talking about the same God as the Hebrew and Christian God. Another marvelous example of Plato's divine inspiration is his mention of Penelope (fol. 67^r), whose story is an allegory of the constancy of the human soul in its pursuit of the ideal.

We should always try to recognize the allegorical meaning of what Plato says. For example, Plato says that there are very few things that are purely good or purely evil; most things are a mixture of both (fols. 65^v–66^r). The right way to interpret this is to notice first that Hermes says (fol. 67^v) that all things are found in the Logos:

> Hermes thinks that goods are seeds of God, and he means by this expression "seeds" the son of God (the Logos).

Hermes also says that no one except God is truly good, and when we say the word "God" we should not mean some other kind of good; nothing except God is truly good. God does not invite us to goodness (fol. 67^v) but draws us to goodness (fol. 68^r).

The major problem with Plato's statement is that we tend to apply it to people. Only God is good, but we speak of good and evil people, as if the term "good" applied to people as well. We think of evil as sin, and, conversely, of goodness as avoiding of sin. But when Plato says that true good and true evil are rare, he cannot mean that wicked people are few, because Augustine and the Book of Esdras tell us that they will be many. But Plato's comment also cannot mean that good people are numerous, for the Bible says that "many are called, but few are chosen", and Augustine also says (*City of god* XXII) that the saved will be few.

Doget then returns to the problem of the definition of the soul (fol. 70ᵛ). Plato rejects the definition of the soul as a harmony, on the ground that the soul must precede the body, but we have already shown that the pre-existence of the soul is impossible. The fact that Socrates raises the question of what the soul is made of (fire, air, memory, etc.) (fol. 72ᵛ), shows that Socrates was living in a primitive period, when people like Democritus and Leucippus tended to interpret the world in purely physical terms. Socrates is right however, in believing that mind is the cause of everything (fol 74ʳ). Aristotle also accepts this view in *De anima* I, but the concept is stated much more clearly in Hermes' *Pimander*.

Turning to the question of how the soul knows (fol 76ʳ), Doget says that Socrates believed that we should not try to look at the truth directly, just as we cannot look directly at the sun; rather we should look at it indirectly, in a mirror. The implication is that Doget too believes this, since he is looking at the mirror of the *Phaedo* rather than at the Bible.

On fols. 78ᵛ–85ʳ Doget calls attention to Socrates' statement that at the death of the body the soul is freed from depravity; Doget confirms this fact by giving a long list of depraved sinners who have no hope of salvation, and ends (fol. 84ᵛ) with another quotation from the *Pimander*, in which Hermes predicts to his disciples that he will be immortal.

Socrates mention of his daemon prompts Doget to explain (fol. 85ʳ) that Apuleius has written a whole book on this subject (*De deo Socratis*), explaining that everyone has a guardian angel. What this probably means, says Doget, is merely the phenomenon of conscience, but Socrates may have had angels in mind since Jerome says that everyone has a guardian angel. What Jerome actually means, of course, is that everyone has two angels, a good one and an evil one.

Socrates also says that the earth is in the middle of the universe (fol. 87ʳ). If this is the case, we must certainly wonder what is holding the earth up. But both Job and Isidore tell us that we have no right to ask such questions. We do know, however, from Macrobius, that the continents are arranged on the earth like a pyramid, with Europe at the top, and Africa and Asia below. Thinking about the continents carries Doget away momentarily into private reverie, where, thinking of *Timaeus* 24E, perhaps, he suggests that perhaps we are all really living after all at the bottom of a huge sea, and only think that we are living on the earth.

The final scene of the *Phaedo*, where Socrates dies, inspires Doget to conclude his commentary with a panegyric in praise of Plato. Borrowing from Augustine's *City of God* VIII, Doget explains that Plato travelled to Egypt and must there have learned from the Hebrew prophets much of what he knew about the true Theology (fol. 91ᵛ). In any case his opinions are nearly divine, and too good for a pagan to keep to himself (fol. 93ʳ). The holiness of Socrates' conception of immortality is shown in the final scene of the *Phaedo*. Socrates' nonchalance about the fate of his body contrasts greatly with the excessive attention that people in contemporary England lavish on the bodies of the dead (fol. 93ᵛ). Socrates' remark about owing a cock to Asclepius shows Socrates' sense of justice and also his idealism, since he wants to rid himself of the things of this world in preparation for the next world (fol. 97ʳ). "How religiously he ended his life." Doget concludes, "his true worth will be rewarded at the Last Judgment" (fol. 97ᵛ; tr. mine).

It is tempting to suppose, in reading Doget's work, that we have crossed a major watershed in the position of Plato in England. Fifty years earlier a Master of Arts at Oxford had criticized one of his teachers for defending Plato's theory of Ideas: "Plato must have been wrong about the Ideas", said the student, "because he also advocated marital communism," (Oxford, Corpus Christi College MS 116, fol. 53ʳ; cited by Robson, 1961, p. 230). Now, here, in Doget, we appear to have moved from that student's medieval position, to the new Renaissance position, in which Plato is called upon to defend Christianity against its traditional enemies: secularism, rationalism, and materialism. But such an interpretation is probably not justified. It would never have occurred to Doget that Christianity needed Plato to defend it, or that Plato was in any way the wave of an anti-Aristotelean future. Doget wrote about Plato only because the *Phaedo* happened to have a safe Christian subject, the immortality of the soul.

The truth is that Doget was not much interested in current events. Writing in the quiet of the King's College Library, to which he later left his books (Munby, 1951), Doget gives no indication that his country was then in the throes of Civil War. The Wars of the Roses between the Yorkists and the Lancastrians had begun in 1455 at the Battle of St. Albans, and had been raging ever since. By 1473 the war was the overriding concern of most Englishmen, from Lands End to Jarrow, but you would never know that, from Doget's pages.

It is therefore hardly surprising that Doget's view of Plato shows little understanding of the reasons for the revival of Plato in Italy; like most other Englishmen of his time, he was willing to give Plato a reading, but only to the extent that the Roman Church approved.

In other manuscript literature of the period, as in Doget, the view of Plato is still thoroughly medieval. For example, in an anonymous English tract of the early fifteenth century Plato is credited with having explained how one can tell, merely by analyzing a person's physiognomy, that he is to be avoided (Oxford, Bodl. MS, Ashmole 1447, item ix.9, pp. 3–5). An equally medieval conception occurs in another anonymous English translation written about 1450, of a medieval Latin romance called *Historia Alexandri Magni de preliis*. In this work Plato appears in connection with a description of Egypt: the author lists Plato among several ancient authors who had visited Egypt and had there acquired exceptional knowledge:

Now somwhat we are aduysed to reherse whiche of the Grekis that were passynge in wysedom & excellent of lernynge, cam ouer in-to Egipte of olde tyme in purpose to here & vnderstande theyr lawes and doctryne. The prelates Egipcyen haue in their sacred bokes of scripture registred of recorde how ther cam fyrst out of Grece in-to Egipte these whos names be here subscrybed: Orpheus, Museus, Melampedes, Dedalus, Homerus the famous poete, and Lygurge the Spartane. And after theym cam Solon of Athenes, Plato the philosopher, Samius Picthogaras, Eudoxus the deuyne, Democritus Abderites, and Mopides Chius.

Of alle these there yet remayneth apparent euydence; of somme ther be ymagis, and of dyuerce ther be placis that toke theyr denomynacion as wel of theym-self as of theyr scyence & connynge whiche they lernyd in Egipte, alle suche thynges as caused theym to be had in wonderful commendacion emonge theyr owne nacion. (Skeat ed., 1886, pp. 128–129).

By-yonde this I fynde remembrid in theyr recordis how Ligurge, Plato, & Solon toke suche lawes as they sawe emonge Thegipcyens & brought theym in-to their contree to the vse and behoef of theyr wele in comyn. Picthogoras also appercevued & lernyd oute of the sacryd bokys & volumes emonge Thegipcyens geometrye and arsmetryke and the transmutacion of sowlis in-to other bodyes. They suppose that Democritus in fyue yere that he was in Egipte lernyd many thyngis in astrologye; and how Inopides was of longe tyme studyously conuersaunt with the prestis Egipcyen which in astronomy had wonder experyence, and how he brought home amonge the Grekis the practyke to knowe the course of the sonne & of other sterris, the zodyake & many other poyntis whiche he had lernyd emonge theym. (Skeat ed., 1886, pp. 132–133).

The "recordis" that the author mentions as his source for this material are nothing more recherché than the standard medieval authorities, Augustine's *City of God*, and Isidore's *Etymologiae*.

The closest that one comes to Plato himself in the manuscripts is the familiar medieval Calcidius *Timaeus*, as quoted in John Boston of Bury's tract *Gladius Salomonis*, of 1460 (Babington ed., 1860, vol. 2, p. 590; quoting *Timaeus* 40D–E and 29D).

A more famous writer of this period whose allusions to Plato are also entirely medieval is John Lydgate (c. 1370–1450). Lydgate was from the age of fifteen a monk of the Benedictine monastery of Bury St. Edmunds, (on his life see Ebin, 1985 and Pearsall, 1970). Although his order did send him to Oxford for two years (1406–1408), the dominant influence in his life was his own chapter library. In Lydgate's time the library at Bury St. Edmunds was the second largest monastic library in England, containing more than 2,000 volumes; only Christ Church Canterbury exceeded it in size. Lydgate based much of his career on imitating or translating into English verse, books that he found in that library.

Lydgate's practice as a translator was very free, and consistently inflating. He had a curious habit of adding allusions to Plato to the works that he translated. This habit can be seen in translations throughout his career, from the earliest to the latest. His earliest translation was one that he made between 1406–1408, probably while he was at Oxford. This was a translation of a French allegorical dream-vision *Les échecs amoureux (Love's Game of Chess*. The original work is a poem of 30,000 lines; from this huge carcass Lydgate cut himself off a manageable chunk, the first 4,873 lines, which he amplified into an English poem of 7,042 lines under the title *Reason and Sensuality*. In this work the poet begins by describing a dream-vision in which he sees a beautiful lady called Nature. After describing Nature at some length, he says that he would like to be able to describe Nature's works as well, but they, unfortunately, are indescribable; not even Plato and Aristotle have succeeded in describing them:

> For this lady at her forge
> Continually produces new things
> That are so marvelous and astonishing
> That no man alive has the brains
> To describe every one of them,
> Not even Aristotle or Plato.
> (*Reson and Sensualyte*, ll. 307–313, ed. Sieper, 1898, p. 9; tr. mine.)

This allusion to Plato is not present in *Les échecs amoureux*: it is Lydgate's own addition, but Lydgate did not himself invent it; in fact, he took it from the *Roman de la Rose* (ll. 16183–16189).

The last of Lydgate's translations (he left it unfinished at his death about 1450), was a version of the *Secretum secretorum*. Under the title *De regimine principum* this work had been popular in England since about 1180, when Gerald of Wales brought it back from Paris (1177–1180) (Goddu and Rouse, 1977; see also Jayne, 1991, pp. 720–722e). Lydgate was making his translation from a French version, and had arrived at line 1,491 when he died. Henry VI, for whom the translation was being made, ordered a man named Benedict Burgh to complete it. Burgh added another 1,239 lines, but he, too, left the work unfinished. Even in its incomplete state the work is useful for our purposes, because in the part that Lydgate himself completed we see once again his habit of citing Plato for padding.

In a section of the work where "Aristotle" is discussing the magical properties of rubies, Lydgate apparently feels nervous about his subject, and inserts a personal disclaimer to the effect that he himself knows nothing about the scientific matters being discussed in this treatise. He seeks to certify his ignorance by stating that he is not familiar "Nother with Plato nor with socratees" (1511 ed. sig. BI^r). I think we may take Lydgate at his word on this subject.

Unlike most of Lydgate's work, *The assemble of goddes*, written about 1420 (STC 17005), was an original work rather than a translation. It is a moral allegory in Middle English verse, set in classical antiquity. Plato is mentioned in the poem only once. The occasion is a banquet given by Apollo for all the other gods and goddesses. Among the guests at the banquet is a group of "sage phylosophyrs" including Plato, Socrates, and Sortes:

56

Thus was the table set rownde aboute
  With goddys & goddesses, as I haue yow tolde.
Awaytyng on the boorde was a gret route
  Of sage phylosophyrs & poetes many folde.
Ther was sad Sychero & Arystotyll olde,
  Tholome, Dorothe, with Dyogenes,
  Plato, Messehala, & wyse Socrates,

57

Sortes and Saphyrus with Hermes stood behynde,
  Auycen and Aueroys with hem were in fere.
Galyen & Ipocras, that physyk haue in mynde,
  With helpe of Esculapion, toward hem drow nere.
Virgyle, Orace, Ouyde and Omere,
  Euclyde, and Albert yaue her attendunce,
  To do the goddys and goddesses pleasaunce.
(Triggs, 1895, ed. pp. 12–13).

Lydgate's most popular work was *The Falle of Princis* (STC 3175). This work, written between 1431 and 1439, was a translation into English verse of a French verse translation (c. 1409) by Laurent de Premierfait (see Ebin., 1985, pp. 60–67) of Boccaccio's *De casibus virorum*. Pynson printed Lydgate's version in 1494.

Boccaccio himself nowhere mentions Plato in the *De casibus virorum*, but Lydgate, by way of embroidering on Boccaccio's text, adds five anecdotes about Plato, four taken from Higden's *Polychronicon* and one from John of Salisbury's *Policraticus*. Thus in Book II (vol. II, p. 285 Bergen ed., 1924–1927) where Lydgate relates the story of King Astriages, who married his daughter to Cambises, Lydgate borrows from Higden's *Polychronicon* the explanation that Astriages made this mistake because he had not heard about Socrates, and therefore supposed that nobility was conferred by blood rather than by divine grace:

In thinking this, he did not take into account the fact
That Socrates, Plato's teacher,
Was of low birth,
And never ruled over any kingdom or region,
But all his life devoted himself

Only to having mastery
Over moral virtue and philosophy.
(Book II, II. 3039–3045, Bergen ed., 1924–1927, Part 1, p. 285; tr. mine).

In book III Lydgate tells the story of the suicide of Marcus Porcius Cato, and once more he borrows some details from Higden's *Polychronicon*:

He had so much self-control
That when he read Plato's book about immortality
(That is, the *Phaedo*), and saw there that
Human souls do not die
But live eternally in either pleasure or pain,
(This is what Plato wrote in his book:
The body can be killed
But the soul lives on eternally.)
This Cato, solid as a wall,
Was not afraid to die,
And killed himself with his bare sword.
(Book III, II. 1264–1274, Bergen ed., 1924–1927, Part 2, pp. 363–364; tr. mine).

Another story for which Lydgate borrows some embroideries from Higden's *Polychronicon* is the story of Calisthenes:

Along with other boys, this Calisthenes
Was sent to school in his youth
In the two schools, one of prudent Socrates
And the other of Plato, which held the key
To the secret mysteries and the divine Ideas.
In these two excellent schools
No one else learned half as much as he did.
These old teachers, these two philosophers
In those days, because of their superior learning, were
Called the two treasure chests of the world,
Or rather the treasurers who kept the two chests.
Because God had ordained
That they should be inspired and
Given the key to all knowledge.
(Book IV. II. 1177–1190, Bergen ed., 1924–1927, Part 2, p. 506; tr. mine).

After rambling on for some time about other matters, Lydgate eventually remembers Calisthenes, and repeats what he has told us:

This tragedy about Calisthenes
Says that in his youth he was
Educated by Plato and Socrates,

Drew abundantly of their milk,
And learned from them to eschew sloth.
But in the end he was dismembered by
Alexander for telling the truth.
(Book IV, II. 1422–1428, Bergen ed., 1924–1927, Part 2, p. 512; tr. mine).

In Boccaccio's section on Cicero, Lydgate once again adds a decorative reference to Plato; this one he takes not from Higden, but from John of Salisbury:

The books of the ancients tell us
That Plato was a fortune-teller and
Had the reputation of being
The very source and well of Rhetoric,
And the mirror of eloquence in his style.
But the Greeks say that Cicero was
Plato's equal in Rhetoric,
Both in particular details and as a whole.
(Book VI, ll. 3123–3129, Bergen ed., 1924–1927, Part 3, p. 758; tr. mine).

The difficulty that English writers experienced in trying to assimilate the new information about Plato that was filtering in from Italy by the middle of the fifteenth century is best illustrated in an English chronicler of the period, John Capgrave (1392–1464). Capgrave was a prolific Austin friar, of King's Lynn, in Norfolk. Although he had apparently heard something about Bruni's translations of Plato, Capgrave's conception of Plato was still basically medieval. In his *Chronicle of England* (c. 1462), written in English, Capgrave begins with the Creation, and when he gets to the year 424 B.C. he gives us the following account of Plato, borrowed erratically from Augustine's *City of God*, VIII:

In this time was Plato disciple to Socrates, in whose bokes was found a grete part of that Gospel. "In principio erat Verbum". When he was take with soudioures and broute to Dionisie the tyrant, he, seing so many aboute the tirant, seide onto him, "What hast thou do that thou nedist so many men?" This Plato mad many bokes and named hem after his maystires. *Themeus* is on; *Phedron* a othir; and third, *Gorgialis*; the IIII, *Pitharas*. And though men feyne mech thing of his death, he was hald in great reverens that thei had doute, whan he was ded, whethir thei schuld a noumbir him amoung the hie goddes or semigoddes.
(Hingston ed., 1858, p. 50).

That Capgrave should have heard of the "*Themeus*" is natural, for the Calcidius translation of the *Timaeus* had been commonly available in England since 1111. But Capgrave's other references must derive from his having heard about the translations by Bruni. The "*Phedron*" is probably the *Phaedo*, which Bruni had translated in 1405. The "*Gorgialis*" is the *Gorgias*, which Bruni had translated in 1409. The fourth work, the "*Pitharas*", is probably a mere fiction, based on the name Pythagoras; but it may conceivably be a confusion for Bruni's translation of the *Phaedrus* (1424).

To summarize the evidence from manuscripts, the principal advance in English knowledge about Plato during the period 1423–1483 was the fact that for the first time it became thinkable in England for individuals to own copies of works of Plato. This does not mean that Plato had become a "popular author": there is still no allusion to Plato in family papers of such prominent fifteenth century families as the Pastons, Celys, and Stonors. Nor did the London scrivener John Shirley (1366–1456) ever make a copy of any work by or about Plato (Doyle, 1961). The few Englishmen who did travel to Italy and acquire copies of Plato's works usually bought Latin translations rather than the original Greek text, and promptly gave their manuscripts to Oxford or Cambridge University for other people to read. Even at the universities such manuscripts attracted very little attention: there was some copying of the *Axiochus*, but apart from the commentary on the *Phaedo* by John Doget, the new manuscripts mainly sat on the shelves and gathered dust. Between 1423 and 1483 the Chrysoloras revival of Plato in Italy did have a number of repercussions in England, but it did not alter significantly the essentially medieval conception of Plato that prevailed there.

B. THE PRINTED BOOKS

So long as books were available only in the form of manuscripts, knowledge about Plato in England remained in the hands of people who had access to manuscripts. As we have seen, that minority was very small. The invention of printing made books available to a very much larger part of the population, but that increased exposure did not at first have much effect on knowledge about Plato. The first book ever printed in England was printed in 1476. From that date to the accession of the Tudors in 1485, England had only one London printer, William Caxton (c. 1422–1491). (There was a printer in Oxford who printed Bruni's translation of Aristotle's *Nicomachean Ethics* in 1479, STC752). During the period 1476–1485 Caxton printed only seven books that contained any allusion to Plato, and all seven books merely perpetuated medieval conceptions of Plato. Thus the general population remained ill-informed about Plato for some time after the invention of printing. Let us now examine Caxton's output in some detail, and see why that was the case.

Caxton was an Englishman who had learned the new technology of printing in Belgium, and had then returned to England to set up a press of his own in Westminster. (On the 107 volumes printed by Caxton see Blake, 1969, 1973, and Painter, 1976. There is a chronological checklist in Painter, pp. 211–215; an alphabetical checklist, showing modern reprints, is in Blake, 1969, pp. 224–239). The seven pre-Tudor books that Caxton printed that involved allusions to Plato were the following:

Table 4. Works involving Plato printed by Caxton

1.	1477	Mubashshir ibn Fatik, *Dicts or Sayings of the Philosophers* (1053 A.D.)
2.	1478	Chaucer, *Canterbury Tales* (c. 1390 A.D.)
3.	1478	Boethius, *Consolation of Philosophy* (c. 400 A.D.)
4.	1482	Higden, *Polychronicon* (c. 1364 A.D.)
5.	1483	Anon., *Court of Sapience* (c. 1430 A.D.)
6.	1483	Honorius, *Mirrour of the World* (c. 1245 A.D.)
7.	1483	Gower, *Confessio amantis* (1390 A.D.)

I have placed in parenthesis after each work its date of origin. As these dates show, every one of these works is medieval. The information that they give about Plato is therefore also medieval. One would never know from Caxton's works that at the very time he was printing these medieval books in England, the *Works* of Plato were being worked on in Florence (Ficino's *Opera Platonis*, Florence, 1484). The only Florentine writer of the time whom Caxton mentions is Poggio Bracciolini, and Caxton mentions him only to point out that Bracciolini owned a manuscript of the book that Caxton was printing, an anonymous commentary on Cato called *Caton:*

> There was a noble clerke named Pogius of
> Florence, and was secretary to Pope Eugenye
> and also to Pope Nycholas, whiche had in the
> cyte of Florence a noble and well-stuffed
> lybrarye whiche alle noble straungyers
> comynge to Florence desyred to see; and
> therein they fonde many noble and rare
> bookes. And whanne they had axyd of hym
> whiche was the best boke of them alle, and
> that he reputed for best, he sayd that he
> helde *Cathon glosed* for the best book of his
> lyberarye. . . doubtles hit must folowe that
> this is a noble booke and a vertuous . . .
> (1483 ed., sig.ii^v)

The work that Caxton printed in 1477 under the title *Dicts or Sayings of the Philosophers* has a very long and complicated history. It was first written about 1049, in Cairo, by a Syrian named Abu'l Wafa Mubashshir ibn Fatik (1019–1097). The original language of the work was Arabic, and its title was *Muhtar-al-Hikam* (*Wise Sayings*). The work contains 23 sections:

1. Seth	13. Aristotle
2. Hermes	14. Alexander
3. Thoth	15. Ptolemy
4. Asclepius	16. Assaron (?)
5. Homer	17. Loqman

6. Solon	18. Eunapius
7. Zeno	19. Mahada-Gis (?)
8. Hippocrates	20. Basil
9. Pythagoras	21. Gregory
10. Diogenes	22. Galen
11. Socrates	23. Miscellaneous authors
12. Plato	

Each section (except two) consists of two parts: first a biographical sketch of the man concerned, and then a collection of quotations and anecdotes that are associated with him. The two exceptional sections are no. 14, on Alexander the Great, and no. 23, on Miscellaneous authors. The section on Alexander is much the longest of the sections, and it differs from all the others in form. It is essentially a straight biography, taken from Pseudo-Callisthenes, who quotes from his hero not brief aphorisms and anecdotes, such as are found in all of the other sections of the *Muhtar-al-Hikam*, but long transcriptions of entire speeches and whole letters, both of Alexander and of the Persian King Darius.

Section 23 of the *Muhtar-al-Hikam* contains no biographical material at all; it is limited to individual quotations from authors not included in the other sections. A number of the quotations in this section are attributed to Protagoras, but most of them are anonymous.

Altogether the *Muhtar-al-Hikam* contains many hundreds of quotations, taken from Jewish, Arabic, and Greek sources. The authors quoted include Christians (Basil and Gregory) as well as pagans, and non-philosophers. The heterogeneous character of the original work was accurately reflected in the title of its first translation in a western language, a Spanish translation made about 1257, entitled *Bocados de Oro* (*Golden Sayings*; modern ed, Crombach, 1971). About 1290, however, in Sicily, this Spanish version was translated into Latin, probably by Giovanni da Procida, physician to Frederick II. Since the Latin translator omitted all the quotations that were not ascribed to philosophers, he gave his version the title *Liber philosophorum moralium*. In this form, as a collection limited to the sayings of philosophers, the Latin version achieved a wide circulation in Europe, sometimes under the title *Placita philosophorum* (ed. Renzi, 1854) or *De dogmatibus philosophorum*. About 1390 this Latin version was translated into French by Guillaume de Tignonville under the title *Les dits des philosophes,* or simply, *Dits moraulx* (ed. Eder, 1915). In England the collection became available in both its Latin and French versions as early as the fourteenth century, but for some reason, in the second half of the fifteenth century the work suddenly became very popular in England; no less than four different translators tried their hands at it:

1450 Stephen Scrope, stepson of Sir John Fastolf, from French; slightly expanded
       and paragraphed in 1472 by Fastolf's secretary, William of Worcester
       (modern eds. Schofield, 1936, and Bühler, 1941,)

c. 1460 Anonymous: from French (Modern ed. Bühler, 1941)

c. 1470 George Ashby; from Latin; very small part of whole
      (modern ed. Bateson, 1899)

c. 1475 Anthony Woodville, Earl Rivers; from French; printed by Caxton, 1477
      (modern ed. Blades, 1901)

Our main concern is with the version printed by Caxton, but before we turn to that, it will be worthwhile to glance briefly at the version by George Ashby (c. 1390–1475). During his active years Ashby had been a civil servant at the court of Henry VI, but about 1470, when he was nearly eighty years old, he decided to devote himself to the writing of "poetry", taking as his models:

> Maisters Gower, Chauucer & Lydgate,
>   Primier poetes of this nacion,
> Embelysshing oure englisshe tendure algate,
> Firste finders to oure consolacion
>   Off fresshe, douce englisshe and formacion
>   Of newe balades, not vsed before,
>   By whome we all may haue lernyng and lore.
> ("Active Policy", ed. Bateson, 1899, p. 13).

The so-called "ballad" form that Ashby admired in his three famous predecessors was the seven-line "rhyme royal" stanza. Using this form in the ponderous style seen above (actually a 7-line stanza of 4-beat pausing metre, rhymed ababbcc). Ashby wrote three works, one for the past, one for the present, and one for the future. Ashby's "poem-for-the-past" was a work called " A Prisoner's Reflections'" describing his experience as a prisoner in the Fleet in 1463. Ashby's "poem for the present" was a homily for the instruction of Henry VI's son, Edward, Prince of Wales, entitled "Active Policy of a Prince". Ashby's "poem-for-the-future", also designed for the instruction of Prince Edward, was called *Dicta et opiniones diversorum philosophorum* (*Sayings and Opinions of Various Philosophers*).

In the poem "Active Policy of a Prince", Ashby begins apologetically, explaining that he is a novice when it comes to writing verse ("Nor of Balades haue experience", 1. 41, ed. Bateson, 1899, p. 14) and that since he has not seen very many collections of quotations, such as the *Glossa Ordinaria*, he will have to speak very personally and briefly:

> Right so though I haue not seien scripture
>   Of many bookes right sentenciall,
> In especial of the gloses sure,
>   I woll therfor kepe true menyng formal,
>   Nor right meche delatyng the rehersall,
>   Thaugh I do nat so wele as thei before,
>   Ostendyng my beneuolence & lore
> (ed. Bateson, 1899, pp. 14–15).

The fact is, however, that Ashby was working from the *Muhtar-al-Hikam*, in its Latin translation, the *Liber philosophorum moralium*. At #43 of the "Active Policy" Ashby quotes and then paraphrases one of the aphorisms from the Plato section of the book:

43

Decet Regem satisfacere de stipendiis
stipendiariis sibi servientibus, alioquin
societas despiciet eum & dominium suum;
hec Plato.

And paie youre men theire wages & dutee,
  That thei may lyue withoute extorcion,
And so wol god trouthe & equitee,
  And therfore take hertili this mocion.
  And in their nedys be their proteccion.
  And so shal youre fame encrece & rise,
    And euery man youre pleasire accomplise.
(ed. Bateson, 1899, p. 22; Latin ed. Franceschini, 1931–1932, p.475).

Similarly, in #43 (ed. Bateson, 1899, p. 23; Franceschini, 1931–1932, p. 429) Ashby quotes and paraphrases an "opinion" of "Pitogoras"; in #51, an "opinion" of Hermes Trismegistus (ed. Bateson, p. 24; Latin ed. Franceschini, 1931–1932, p. 405); and in #100, an "opinion" of Socrates:

100

Facias aliis quod tibi vis fieri & non facias aliis
Quod tibi non vis fieri; hec Socrates.

If forgoten be al lawe positife
  Remembre the noble lawe of nature,
Obseruyng it al daies of your lif,
  And ye shal kepe equite iust & suer,
  As to ministre to iche Creature
    Suche misericorde, iustice & eke grace,
    As ye wold be doon to in semblable case.
(ed. Bateson, 1899, pp. 34–35; Latin ed. Franceschini, 1931–1932, p. 458).

The fact that this statement is a paraphrase of the Golden Rule from Matthew 1:7–8, and therefore could not have been made by Socrates did not trouble Ashby; he was simply following his Latin source.

Having discovered, in the "Active Policy", what a rich mine the *Liber philosophorum* was, Ashby then worked that mine more ambitiously. Ashby's next work, called *Dicta et opiniones diversorum philosophorum* consists of 181 quotation from the *Liber philosophorum moralium*. To each quotation Ashby gives the same treatment he had invented for the "Active Policy": first he assigns a number, then he quotes the Latin verbatim, including the name of the section from which he has taken it (e.g. "hec Aristoteles", "hec Socrates"). Finally, he composes a paraphrase-meditation on the saying in crude English verse. A typical example is the following, advising the prince to select his servants from among old trusted members of the royal household (such as himself):

34

Decet Regem ad sua seruicia suscepere quem
priusquam regnaret bonum et fidelem cognouit.
Cum Rex postquam regnauerit non valet eos
bene cognoscere quia omnes ei postmodum
adulantur & honorantur eundem; hec Socrates.

A kynge sholde take of his olde acquaintance,
  His familier servauntes vertuous,
That he knewe before his Regne of Substance,
  Wele disposed, trewe, not malicious.
When he reigneth, eche man wolbe Ioyous
  To glose hym, to please hym with al circumstance:
  Harde it were to knowe than their variance.
(ed. Bateson, 1899, p. 53; Latin ed. Franceschini, 1931–1932, p. 460).

As this example shows, the criterion that Ashby used in selecting aphorisms to translate was essentially political: he chose selections that would provide useful advice for his young Prince. Thus among other sage warnings Ashby selects statements advising that rulers should avoid appearing drunk in public (#54, ed. Bateson, 1899, p. 59; Latin ed. Franceschini, 1931–1932, p. 482) and avoid a reputation for favoritism (#73, ed. Bateson, 1899, p. 65; Latin ed. Franceschini, 1931–1932, p. 477).

Passage #34, which I have just quoted, is characteristic of Ashby's work in another way as well, namely, that if he cannot find a passage in the Latin text that will serve for the lesson he wishes to teach, he makes one up himself. Thus in #34 only the first Latin sentence comes from the *Liber philosophorum*; the second, Ashby invents. Other inventions include the following two, "attributed to Plato":

57

Qualis Rex, talis populus. Cupiditates
& hominum voluntates reperiuntur iuxta
Regum cupiditates & voluntates ipsorum;
hec Plato.

Suche as the kynge is, suche bene al other,

Bothe in wille & also in couetise;
The toon may not be withoute the tother;
  For the kynge hathe the charge theim to supprise,
  That wolde surmonte, or in vices arise.
    The kyng may make his people as hym liste,
    Either evil or vertuous & iust.
(ed. Bateson, 1899, p. 60; not in Franceschini, 1931–1932).

73

Non iudices priusquam vtrosque audias contendentes; hec Plato.

In any striff, make neuer iugement
  Til ye haue herde boothe parties wisely,
Leest after ye haue cause to repente,
  For lack of Foresight and serching treuly.
  A kynges worde muste nedys stand iustly;
    Therfore in al thing be wele approved,
    That nought eschape, digne to be reproued.
(ed. Bateson, 1899, p. 65; not in Franceschini, 1931–1932).

I have described Ashby's little English poems as "paraphrase-meditations", for they are not really translations of their Latin epigraphs, or even very close paraphrases. An example is #66, where Ashby attributes to Hermes Trismegistus a statement that does not appear in the original Latin text. In the poem that elucidates this text Ashby represents Hermes as alluding to Jesus Christ, about whom Hermes (fl. 4000 B.C.) could hardly have known.

66

Qui deficit in eo quod tenetur Creatori
suo, quanto magis deficit in omnibus aliis
bonis operibus. Hec Hermes

He that lackythe for to do his duetie
  To al myghti Iesu, oure creatour,
In all tymes of his necessite,
  And displeasith ofte owre Sauiour,
Standyng owte of goddes loue & fauour,
    Must nedis lakke myche more other goode werke,
    Wytnessyng hermes, the noble, goode clerke.
(ed. Bateson, 1899, p. 63).

Of Ashby's 181 "sayings", 39 are attributed to Plato, 39 to Hermes, 24 to Socrates,

36 to Aristotle, and the remaining 43 to other authors. Since Ashby includes so many "sayings" from Plato, an English reader might have supposed himself to be learning a great deal about Plato from Ashby's book. But almost nothing in the book can be regarded as historically accurate. Quite apart from his own mistakes and inventions, most of the attributions to Plato in his source, the *Liber philosophorum*, were also inaccurate. For example, in the section on Alexander in the original *Muhtar-al-Hikam* there are many anecdotes concerning Alexander's conversations with Aristotle. The historical reason for this was that Aristotle was Alexander's tutor. In the Spanish and French translations of the *Muhtar* these anecdotes are reported correctly, but in the Latin version the translator evidently grew bored with anecdotes about Aristotle and decided to put Plato in instead, from time to time. Thus in the Latin version the name Plato is substituted for Aristotle in the following anecdote:

> Alexander the Great once asked Plato
> to define for him the proper activities
> of a good ruler. Plato replied. "Every
> night he should make plans for what is
> best for his people, and every day he
> should put those plans into effect".
> (ed. Franceschini, 1931–1932, pp. 527–528; paraphrase mine).

Errors of this kind are by no means confined to the Latin translation of the *Muhtar-al-Hikam*; they occur in all the other translations as well. One has only to compare the two fifteenth century English translations that are printed side by side by Bühler to see how much error could be introduced by different translators, even when they were working from the same version. When one multiplies this by the welter of incompetent linguists and ignorant scribes who had had a hand in the text tradition of the *Muhtar*, one realizes that Ashby was not such a fool as he seems. The degree of confusion about Plato that prevails in all the fifteenth century versions of the *Muhtar* may be seen in a statement that appears in four manuscripts of the Scrope translation. Speaking of Socrates, these manuscripts report that Socrates had a teacher named Timeus, and that Socrates himself was the author of:

> a booke he made of the perpetuite
> of the soule that is called *Plato*
> *in Thimeo*, translated out of Greek
> into Latyn tung bi Marcus Tullius.
> (ed. Bühler, 1941, p. 73n)

If these statements reflect Stephen Scrope's conception of Plato, he obviously had things badly confused: Timaeus Locris was a Pythagorean philosopher roughly contemporary with Plato; he was not a teacher of Socrates. Plato, not Socrates, wrote a dialogue on the immortality of the soul; it is called the *Phaedo*, not the *Timaeus*; Socrates wrote no books at all. Plato was the author of the *Timaeus*, not part of its title. Scrope does make one accurate point: Cicero did translate the *Timaeus* from Greek into Latin.

Caxton's version of the *Muhtar-al-Hikam*, published in 1477, inherits all of the long accumulation of errors of which Ashby and Scrope remind us, and to them adds new errors of its own. Caxton's version, called *Dicts or Saying of the Philosophers*, is an edition of an English translation by Anthony Woodville, Earl Rivers, who paid Caxton to print it. Rivers, like Scrope, made his translation from the French of Tignonville. Rivers' version is more readable, because less literal, than Scrope's, but Rivers was plainly bored by the task, and butchered the text with deletions. For example, he specifically acknowledged to Caxton that the had left out most of the letters from the Alexander section because he thought them inappropriate to the character of the rest of the book as a collection of aphorisms. His many other deletions from the text Rivers tried to cover by asking Caxton (who was an experienced translator from French) to check the translation with the French, and correct any errors (Caxton, Epilogue, Blake ed. in *Caxton's Own Prose*, 1973, pp. 73–76).

Caxton claims that he did check Rivers' translation, but the only omission that he noticed was a deletion from the section on Socrates. In the omitted passage Socrates had said some very unkind things about the female sex. Caxton explains apologetically that he cannot imagine why Rivers left out the passage, unless he feared that it might offend some of his feminine friends, or perhaps it was only that a passing breeze happened to blow away the page that Rivers was translating at that moment. In any case, continues Caxton, the reason why Socrates had such a low opinion of women was that he was "a Greke boren in a ferre contre from hens"; certainly no English woman ever had such faults as Socrates complains of (Blake ed., 1972, p. 74). In any case, for the sake of completeness Caxton thinks that the offending passage ought to be made available to readers (Blake ed., 1973, p. 76), so he has translated the passage from the French himself; but he has printed it in an appendix at the back of the book, in order not to offend his employer, Rivers, who can easily cut out those pages from his copy if he wishes. (In Blake's ed. Caxton's translation of the deleted passage appears on pp. 75–76). Caxton does not mention in his epilogue that among many other deletions, Rivers also omits from his translation several other pages from the Socrates section and several more from the Plato section (See Schofield ed. of Scrope tr., 1936, p. 33).

In the reduced form in which it appears in Caxton's edition of the *Dicts*, the Plato section occupies pp. 55–63. (My pagination refers to the 1901 facsimile ed.; Caxton's original was not only unpaginated and unfoliated, but unsigned as well, and the facsimile ed. by William Blades, 1877, provides no guidance.) Caxton's version devotes two pages (pp. 55–56) to Plato's life, stating that Plato was a pupil of Socrates, taught at Athens, travelled in Egypt, lived to the age of 61, and wrote 56 works. The errors in this account (Plato died at 81 and left 36 works) are not Caxton's; they go all the way back to the Latin version (ed. Franceschini, 1931–1932, p. 462).

The remainder of Caxton's section on Plato (pp. 56–63) consists of about 180 sayings culled by Rivers from the French version that he was following. Rivers usually ties these pieces together with the phrases, "And said", as in these examples:

And said dispraise not a litill thing,
    for or it may encresse.
(1901 ed., p. 60)

And said he that can not nor wil gouerne
    him self is not able to gouerne many other.
(1901 ed., p. 61)

And said our lorde accepteth him for noble
    that doth goode werkis, though he be
    peasible of litle wordes.
(1901 ed., p. 61)

And said haue in mynde the daye that thou shal
    be called to thy Jugement.
(1901, ed., p. 62)

The Christian character of the last two of these examples shows how little either Rivers or Caxton cared whether these quotations were authentically Platonic or not.

In addition to the section devoted specifically to Plato, Caxton's *Dicts* contain dozens of other allusions to Plato distributed as anecdotes among the sections devoted to other men. In the section on Socrates (1901 ed., pp. 40–55) Caxton reports that once, when Plato was about to go on a trip and asked Socrates for advice, Socrates replied as follows:

Don't trust anyone you know.
Don't have anything to do with anyone you don't know.
Never leave the main highway.
Never walk barefooted.
Never travel at night.
(1901 ed., p. 45; paraphrase mine).

In another anecdote in the Socrates section Caxton reports that Plato once sent a message to Socrates saying that he would sign up as a student of Socrates if Socrates could answer satisfactorily the following three questions:

1. What kind of man is the most to be pitied?
2. What makes a man's business affairs go wrong?
3. What is the best way to earn a reward from God?

To these questions Socrates gives the following answers, mixing English politics, Small-Business-Administration practicality, and Christian piety in a way quite impossible to the historical Socrates:

1. There are three kinds of men who are to be pitied:

     a. a good man under the domination of an evil one

     b. a wise man under the domination of a fool

     c. a generous man under the domination of a miser

 2. What makes business affairs go bad is:

     a. failure to heed good advice

     b. failure to use all the means at one's disposal

     c. unwillingness to commit one's personal resources

 3. God rewards those who

     a. obey him

     b. avoid sin

(1901 ed., p. 49; paraphrase mine).

It is obvious that in Caxton's mind Socrates was just as Christian as Plato.
In the section on Aristotle in Caxton's *Dicts* (1901 ed., pp. 64–76) there are still
more anecdotes about Plato; I quote only one:

> And Platon rebuked him bicause that he wrotte his sciences in bookis, to whom
> he said in excusing him, that it is a thing knowen and notified ynowe that all thoo
> that loueth science ought to do nothing that shulde cause the losse of her. And
> therfore it is good to compose and make bookis by the whiche science shalbe
> lerned, and whan our memorie shal fayle it shalbe recouered by meane of bookis.
> (1901 ed., p 66).

In this passage we hear neither Plato nor Aristotle, but Caxton himself speaking, and
speaking seriously. For the most part, however, Caxton's version of the *Dicts* is little
more than a jestbook, a collection of amusing fictional anecdotes, and the picture of
Plato that it presents is that of a clever inventor of one-liners. Few English readers
were yet in a position to suppose that there was anything wrong with that picture.

    The fact that it was the *Dicts or Sayings* rather than some other collection that became
the first commonplace-book printed in England had important consequences for the
status of Plato. In the year that Caxton printed the *Dicts* (1477) his other possible choices
among philosophical commonplace-books by Englishmen were the following:

John of Salisbury, *Policraticus* (1159)

Walter Burley, *De vita et moribus philosophorum* (1345)

John Whethamstede, *Granarium* (c. 1465)

    Caxton's preference for the *Dicts* over any of these others was based only on the
fact that the *Dicts* was available in English, whereas the others were not. But English
knowledge about Plato would have been significantly better off if Caxton had picked
almost any of the three works on this list. Salisbury, Burley, and Whethamstede all
provided much more accurate biographical and philosophical information about Plato
than did the *Dicts* (for the works by Salisbury see Jayne, 1991, pp. 637–711; for
Burley see Jayne, 1993, pp. 120–123; for Whethamstede see the discussion on pp.
22–25 above).

In 1478 Caxton printed two works by Geoffrey Chaucer: his *Canterbury Tales* and his translation of Boethius' *Consolation of Philosophy*. Geoffrey Chaucer (c. 1340–1400) was a London civil servant who wrote poetry in his spare time. Nothing in his life led him naturally to Plato. He was born into the world of affairs in London; after spending most of his youth (c. 1357 to c. 1374) as a court-functionary to three members of the royal family (Prince Lionel, King Edward III, and John of Gaunt), he was appointed Controller of Customs (1374–1386); he also served (1389–1391) as superintendent of the Royal Public Works Department. In his early years he travelled constantly, especially to France and Italy, but that was a century before the rediscovery of Plato in Italy, and there is no evidence that he learned anything more about Plato on the continent than he did in his daily London routine of watching out for corruption among customs officers, and graft among building inspectors.

The main body of Chaucer's work consists of seven long narrative poems and twenty-one short lyrics. He also made a number of translations, including part of *Le Roman de la Rose*, the whole of Boethius' *Consolation of Philosophy*, and Messahala's *Composition and Operation of the Astrolabe*. Chaucer refers to Plato twenty-one times, but in only three of his works, the *House of Fame* (c. 1375, the Boethius translation (1380), and *The Canterbury Tales* (1390). I believe that all of these allusions are based on secondary sources, and that Chaucer had never read any work of Plato (for other views see Grennen, 1984; Takada, 1944).

Chaucer's first extensive exposure to Plato may have occurred about 1368, when he translated part of the *Roman de la Rose*. Plato does not appear in the parts of the poem that Chaucer translated (ll. 1–5154 and 10679–12360), or in the part that he used later in the "Monk's Tale" (ll. 5829–6901). Plato does figure prominently in other parts of the *Roman de la Rose*, and since Chaucer is very likely to have read the entire poem, he was no doubt aware of its allusions to Plato, but we need not examine them here.

About 1380 Chaucer translated the whole of Boethius' *Consolation of Philosophy* into English. Although he obviously knew about the French translation of the same work by Jean de Meun, Chaucer had none of Jean de Meun's scholarly familiarity with the commentators on Boethius' work, writers such as Guillaume de Conches and William of Aragon (See Minnis, 1981, pp. 324, 354). Chaucer translated Boethius' work directly from Latin, and he mentions Plato only in the places where Boethius himself does so:

1. Socrates, Plato's teacher, died an innocent martyr.
   (I. pr. 3, 25–27)
2. States are happiest when ruled by philosophers.
   (I. pr. 4, 27–32)
3. Wise men should accept responsibility for ruling.
   (I. pr. 4, 33–35)
4. Men should seek God's help through prayer.

(III. pr. 9, 191–193)

5. Learning is a recollection of innate knowledge.
   (III. m. ll, 43–46, and III. pr. 12, title and ll. 1–8)
6. Names should correspond to the things they mean.
   (III. pr. 12, 205–207)
7. Only wise men deserve to do as they like.
   (IV. pr. 2, 257–259, and V. pr. 6, 95–97)
8. Plato believed the world to be coeternal with God.
   (V. pr. 6, 51–56)

These ideas Boethius derived directly from the text of Plato, as follows:

Phaedo (#1)	*Cratylus* (#6)
Republic (#2,3)	*Gorgias* (#7)
Meno (#5)	*Timaeus* (#4, 8)

(For fuller discussion of Plato in the *Consolation of Philosophy*, see Jayne, 1991, pp. 249–257). But Chaucer had no way of knowing that this was the case. The only dialogue that he appears to have heard of is the *Timaeus*, but he cannot have read that work, for he refers to it in the same incorrect way that the work is referred to in most English medieval library catalogues. Because the work was known only in Calcidius' translation, which was accompanied by a commentary, it was commonly catalogued as if it were only a commentary, "Plato's *In Thimeo*". This is the title that Chaucer uses as well; in the one place where he refers to it, he says:

> . . . it liketh to my disciple Plato in his book of *In Thymeo* that in ryht litel thynges men schulde byseche the help of God.
> (Bothius tr. III. pr. 9, 189–192).

The *Timaeus* passage referred to is 27C, but Chaucer mentions the *Timaeus* only because Boethius does.

As a footnote to Caxton's edition of Boethius I should point out that Caxton need not have reached all the way back to Chaucer for an English translation of that work. A much more scholarly English translation of Beothius had been written in 1410 by John Walton, at the Augustinian Abbey of Osney, in Oxfordshire. Caxton probably did not know about Walton's translation, which was not published until 1525, and even then printed only in a monastery at Tavistock. Like Chaucer, Walton mentions Plato only in the places where Boethius mentions him. Caxton's ignorance of Walton was therefore inconsequential so far as the history of Plato is concerned (on Walton's version see Minnis, 1981, pp. 343–347).

About 1390 Chaucer completed his masterpiece, *The Canterbury Tales*. In this work, too, his allusions to Plato show that he was entirely dependent for his knowledge of Plato on secondary sources. In the General Prologue to *The Canterbury Tales* Chaucer repeats a commonplace that he had found in Boethius, that Plato thought that names should correspond with their referents:

Eek Plato seith, whoso kan hym rede,
The wordes moote be cosyn to the dede.
(*CT*. Gen. Prol. ll. 741–742).

Chaucer repeats the same commonplace in the "Manciple's Tale",

The wise Plato seith, as ye may rede,
The work moot nede accorde with the dede.
(*CT*, Manc. Tale, ll. 207–208).

The remaining allusion to Plato in *The Canterbury Tales* is more interesting; it occupies a whole sub-narrative of the "Canon's Yeoman's Tale". The yeoman, it will be remembered, devotes his turn as story-teller to exposing the frauds of his former employer, an alchemist. Toward the end (ll. 1448–1471) the yeoman tells a story about an alchemist named Plato, whose student once asked him to reveal the secret of the philosopher's stone:

Also ther was a disciple of Plato,
That on a tyme seyde his maister to,
As his book Senior wol here witnesse,
And this was his demande in soothfastnesse:
"Telle me the name of the privee stone".
(*CT*. Can. Yeo. Tale, ll. 1448–1452).

Plato then explains that the name of the stone is "Magnasia" (l. 1455). "What is that?" asks the student, and Plato replies, "a kind of water that is made of all four elements" (ll. 1459–1460). The student then naturally asks, "Where can I find that kind of water?" But Plato replies, "I won't tell you. All philosophers are sworn not to reveal that to anyone, and it is not written down in any book, because Christ does not want it known":

"Nay, nay" quod Plato, "certein, that I nyl.
The philosophres sworn were everychoon
That they sholden discovere it unto noon,
Ne in no book it write in no manere.
For unto Crist it is so lief and deere
That he wol not that it discovered bee. . ."
(*CT*, Can. Yeo. Tale, ll. 1463–1468).

Chaucer took this story from an alchemical work call *Senior's Chemical Table* (*Senioris Zadith Tabula chemica*: see Ruska, 1937), where the story is told of Solomon, not Plato. Chaucer's selection of the name Plato suggests that he may have known of a work called *Plato's summa alchemiae* (see Appendix 1, 85).

It seems hard to imagine today that a man as well-read as Chaucer could have thought that Plato was an alchemist, but he probably did. To most medieval Englishmen Plato was a "philosopher", but only in the medieval sense of that term, which meant essentially "scientist". Since science included alchemy, magic, astrology, and medicine, as well as cosmology, astronomy, and other studies of the physical world, it was natural for a medieval Englishman to suppose that the same author who wrote a treatise on cosmology (the *In thymeo*) could have written others on alchemy and medicine as well (Curry, 1960).

Chaucer's conception of Plato as having been a scientist of some sort, with special expertise in astrology and alchemy, was probably the commonest view of Plato among educated laymen in England between the twelfth and sixteenth centuries. Evidence of Plato's association with astrology may be seen in an English manuscript of the early fifteenth century which begins:

> Here begynneth the art of Ptholome,
> Plato, and Pictagore.
> (Oxford, Bodl. MS Ashmole 396, fol. 200^r).

The manuscript is a collection of notes on astrological matters. Plato's association with alchemy may be seen in another English manuscript of about the same period containing a number of tracts on alchemy; one of these tracts is entitled:

> *Compendium of Alchemy from Plato's Book*
> *On the Four, that is, the Four Elements.*
> (Oxford, Bodl. MS Ashmole 1416, item 36, fols. 109–113).

The passage in the *Timaeus* where Plato discusses the four elements is 48B–51D (Calcidius tr., 1975; Waszink ed., pp. 45–49). In the same alchemical manuscript with the *Compendium of Alchemy* is a brief "saying" in which Socrates is represented as explaining to Plato the fact that sulphuric acid is a powerful solvent (Oxford, Bodl. MS Ashmole 1416, item 57, fols. 147–148).

Chaucer's *House of Fame* is a long narrative poem written about 1375. In this poem Chaucer cites Plato twice, in both cases as an authority on scientific matters. In the first instance Chaucer reports that all scientists agree that everything seeks its natural place in the world:

> Loo, this sentence ys knowen kouth
> Of every philosophres mouth,
> As Aristotle and daun Platon,
> And other cleryks many oon.
> (*HF*, ll. 757–760).

In the second passage Chaucer explains that just as water and earth are inhabited by various creatures, so the element of air is also:

> Of which that speketh Daun Plato
> (*HF*, l. 931)

Some modern scholars (e.g. Grennen) have concluded from these allusions that

Chaucer must have read the *Timaeus*, but I think that very unlikely. The first of these allusions Chaucer probably took from Augustine's *Confessions*, XIII. 9, and the second from Augustine's *City of God*, VIII. 15.

In 1482 Caxton printed one of the great reference works of the English Middle Ages, the *Polychronicon* of Ranulf Higden. Higden (d. 1364) was a Benedictine at the Abbey of St. Werbrugh in Chester (Taylor, 1966). Writing in the late 1320's for his fellow monks, sequestered in that far corner of England, Higden set out to explain what the outside world was like, not merely in his own day, but throughout all time since the Creation, and not merely in England, but throughout the globe. The naiveté of Higden's project may best be appreciated by realizing that he had never set foot outside of Chester himself; the lighthouse beam of revelation that he proposed to throw upon the outside world was powered only by a few encyclopedias that happened to be in the Abbey library. Yet Higden's book enjoyed a phenomenal popularity: the entire seven books were translated into English in 1387, and again in the fifteenth century, and the work was printed in England in both the fifteenth and sixteenth centuries. The key to Higden's success was that he was a born entertainer: his book is composed primarily of gossipy anecdotes about famous people of history.

Higden's work has seven "Books" because, as he modestly explains, the Creation of the world took seven days. Book I describes the geography of the globe. Book II covers roughly the first five of the traditional six ages of the history of the world, that is, from the Creation to classical times. Books III-V cover the period of Greek and Roman antiquity, and Books VI and VII are on England.

In accordance with this plan, Higden's discussion of Plato falls in Book III (ch. 23). This chapter, grandly entitled "On the Life and Opinions of the Philosopher Plato", is relatively long (vol. III, pp. 340–359 in the Rolls Series ed., 1871). Its biographical anecdotes, such as the stories of the bees, the swan, and the fishermen (III, 350–353), show that it has been lifted almost entirely from John of Wales' *Compendiloquium* (see Jayne, 1993, pp. 104–107). Higden does not acknowledge John of Wales as his source; he merely cites as his own the sources that John cites, including John of Salisbury's *Policraticus*, Valerius Maximus, and Salisbury's mythical Flavianus (*De vestigiis et dogmatibus philosophorum*). Thus even when Higden points out that Augustine respected Plato (in *City* Book XVI, ch. 20 and *Conf.* Book VII), because Plato held so many views in keeping with the prophets and with the Gospel of St. John, Higden is merely following John of Wales.

In addition to the chapter that he devotes entirely to Plato, Higden also cites or quotes Plato frequently elsewhere in Books II, III, and IV of his work. In the prologue to Book II (II. 181) he mentions that Plato says that men follow the habits and manners of the animals that they resemble. In ch. 9 of Book II (II. 280–281), Higden reports that Plato says in the *Philosopher* (i.e. the *Epinomis*) that many poets have been seduced by the desire for money and power to put their special talents to wicked uses; Higden correctly gives as his source for this reference Isidore, *Etymologiae*, Book 8.

In chapter 18 of Book II (II. 374–375). Higden says that Plato wrote the myth of Er (*Republic* XIII) to show the immortality of the soul. In chapter 33 of Book II, on the seven liberal arts, Higden mentions Plato twice, saying that Plato was a student of Socrates (III. 64–65), and that it was Plato who first divided the field of science into the four subjects of arithmetic, geometry, music and astronomy (III. 62–63). In Book III, chapter 12, "On the Other Philosophers", Higden says that the followers of Plato were called "Platonists" (III. 214–215), that Plato established his school in a ruined villa called Academia, near Athens (III. pp. 216–217)); that, just as Thales specialized in science, so Socrates specialized in Ethics, and Plato in Logic (III. 218–219); that Plato's philosophy is said to have been the most perfect of all (III. 218–219; based on Isidore 8.6); and that Plato said that God combines being, intellect, and life (III. 220–221). This last idea had been made familiar to the Middle Ages by the *Divine Names* of Pseudo Dionysius, but Higden probably took his reference from John of Salisbury's *Policraticus*. In chapter 16 of Book III "On the Law of the 12 Fables", Higden says that the art of Logic, according to Boethius, was founded by the god Pan, but systematized by Plato (III. 250–251). Higden devotes a long section to Socrates (Book III, ch. 18, pp. 275–387), including (III. 274–275) the information that Socrates was the teacher of Plato, and that Calcidius says, in his commentary on the *Timaeus*, that Socrates had a daemon (III. 276–277); that Plato's students envied him (III. 288–289); and that Plato was the best of Socrates' many students (III. 290–291). In Book III chapter 41, on Caesar's war with Pompey, Higden tells us that when Marcus Porcius Cato heard of the death of Pompey, he read Plato's *Phaedo*, and having learned from that book that his soul was immortal, committed suicide, in spite of the protestation of his friends (IV. 200–210). In Chapter 28 of Book IV, "On Julian the Apostate" Higden reports that in the war against the Persians Julian had to kill the King of Ctesiphon because that king refused to surrender, thinking that he was invincible because the soul of Alexander the Great had transmigrated into him, "according to the opinion of Pythagoras and Plato". (V. 174–175).

The printing of the gigantic *Polychronicon* must have involved   assembling an exceptionally large staff, and the need to keep that staff busy may explain why in the following year (1483) Caxton printed two encyclopedias, and Gower's enormous *Confessio   amantis*. The least ambitious of these three works was an anonymous English poem of 340 rhyme royal stanzas, called *The Court of Sapience* (for date of printing see ed. Harvey, 1984, p. xiv). In this poem Plato first appears in a passage in which the poet is trying to explain that Philosophy may be divided into three fields: Physics, Ethics, and Logic:

229

Millesius, one of the sages sevene,

In Grece fyrst drewe, as in the craft of kynde,
By his reason the causes of the hevene,
And of eche thyng the nature gan he fynde;
Than come Plato, a worthy clerke of kynde;
For natural art sought oute geomatrye,
Arsemetryk, musyk, and astronomye.

230

Dame Ethyca, pryncesse of polycye,
Good Socrates fyrst founde for governaunce,
To knowe vertu and conne lyve honestly;
And four ladyes he sought, ful of pleasaunce,
To serve Dame Ethyke with obeysaunce,
Whoos names ben Prudence and Ryghtwysenes,
Dame Fortitude and Temporaunce I gesse.

231

Than fond Plato the lady Racyonal,
Whiche, whan that kynd and vertu knowen bene,
Techeth eche man by reson specyal
To understonde the subtyl strengthe and clene
Of kynd and vertu, what they wold and mene.
Than sought he oute Dame Dyalectyca
To serven her with Dame Rhetorica.
(ll. 1597–1617, 1480 ed., sigs. dl^v–d2^r, ed. Harvey, 1984, pp. 54–55).

The *Court of Sapience* was written between 1430 and 1460 (ed. Harvey, 1984, p. xxiv), but the substance of this passage is much earlier, for it derives from Chapter II. xxiv of the *Etymologiae* of Isidore, who in turn is merely echoing Augustine, *City of God*, VIII.3, where the point made is that the founders of the respective branches of Philosophy were as follows:

Physics	Pre-Socratics
Ethics	Socrates
Logic	Plato

In the *Court of Sapience* the founder of Physics is said to have been Millesius, but the poet is not really sure about Plato, for a few lines further on, he notices a group of Natural Scientists sitting in the "goodly parlor" of Dame Science, and he includes Plato in this group as well:

240

Arystotyl, Averous, Avycenne,
Good Algazel, Galyene, Apollynus,
Pyctagoras, and Plato with his penne,

Macrobius, Cato, Boecius,
Rasius, Isake, Calyxte, Orbasius,
Salustius, Theophyl, Ypocras--
With many mo whoos names I lete pas.
(ll. 1674–1680, 1480 ed., sig, d3ʳ, ed. Harvey, 1984, p. 57).

The other encyclopedia that Caxton printed in 1483 had a much longer history; it was an old medieval work that Caxton had found in a French prose text, and which he had translated into English under the title *The Mirrour of the World*, in 1480.

The original work from which Caxton's *Mirrour of the World* derives was a Latin encyclopedia called *Imago mundi*, written about 1110 by an Englishman who wrote under the pseudonym Honorius (c. 1090–c.1156), (on Honorius see Garrigues, 1983; modern ed. of *Imago mundi* by Flint, 1983). The *Imago mundi* was an attempt to modernize Bede's *De natura rerum*, using as supplementary materials Isidore's *Etymologiae*, and Pliny's *Natural History* (see Jayne, 1991. pp. 345–353). Honorius' own work is organized in three books:

Book I   The World
             A. Geography
             B. Meteorology
             C. Astronomy
Book II   Time
Book III   Human History (a chronology)

Honorius mentions Plato only twice in the *Imago mundi*; one is a reference to Atlantis:

Among the Hesperides islands was that huge island larger in size than Africa and Europe, which, according to Plato, sank into the ocean. . .
(Book I, ch. 36; ed. Flint, 1983, p. 66; tr. mine).

Plato's allusion to Atlantis occurs in *Timaeus* 24E, but Honorius took his reference from Pliny (Rackham tr., 1938–1963, vol. 1, pp. 334–337). The other reference to Plato occurs in a chronology of world history that he transcribed from Isidore's *Etymologiae*, V.39.20 (ed. Lindsay, 1911):

Fifth Age
Reign of the Babylonians
. . . The Seven Sages. . .
Reign of the Persians
. . . Pythagoras . . . Socrates . . . Plato . . . Aristotle . . .
Reign of Alexander the Great
(Book III, ed. Flint, 1983, pp. 137–138; tr. mine).

Honorius' *Imago mundi* was widely used, both in Latin and in several vernacular translations. One of the latter was a translation into French verse written about 1246 by Gossuin of Metz. Gossuin retained Honorius's title, calling his work *L'image du monde*, but the work itself he drastically modified.

Of Honorius' original work Gossuin uses only the geographical and astronomical material from Book I. To this he prefaces a long section on the Creation and the nature of Man, and adds at the end a section on the study of Philosophy. Even the material that he retains from Honorius, Gossuin greatly alters, adding new material from several other works, especially Ptolemy's *Almagest* and Nequam's *De naturis rerum*. Gossuin took the trouble to write his work twice, first in French verse, and then over again in French prose (see Prior ed., 1987). Toward the end of the fifteenth century the prose version was rewritten in dialogue form under the title *Livre des secrets aux philosophes* (Klibansky, 1981, p. 63).

The work that Caxton printed in 1483 under the title *Mirrour of the World* (STC 24762) was an English translation, by Caxton himself, of the French prose version of Gossuin. Caxton's translation greatly inflates Gossuin's text throughout, but the allusions to Plato in Caxton's version are all from Gossuin's text. One of Gossuin's allusions he had taken from Honorius; this was the allusion to Atlantis, but in Caxton's florid prose the reference is barely recognizable:

> Another yle is in this contre so grete as the wyse Plato witnesseth the whiche in his tyme was a clercke of right grete renomee, whiche hath more of pourpris and space than alle Europe and Affryke conteynen. But sith the tyme of Plato it was in suche wyse destroyed and broken, lyke as it plesid our lord, that it sanke down in to Abisme for the grete synnes that they commysed that were dwellars and inhabitauns therein.
>
> (*Mirrour of the World*, Part II. ch. 13; 1483 ed. sig. gii^v–giii^r; ed. Prior, 1966, pp. 95–96; from Gossuin, ed. Prior, 1966, pp. 131–132).

In addition to this passage about Plato, carried over from Honorius, Gossuin had added five new passages about Plato. The first occurs in Part I, chapter 14 on the Creation:

> And first of alle saith Plato, which was a man of grete renommee, that nature is an ouer puissance or myght in thinges that she maketh to growe lyke by lyke after that that euerych may bee. And this may be vnder-standed by one man that engendreth another, and by bestes, by plantes and by seedes the whiche after their semblaunces growe, and after their facion. And lo this is that that the wise Platon saith whiche was a grete clerke.
>
> After hym saith Aristotle, that this was a yefte comen fro the hye prynce, whan he gaf vertu to the firmament and to the sterres for to meue and to be and that without God suche power ne myght not be gyuen, as the thynges that have power to remeue, to bee and to meue. Aristotle that saith this studyed in many a book treatyng of nature. Many other philosophres ther were that said that nature proceded of vertues of hete which causeth alle thinges to growe and nourisshe. But for this present tyme I passe ouer for to speke of other matere. Tho philosophres ensieweth better Plato than Aristotle; thus said they that them semeth.

(*Mirrour of the World*, Part I, ch. 14; 1483 ed. sig. dii^v–diii^r; ed. Prior, 1966, pp. 46–47; from Gossuin, ed. Prior, 1966, pp. 88–89).

The passage attributed (in the first sentence) to Plato, is actually in the *Asclepius* of Hermes Trismegistus (sect. 4; Copenhaver tr., 1992, pp. 68–69).

The next allusion occurs in Part III, chapter 10, where Gossuin lists as the great students of the seven liberal arts after Noah: Shem, Abraham, Plato, Aristotle, Boethius, and Vergil. The great glory of Plato, according to Gossuin, is that he recognized that God is the Creator, and is a Trinity of Father, Son, and Holy Ghost, with attributes of power, wisdom, and goodness:

> And after cam Plato the sage and right souerayn in philosophye, and his clerke named Aristotle the wyse clerke. This Plato was the man aboue al them of the world in clergye the most experte of them that were to fore or after hym. He preuyd first that ther was but one that was only souerayn, whiche all made & of whom alle good thinge cometh; yet his bookes approue hyely that ther ne is but one souerayn good, that is our lord God whiche made alle thynges. And in this only veryte he preuyd the right trouthe; ffor he preued his power, his wisedom and his goodnes. Thise thre bountees reclayme alle crysten men, that is the fader, the sone, and the holy goste. Of the fader he sayde the power and puissance; of the sone, the Sapyence; and of the holy gost, the bienueullaunce. And Aristotle, whiche cam after hym, holdeth plente of thynges nyghe to hym, & knewe the thynges that he had sayd, and ordeyned right wel the science of logyke, ffor he knewe more therof than of other sciences. Thise two notable clerkes fonde by their wysedom and connyng thre persones in one essence, and preuyd it; but they put it not in latyn, ffor bothe two were paynems, as they that were more than thre hondred yere to fore the comynge of our lord Jhesu Cryste. And alle their bookes were in grekyssh lettres.
> (*Mirrour of the World*, Part III, ch. 12; 1483 ed. sig. liii^{r-v}; ed., Prior, 1966, pp. 156–157; from Gossuin, ed. Prior, 1966, pp. 182–183).

After praising Vergil's knowledge of astronomy at some length, Gossuin then turns to the importance of travel, and cites Plato as a famous example:

> The philosophres, that wel coude vnderstonde this world, had moche leuer to suffre trauaylles and mesayses for to lerne than tendende to worldly honours; ffor they helde for more dere and worthy the sciences and the clergyes than alle the seygnouryes of the world.
> Plato, whiche was a puissaunt and a recommended maistre of Athenes, left his noble estate and his place, by cause he wolde of suche renommee lyue, that he serched many londes and contrees. And had leuer haue payne, mesayse and trauayll for tenserche trouthe and for to lerne science, than for to haue seygnourie and domynacion in the world, ne renommee for to be maister; ffor he wold saye nothyng but yf he were certayn therof, ffor ony vayne glorye of the world.

(*Mirror of the World*, Part III, ch. 15; 1483 ed. sig. lvii^v; ed. Prior, 1966, p. 164; from Gossuin, ed. Prior, 1966, p. 188).

Gossuin may have taken this reference from Macrobius' *Commentary on Scipio's Dream*, but the allusion to Plato's travels to Egypt was a commonplace, from St. Augustine onward.

The fourth passage about Plato occurs in Part III, chapter 16, beginning with the title:

> What thynge is philosophye and of thanswer that Plato made thereof. Veray Philosophye is to haue knowlech, of god and fyn loue of sapyence, and to knowe the secretes and ordinaunces of dyuyne thynges and of humayne ffor to knowe god and his power, and what a man ought to be so that he myght conduyte hym that it myght be to god agreable. Who that wel knewe god and his mysteryes, he shold wel conne entierly philosophye.
>
> Alle they ben good philosophres that of them self haue knowleche. Of whom Plato answerd to somme that demanded hym in commun, and sayd to hym that he had lerned ynowh and neded nomore, ffor he had estudyed alle his time for to lerne; and it was sayd to hym: "Maystre, it is wel in yow for to saye to vs somme good worde procedyng of hye entendement, as ye haue don other tymes." Thenne Plato, how wel that he was the most experymented of all other, answerd sayeng, as in his herte troubled, that he had nomore lerned sauf as moche as he that felt hym self lyke vnto a vessel that day and nyght is all voyde & empty. Thus moche answerd Plato and nomore, how wel he was at that tyme the most grete clerke that was knowen in alle the world, and of moche perfounde science.
>
> (*Mirrour of the World* Part III, ch. 16; 1483 ed. sig. mi^r; ed. Prior, 1966, pp. 166–167; from Gossuin, ed. Prior, 1966, 59, 190).

The *Mirrour* closes with a recapitulation which includes a repetition of the author's praise of Vergil and Plato as authorities on science:

> In the thirde partye ye haue herde how the day & nyght come; and of the mone & of the sonne, how they rendre their lyght, and how eche of them leseth their clerenes by nyght & by day somtyme, & of the Eclipses that thenne happe, wherby the day bycometh derke; and of the grete eclypse that fylle atte the deth of our lord Jhesu Cryste, by whiche saynt Dionys was after ward conuerted; & of the vertue of the firmament & of the sterres, & how the world was mesured, & the heuen & therthe; of the kynge Tholomeus & of his prudence; of Adam & of somme other; and how clergye & the vii sciences were kepte ayenst the flood, and how all this was founden agayn after the flood; and of the merueylles that Virgyle made by his wytte & clergye; and for what cause moneye was so named & establisshed; and of the philosophres that wente thurgh the world for to lerne; what thinge is philosophye & what Plato answerde therto; how moche the erthe, the mone & the sonne haue of gretenes, euerych of hym self; & the stages of the

sterres, of their nombre, & of their ymages; the heyght & gretenes of the firma-
ment, & of the blew heuen whiche is aboue that; & of the heuene crystalyn, & of
the heuen Imperial.
(*Mirrour of the World*, Part III, ch. 24; 1483 ed. sig. nii^v; ed. Prior, 1966, pp.
182–183; from Gossuin, ed. Prior, 1966, pp. 202–203).

Caxton's last pre-Tudor book was the *Confessio amantis* of Gower, printed in 1483.
John Gower (c.1330–1408) was a London civil servant (Fisher, 1964).
In his spare time he wrote thousands and thousands of lines of insufferable verse, in
three different languages, Latin, French, and English. In his Latin poems he does not
mention Plato. In his major French poem, *the Mirrour de l'omme*, (c.1381), Gower
invokes the authority of Plato twice, in both cases ignoring the facts, in favor of the
relentless didacticism that led Chaucer to call his friend "Moral Gower":

> Plato tells us plainly
> That virtue requires
> Each according to his rank
> By rule and governance
> To live properly
> Toward God and man.
> (11. 15205–15210; Macaulay ed. *Complete Works*, vol. 1, The French Works, p.
> 176; tr. mine)

and again:

> Prudence applies to all,
> Word, deed, and thought.
> As Plato says, the wise man
> Follows the straight line
> Of reason, never doing anything
> Contrary to God's will.
> (11. 15235–15240; Macaulay ed. *Complete Works*, 1899–1902, vol. 1, The French
> Works, p. 177; tr. mine).

Elsewhere in the poem Gower also refers to Socrates and his scolding wife (11.
4168–4176; Macaulay ed. *Complete Works*, 1899–1902, vol. 1, The French Works,
p. 51).

The work of Gower that Caxton chose to print in 1483 was naturally one of Gower's
English works, the *Confessio amantis* (first version, completed in 1390; see Fisher,
1964, p. 116). This work is a verse anthology of stories illustrating the Seven Deadly
Sins. The Latin title derives from the frame–device: the stories are told by a lover
who is confessing his sins to a priest. The priest, however, is a priest of Venus, not of
Christ. A work with this kind of design did not naturally invite attention to Plato, and
in the whole 34,000 lines of the poem Plato is referred to only twice. The first allusion occurs in a passage about Ulysses. To our surprise, Gower reports that Ulysses

was as learned in Rhetoric as Cicero, and in Philosophy as Plato (Book VII, 1. 1404; Macaulay ed. *Complete Works*, 1899–1902, vol. 3, p. 205). Even more surprising is the narrator's second allusion, in the following book, where he says that among the famous lovers of the world, along with Tristan, Cleopatra, and Penelope, were "Sortes and Plato" (Book VIIII, 1. 2718; Macaulay ed. *Complete Works*, 1899–1902, vol. 3, p. 460). The name Sortes (originally a mis-transcription of the name Socrates) was conventionally used in paradigms in the study of Logic (see Pflaum, 1931).

Important though Caxton was to the history of printing, his influence on knowledge about Plato was entirely regressive. Because of his insistence on printing works in the English language, he inadvertently perpetuated the medieval conception of Plato rather than the new one that was coming in from the continent. Thus so far as most Englishmen were concerned, Plato remained merely a legend; the numerous seeds from the Chrysoloras revival of Plato fell on stony ground in England, and the promising pre-Tudor revival of Plato came to nothing.

PART II

THE TUDOR PHASE (1485–1603)

CHAPTER 4

THE PLETHO REVIVAL OF PLATO IN ITALY

A. In Rome (1439–1487)

The second major movement toward the revival of Plato in Italy was the work of another Greek visitor, Giorgios Gemisthos Pletho, a monk from the monastery of Mistra in the Greek Peloponessus (on Pletho see Masai, 1954, 1956). Pletho came to Florence in 1439 as a delegate to the Church Council that convened at Florence in that year. That Council had been called for the great purpose of trying to reconcile the Eastern and Western branches of the Church, but the practical business of the Council involved trying to reach compromise on small technical differences such as the *filioque* clause in the Creed, and the date of Easter (Gill, 1965). The Council had originally convened at Basle (April, 1437), but had subsequently moved to Ferrara, and from there, in January, 1439, to Florence. The Council wound up its business by issuing the Decree of Union in June, 1439. Pletho then returned to Mistra, but during his six months in Florence he had had a dramatic effect on the revival of Plato in Italy. So far as England was to be concerned, the most important influence of Pletho was his impact on the Medici family in Florence, but Pletho also had a powerful impact on some of his colleagues among the Greek clerics in Rome, and we must examine that episode before we move on to the Medici phase of Pletho's influence.

Not all of the delegates to the Council of 1439 were centrally involved in the inner circles where the actual business of the Council was transacted. The minor Greek Delegates naturally congregated to themselves because of the fact that they were foreign visitors in a country where the spoken language was Italian. In order to amuse themselves, some of these Greek clerics debated with each other on a topic that they had been debating in Greece before they came, namely, the relative superiority of Plato to Aristotle. The clerics who favored Plato opposed reunification, whereas the clerics who favored Aristotle favored reunification, but the Plato-Aristotle debate in Italy really had nothing to do with the problem of Church organization. The terms of the debate were set by Pletho, who contended that Plato was superior to Aristotle. Pletho believed that he could show that Plato's theology was a universal theology that had been held by every important ancient culture. As a way of presenting these views to his colleagues, Pletho gave a series of lectures in Greek; he then condensed these lectures into a Greek tract that is now known by its Latin title, *De differentiis Platonis et Aristotelis*. This tract was answered in 1444 by Giorgios

Scholaris, in a counter-tract favoring Aristotle. A counter-tract favoring Plato was then written in 1449 by Theodore of Gaza, and in turn was answered by a tract favoring Aristotle, written by George of Trebizond in 1450. In 1457 George of Trebizond wrote another, more vicious tract attacking Plato, and this was answered in 1459 by Cardinal Giovanni Bessarion. Thus Pletho's initial salvo caused a whole tract-war, in which all of the participants were Greek clerics, and most of the tracts were written in Greek. Eventually the debate also produced Latin translations of several dialogues of Plato and two important treatises written in Latin for Italian readers, and involved major figures in Spain and Germany as well. (The episode has been studied in detail by a number of scholars; see especially Monfasani, 1976, 1984; Hankins, 1990, pp. 163–263; Mohler, 1923–1942; Cammelli, 1941–1954; Masai, 1956; and Purnell, 1971).

Among the participants in this debate we need to discuss in detail only Pletho, Trebizond, and Bessarion. In the *De differentiis Platonis et Aristotelis*, Pletho compares Plato with Aristotle on twenty specific issues, of which the following are the most important:

Table 5. Plato in Pletho

Issue	Plato	Aristotle
1. God as creator	God is creator	God is first mover
2. God	God exercises providence	God is not providentiary
3. Being	one kind only	ten kinds
4. Genus and species	prior to individuals	secondary to individuals
5. Matter	one part of universe	throughout universe
10. History of soul	pre-exists in heaven; descends into body	exists only in body
11. Immortality	soul is immortal	soul is mortal
12. Virtue	abstract qualities	mean between extremes
13. Summun bonum	knowledge of good	pleasure of contemplation
14. Heavens	made of fire	made of quintessence
17. Art	two kinds, divine and human	art is imitation of nature
18. Determinism	soul has free will	all effects are determined by causes
20. Ideas	separate existence	exist only in particulars

(PG 160: cols. 889–934).

Pletho's point in the treatise is that in every case Plato's position is the main-line position taken in the universal Theology found in all major cultures, whereas Aristotle's position is deviant and eccentric (on Pletho see also Hankins, 1990, pp. 193–217, 436–400).

The treatise that George of Trebizond published in 1458 in Latin under the title *Comparatio Platonis et Aristotelis* is a long and vitriolic attack on Plato, excoriating him on three main charges. In Book I Trebizond criticizes Plato on the ground of method: Plato is ignorant, interested only in words, not things, weak in mathematics, inconsistent, unsystematic, and irresponsible; worst of all, he relies on fiction rather than on reason to make his points. Aristotle, on the other hand, is logical, learned, well-versed in mathematics, and systematic; he presents a consistent and comprehensive system in a responsible and philosophical way. In Book II Trebizond turns to Plato's Theology; the inferiority of Plato's views as compared to those of Aristotle may be seen in the following opinions:

> Plato believes in many gods rather than in one God only.
> Plato believes that the world was created by an intermediate creature, not directly by the will of God.
> Plato believes that the world was created not *ex nihilo*, but as a part of the nature of God.
> Plato speaks about the faculties of the soul only figuratively.
> Plato does not believe that the active-passive distinction applies to the soul as well as to the body.
> Plato believes that individuation occurs among disembodied forms rather than only among individual physical objects.
> Plato believes in the pre-existence of the soul.
> Plato does not believe in divine Providence.
> (1523 ed. sigs. a3ʳ–4ᵛ; tr. mine).

Waxing to his theme, Trebizond devotes the third book of his treatise to attacking Plato's personal life. He begins by painting a lurid picture of the homosexuality of Plato and Socrates, as shown in the *Phaedrus* and the *Symposium*. Plato's sexual promiscuity is then further demonstrated by his advocacy (in the *Republic*) of treating women as common property. Plato was also guilty of the sins of envy, pride, and levity. His political writings have already ruined Greece and may ruin the West:

> Read him! Read him yourself, if you don't believe those who have read him! . .
> Read the book that is entitled *On Desire* (i.e. the *Symposium*). It is a creation of the Devil; it dares to describe the blessed life as a life in which some god has melted lover and beloved into one person. What can I say? Whom can I call on? Who will be my witness? Platonic love is pure lust, base, and wicked. Imagine; here is a man in the arms of his boy-lover, and they call him the prince of philosophers! They admire him, and seek him out. They praise him to the stars. Why? Can you think of any reason other than that they, too are involved in this wicked love? Certainly not.
> (1523 ed. sigs. N5ʳ⁻ᵛ; tr. mine).

Not content with these charges, Trebizond goes on to try to blacken Plato's reputation further by identifying Platonism with Epicureanism, on the ground that Plato emphasizes the belief that desire is a good thing:

There were two monsters who were Plato's closest disciples, Epicurus and Mohamet. . . Epicurus thought that pleasure was the *summum bonum* for man, but by pleasure he meant only erotic pleasures of the flesh. Epicurus' ideas are so wicked that they are not even found in his own writings, but are reported only in the writings of others (i.e. Lucretius). . . Epicurus' sect, which was very large, was obviously as much devoted to boy-love as Plato's was, but the Epicureans were accustomed to saying that pleasure was dearer to them than it was to the Platonists because Plato concealed rather than revealed his love. But just as the pleasures of the flesh were desirable to the Epicureans, so Plato, too, did not hesitate to cast his gaze on nude bodies, in order that he might enjoy the body as well as the soul. Just as the root is more important than the branch, so is Platonism more reprehensible than Epicureanism.

(1523 ed. sigs. T6^r-v^; tr. mine).

Plato is not merely reprehensible, however; he is a threat to world civilization. The immediacy of that threat may be seen in the work of Pletho in Florence, and if we are not careful, a fourth Plato will appear among us, with his dangerous creed of "trust your desires" (1523 ed. sigs. T3^v^–X2^v^; paraphrase by Monfasani, 1976, pp. 158–159; on Trebizond see also Hankins, 1990, pp. 163–208).

The vicious tone of Trebizond's treatise immediately (1459) provoked Cardinal Giovanni Bessarion of Nicaea (c.1395–1472) into writing a rejoinder in Greek, called in Latin *In calumniatorem Platonis*. On reflection, however, Bessarion realized that in order to counter Trebizond's charges adequately he would have to translate his work into Latin, so he employed a young clerk at the Curia, Niccolò Perotti, to translate it for him (Monfasani, *Rinasc.* 1981, and *RPL*. 1981). By the time the work finally appeared in print, ten years had passed: it was not published until 1469.

Bessarion organizes his reply in three main sections, corresponding to Trebizond's. In the first he defends Plato's rhetoric and logic, his knowledge of the natural sciences, and his mathematical skills. In the second he takes up Trebizond's criticism of Plato's Theology, answering them as follows:

Plato did believe in the unity of God, as is shown in the *Parmenides*. Plato also believes in the Trinity; the seventh letter shows that what Plato calls God, the Angelic Mind, and the World Soul is the Trinity.
Plato believes that the world was created (as in Genesis); whereas Aristotle believes that the world is eternal.
Plato believes in the immortality of the soul.
Plato believes in providence and free will; he distinguishes between intelligibles and sensibles; sensibles are governed by necessity; intelligibles, by free will.
Plato believes that the four elements can be described mathematically.

Turning to the last of Trebizond's charges, those against Plato's moral character, Bessarion says that Trebizond's charge is naive because it attributes to Plato the opinions of the speakers in the dialogues, whereas in the *Laws* Plato specifically provides ordinances against pederasty. Plato recognizes the existence in men of both earthly and heavenly love; this recognition he shares with such unexceptionable authorities as Solomon and Dionysius the Areopagite. Bessarion's work is an impressive defense of the classical view of Plato's life and thought (on Bessarion see also Hankins, 1990, pp. 208–263, 441–444).

Far from expediting the revival of Plato, the debate among the Greek clerics greatly delayed it. For one thing the debate itself did not settle one way or the other the superiority of Plato or Aristotle. More seriously, because most of the tracts involved were written in Greek, the debate did not much engage anyone except the combatants themselves. Most crucially, because the debate was centered at Rome and involved important members of the Church hierarchy (Bessarion was not only a Cardinal, but also papal secretary to Nicholas V), the debate placed the question of Plato's legitimacy under the direct scrutiny of the Church. The glare of that arena caused Bessarion to delay for 10 years his reply to George of Trebizond, and Bessarion's tract in turn caused Ficino to delay for 15 more years the publication of his translation of the *Opera* of Plato.

Even so, the debate among the Greek clerics did generate some new interest in Plato, including Latin translations of at least 6 dialogues:

Gorgias (1446)	Theodore of Gaza
Laws (1451)	George of Trebizond
Epinomis (1451)	George of Trebizond
Parmenides (1459)	George of Trebizond
Alcibiades II (1467)	Niccolò Perotti (clerk of Bessarion)
Axiochus (1475)	Rudolf Agricola (student of Gaza)

A further consequence of the Roman phase of the Plato revival was the spreading of interest in Plato to two other countries that had previously been largely unaffected by the revival, namely Spain and Germany. The agent of the Spanish connection was Fernando de Córdoba (c.1425–c.1486). Fernando was endowed with a photographic memory, and was accordingly regarded as a prodigy. By the age of 18 he had acquired two doctorates and was serving in the retinue of Alfonso V at Naples. In 1445 Fernando went to Paris, where his unnatural gifts excited much admiration at Court, but much alarm at the Sorbonne. On the grounds that Fernando was some kind of devil or anti-Christ, the Sorbonne theologians hounded him back to Italy. In 1463 Fernando found a protector at Rome in the person of Cardinal Bessarion, who was happy to use Fernando's skills to assist him in his Plato-controversy with Trebizond. Bessarion assigned to Fernando the task of collecting all the favorable references to Plato in the Church Fathers and in the major pagan authorities Cicero, Seneca, Aulus Gellius, Apuleius, and Macrobius. The collection that Fernando produced is called *De laudibus Platonis*. It was never published, and survives in only one manuscript (Rome, Vallicelliana MS 1.22, fols. 1–21, Bonilla y San Martin, 1911, p. 89). Bessarion also assigned Fernando another project in connection with the Trebizond episode: to make a point-by-point comparison between the philosophies of Plato and Aristotle. The work that Fernando produced on this subject was apparently called *De duabus philosophiis et praestantia Platonis supra Aristotelem*; it has not survived, but may be embedded in Bessarion's own subsequent work, *In calumniatorem Platonis*. Fernando died at Rome about 1486, but his knowledge of Plato may well have had some influence in Spain, where later, Ficino was to attract numerous writers to Plato, including Leo Hebreus, Garcilaso, Luis de Léon, Montemayor, and Lope de Vega (for Bibliography on these writers see Jayne tr. Ficino's *De amore*, 1985, pp. 201–203; on Fernando de Córdoba see Bonilla y San Martin, 1911; Carreras y Artau, 1943).

The repercussions in Germany of the Roman debate about Plato and Aristotle may be seen in Nicholas of Cusa (1401–1464). Nicholas Krypffs, to use his proper name, was born at Cues, on the Moselle River. He ran away from home as a child, and was educated at Deventer by a Dutch order of Mystics, the Brothers of the Common Life. It was the Brothers who gave him his name, Nicholas Cusanus, and who introduced him to the works of Pseudo-Dionysius and Meister Eckhardt, thus establishing his lifelong interest in mysticism. From Deventer the Brothers sent Cusanus to Padua to be educated in Canon Law. He then returned to Germany to take a post in the secular clergy. In Germany he caught the eye of the Papal Legate to Germany, Cardinal Giordano Orsini, who took him on as his personal secretary. In 1437 Orsini was put in charge of the Council of Basle, and Cusanus accompanied him to Basle. But when the Council moved to Florence in 1439, Cusanus was sent by the Pope on a special mission to Constantinople to work on the problem of reunification, behind the scenes. It was on his way back from Constantinople to Venice, Cusanus tells us, that he conceived the plan for his major work, the *De docta ignorantia*. When Cusanus returned to Rome, he remained in the service of the Pope, and in 1448 became a Cardinal himself. His participation in the College of Cardinals introduced him to Cardinal Bessarion, and thus Cusanus became aware of the debate between Bessarion and Trebizond (on Cusanus see Gandillac, 1976; Marx, 1905; Stinger, 1985; Vansteenberghe, 1920).

Cusanus could not read Greek, and took little interest in the niceties of that debate, but he did become interested enough in Plato to acquire a copy of Trebizond's translation of Plato's *Laws*, and a copy of Traversari's translation of Diogenes Laertius. In 1459 Cusanus commissioned Trebizond to translate another dialogue of Plato for him, the *Parmenides*. Trebizond undertook the translation very reluctantly. He seems to have been unaware that the work had already been translated into Latin once before: William of Moerbeke had translated the *Parmenides* about 1286, as part of his translation of Proclus' *Commentary* on that dialogue (Klibansky, 1984, p. 32). Cusanus himself owned a copy of Moerbeke's translation of the *Elements of Theology* of Proclus, and it seems strange that Trebizond made no use of Moerbeke's translation of the *Parmenides*, but he apparently did not.

In 1456 Cusanus left Rome to serve as Bishop of Brixen; it was in that position that he finally found time to write his *De docta ignorantia* (1440). This work has three parts: I. on God, II. on the universe, and III. on Christ. Cusanus rarely finds occasion to mention Plato except in the medieval way as a paradigm, along with Socrates, in syllogisms about genus and species (e.g. Book III, ch. 13, p. 154 Hopkins tr., 1981). But he does cite from Calcidius (Ch. 330) the theory that there is no one Idea of all things, (Book I, ch. 17, p. 69 Hopkins tr., 1981), and in Book II, on the universe, he does cite two opinions of Plato: that the theory of Ideas derived from a comparison of similarities (p. 102) and that Plato referred to the universe as an animal (pp. 118, 122).

The chronology of the repercussions in Rome of Pletho's visit is given in Table 6. Of the works noticed in the chronology not one can be placed in England before the Tudor period. The earliest that any of them appears in England is a copy of Bessarion's *In calumniatorem Platonis* (Rome, 1469) owned by James Goldwell at All Souls, Oxford, in 1499 (Emden, 1957–1959, vol. 2, pp. 783–786).

Table 6. Chronology of the Pletho revival in Rome

1439	Pletho *De differentiis*; Cusanus owned 8 dialogues of Plato; Council ends; Decree of Union; diaspora of Greeks; Bessarion, Trebizond to Rome; Gaza to Ferrara; Scholarios to Constantinople; Pletho remains in Florence; Cusanus in Rome
1441	Argyropoulos arrives in Padua
1444	Scholarios replies to Pletho; Fernando in Naples
1446	Gaza tr. *Gorgias* and lectures on it at Ferrara; Fernando in Genoa
1447	Nicholas V elected; Trebizond tr. Eusebius *De Praeparatione*
1449	Gaza at Rome, as ally of Bessarion against Trebizond
1449–50	Gaza and Trebizond quarrel; Pletho replies to Scholarios
1450–51	Trebizond tr. *Laws*, *Epinomis* for Nicholas V at Rome
1452	Nicholas V turns against Trebizond, who flees to Naples
1453	Turks take Constantinople
1455	Nicholas V dies; Trebizond returns to Rome
1456	Trebizond attacks Plato in *Protectio*
1457	Trebizond writes *Comparatio* at Rome
1458	Trebizond publishes *Comparatio* at Rome
1458	Cusanus at Rome acquires Trebizond tr. of *Laws*; commissions tr. of *Parmenides*; acquires Traversari tr. of Diogenes Laertius; Argyropoulos tr. and comments on *Meno*
1459	Trebizond tr. *Parmenides* for Cusanus; Bessarion writes ICP at Viterbo; asks Gaza's help
1460	Pletho dies
1462	Pietro Balbi tr. Proclus *Theol. Platonica* for Cusanus
1463	Fernando joins Bessarion; writes *De duabus philosophiis*
1467	Fernando writes *De laudibus*; Palmieri, Trebizond reply; Perotti tr. *Alcib.* II and *ICP* for Bessarion at Rome
1469	Bessarion publishes *ICP* at Rome; Apuleius *De deo Socratis* and *De dogmate* printed at Rome with Albinus; Argyropoulus tract against Trebizond
1472	Bessarion, Trebizond dies
1475	Agricola (student of Gaza) translates *Axiochus*
1487	Argyropoulos dies

B. In Florence (1439–1499)

Pletho was in Florence for only six months: January to June, 1439. (Marcel, 1958, p. 156). Yet, according to Ficino, during that brief period Pletho was able to persuade the head of the Florentine Republic, Cosimo de' Medici (1389–1464), to become a major sponsor of "Platonic theology" in the West (Ficino, *Opera*, 1576, pp. 1534, 1537). That such a transaction could have taken place in anything like the terms described by Ficino seems very unlikely. Pletho was eighty–four years old, a poor provincial monk who spoke no Italian. Cosimo de' Medici, on the other hand was fifty years old, a rich and powerful banker-politician who scorned most clerics and spoke no Greek. Moreover, Pletho was in Florence as one of the Greek's delegates to a Church Council whose business had nothing to do with Plato, and Cosimo's own interests were anything but Platonic (see Hankins, *JWCI*, 1990). Considering the heavy odds against Cosimo's having had any close personal relation with Pletho, it may well be, as Hankins has argued (1990, pp. 436–440) that the main, perhaps only, vehicle of Pletho's influence on Cosimo was his gift to Cosimo of a manuscript containing the *Works* of Plato.

On the other hand, Pletho would have not given Cosimo such a manuscript if he had not supposed that Cosimo had some sense of its value, and Pletho could easily have heard that Cosimo did know something about Plato, for in 1427 Leonardo Bruni had dedicated to Cosimo a Latin translation of Plato's *Letters*, and in 1435 had translated part of the *Symposium* for Cosimo. In any case, even though Ficino's account of the matter is no doubt grossly foreshortened (it did take Cosimo twenty years to get around to hiring a translator of his manuscript), the fact remains that Cosimo did eventually underwrite a translation of Plato, did provide the manuscripts for the translation, and did dictate the terms under which the translation was made. Those terms, however and whenever Cosimo arrived at them, turned out to be in accord with Pletho's conception of why Plato's *Works* were important in the first place, namely, that Plato was an important link in a long chain of authorities who espoused a universal religion, a religion that was the ancestor of Christianity, and had followers in every major pre-Christian culture (see also Field, 1989; Purnell, 1986).

This universal religion was a form of monotheism in which the one God was believed to have created the world by stages, first intellectual, then spiritual, and finally material. The universe thus consists of a full hierarchy of non-physical (intelligible) beings, spirits, and ideas between the physical (or sensible) world and God. Creation, however, should be thought of as a continuing process, for the universe is in a constant state of emanation outward from God to matter, and inward from matter to God. The human soul participates in this process, emanating from God into a physical body and eventually returning to God. That this religion is an ancestor of Christianity, can be seen in the fact that it preaches a tri-une, benevolent God, who created the world and rules it by his providence, and who created man in his likeness, with an immortal soul capable of eternal happiness with God after the death of the body.

The principal proponents of this religion, according to Pletho, were the following:

Zoroaster	Plato
Hermes Trismegistus	Dionysius Areopagite
Hesiod	Plotinus
Homer	Porphyry
Orpheus	Proclus
Pythagoras	

(Ficino give versions of this list in eleven different passages of his works: e.g. *Opera*, 1576 ed. pp. 156, 386, 1134–1135, 1233, 1836; Marcel, 1958, pp. 602–641, Hankins, 1990, pp. 459–464). Although Plato was only one of the transmitters of the universal theology, he was one of the most voluminous, and Pletho therefore called this universal religion the "Platonic Theology", and referred to all of its authorities, even if they preceded Plato, as "Platonists".

That such a theology should have appealed to Cosimo is not inherently improbable. It was not a theology of renunciation and despair like the theology of the Church of Florence, but an enthusiastic theology of celebration and vitality. It embraced the pagan deities as life-enhancing symbols, praised the beauties and possessions of this world, and advocated that one enjoy and appreciate them.

Thus even if it was not Pletho himself who persuaded Cosimo to see to it that the Greek authorities of this long tradition were made available to the West in Latin translation, it was something very much like a proposal that Cosimo kept in the back of his mind for twenty years while he gradually acquired copies of the authorities on Pletho's list, and looked for someone who could translate them all into Latin (Marcel, 1958, pp. 149–160). It was not until 1458, when Cosimo was nearly seventy years old, that he finally found his man, Marsilio Ficino (1433–1499).

Ficino's credentials for such an undertaking were not very impressive. He was an unemployed, hunch-backed university-drifter, whose knowledge of Greek was only rudimentary. His principal asset was that he was the son of Dr. Dietifeci, Cosimo's physician. In part Cosimo hired Ficino as a personal favor to the boy's father, who had supported his son through seven years at the university and was finding him more and more difficult to handle. The father had enrolled Ficino at the University of Florence (the Studio) in 1452 (Marcel, 1958, p. 177), and Ficino had chosen as his major, Philosophy. At the Studio, to study Philosophy meant to study Aristotle, but Ficino was more interested in Platonists.

As early as 1454 Ficino had begun making copies for himself of various Platonic source materials. The first was a copy of Calcidius' translation of the *Timaeus* (Kristeller, *Suppl.* I, 1937, p. liv). In 1455 he made a copy of another Platonic work, the *Theophrastus* (c.484 A.D.) by Aeneas Gazaeus (450–534 A.D.), in a Latin translation by Ambrogio Traversari. This treatise, which is written in the form of a Platonic dialogue, summarizes opinions on the subject of the immortality of the soul. Every successive civilization, says Gazaeus, has believed in the immortality of the soul, from the Chaldaeans and Egyptians to the Greeks, including Pythagoras, Plato, Plotinus, Porphyry, Jamblichus, and Proclus. This shows that the Christian doctrine of immortality has a long lineage, but it also shows that the Christian doctrine is much superior to its predecessors (Ficino's copy of the work is now Florence, Riccardiana MS 709, fols. 134–183; see Kristeller, *Studies*, 1985, pp. 164–165).

In 1456 Ficino compiled still another Platonic source work, a list of passages concerning the theory of love (see p. 75 below). Shortly thereafter, Ficino undertook to write a comprehensive *Introduction to Platonism (Institutiones ad Platonicam disciplinam)*. This work (now apparently lost), he proudly presented for approval to his mentor in Platonic studies, Cristoforo Landino. Unfortunately, Landino was not impressed, and told Ficino to go away, learn some Greek, and read some Plato before he attempted to write on that subject. (Ficino, *Opera*, 1576 ed., p. 929). The University authorities were even less charitable than Landino about Ficino's work; they thought it smacked of heresy, and they advised him to seek counselling from the Chancellor of the University, Archbishop Antonino. According to one account (Acciaivoli's) the Archbishop merely advised Ficino to read Aquinas' *Contra Gentiles* (Marcel, 1958, pp. 210–212), but according to another (Della Torre's, 1902, p. 575) the Archbishop advised Dietifeci to send his son away to medical school.

Ficino's own reaction to his setback was at least partly constructive; he did set out to learn some Greek; he copied out an entire Greek-Latin phrase-book that listed useful phrases under 63 subject headings (Ficino's copy still survives; it is now Florence, Laurenziana MS Ashburnham 1439; ed. Pintaudi, 1977, who dates Ficino's copy at 1456). In addition Ficino may have taken some lessons in Greek from the Archbishop's secretary, Francesco da Castiglione (Kristeller, *Studies*, pp. 198–200).

But in part Ficino's reaction was also rebellious; technically he obeyed orders by putting aside the Platonists, but he deliberately chose in their stead a far more heretical school of Greek philosophers to study; the Epicureans. For the summer of 1457 he managed to get himself invited to the villa of a friend, where he composed a bold little essay on the Epicurean subject of desire (*De voluptate*). (Marcel, 1958, pp. 219–226). By the spring of 1459 Ficino's father was at the end of his rope with the boy, and he ordered Ficino to enroll in the medical school at Bologna for the following fall term. Ficino, who was then twenty-six, confided to a friend that he had no intention of doing any such thing (Kristeller, *Supp.* II, 1937, pp. 84–85).

Marcel hypothesizes (pp. 233–240) that Ficino attended medical school at Bologna for three years (1459–1462), but there is no record of his having enrolled there, and I think that we should accept what Ficino himself tells us, namely, that at that hopeless impasse in 1459, when his father had laid down the law about going to medical school, Cosimo de' Medici intervened, and rescued Ficino by hiring him as his translator for the Plato project (Kristeller, *Suppl.* II, 1937, 87–88).

Ficino tells us that being rescued from his father was like being given a "second life", but what actually happened to him sounds more like being sold into slavery. Cosimo intended to get some work out of this boy, and his first step was to move Ficino out of Florence to a farm at Celle, a half-day's journey out in the country. There Ficino was to eat, sleep, and work undistracted, either by Florentine social life, or by meddling advice from the pedants at the university. Ficino was to bring to Cosimo in person each batch of work as he completed it. Cosimo provided Ficino with Greek texts of some of the works to be translated, but Cosimo had the wit not to paralyze Ficino by revealing the full enormity of his assignment all at once. What Cosimo intended was that Ficino should translate first all of the major Platonists before Plato, then Plato, and then all of the major Platonists after Plato (Ficino, *Opera*, 1576 ed., p. 1537). Anyone who has ever tried to translate a single hymn of Orpheus, a single dialogue of Plato, or a single page of Proclus' *Elements of Theology* will realize that what Cosimo had in mind was nothing less than the work of an entire lifetime. Ficino was right in seeing his new post as a second life, but it was a life that was being taken away from him, not one that was being given to him.

We do not know exactly in what order Ficino finished all of the translations on his list, but by the end of the first three years, that is, by the Spring of 1462, he had certainly finished at least the following:

Hymns of Orpheus, Homer, and Proclus
Aphorisms of Zoroaster, with Pletho's Commentary
Theogony of Hesiod
Argonautica of Orpheus
(Ficino, *Opera*, 1576 ed., p. 933 and Florence, Laurenziana MS Plut. 36, 35)
and probably the following as well:
Theon of Smyrna
Jamblichus, *De mysteriis*
Plutarch (selections)
Albinus, *Isagogue*
Speusippus, *Definitiones*
(Kristeller, *Suppl*. II, 1937, p. 104; Marcel, 1958, p. 605; Florence, Laurenziana, MS 85, 9).

In August, 1462, he received a letter from his father, telling him that Cosimo was sufficiently impressed with his progress that he was making arrangements for him to move back to Florence. But by then Ficino had got used to his routine at Celle, and decided to stay on there; so his father arranged to rent out for extra income the house that Cosimo had given Ficino in Florence.

By the following April (1463) Ficino had certainly finished the following additional work:
Hermes Trismegistus, *Pimander*
(Kristeller, Suppl. I, 1937, p. cxxxix; and Florence, Laurenziana MS Plut. 71, 33)
and probably the following as well:
Proclus, *Elements of Theology*

Proclus, *Commentary on Alcibiades I*
Pseudo-Dionysius, *Divine Names*
Pythagoras, *Golden Verses, Symbols*
Hermias, *Commentary on the Phaedo*
(see *De amore*; tr. Jayne, 1985, pp. 3–5; Allen, 1980).

In April, 1463, having completed all of the pre-requisite works, Ficino turned at last to the *Works* of Plato (Kristeller, *Suppl.* I, 1937, cxxxix). Cosimo had provided him with two manuscripts of the Greek text of Plato to work from; one that belonged to Cosimo (now Florence, Laurenziana MS 85,9), and another that Cosimo had borrowed from Amerigo Benci for the purpose (Gentile, 1984, pp. 28–30; 1987). Cosimo had also given Ficino a list of the first ten dialogues he wanted translated:

1. *Hipparchus*   On the desire for money
2. *Amatores*   On philosophy
3. *Theages*   On wisdom
4. *Meno*   On virtue
5. *Alcibiades I*   On human nature
6. *Alcibiades II*   On prayer
7. *Minos*   On law
8. *Euthyphro*   On holiness
9. *Parmenides*   On God
10. *Philebus*   On the *summum bonum*

(The translations are in Oxford, Bodleian, MS Canon class. lat. 163).

Starting in April, 1463, and working at the rate of about a dialogue a month, Ficino completed the first five dialogues on Cosimo's list by the end of the summer and promised the other five before Christmas. But Ficino fell behind, and when the Christmas season arrived, he had finished only nine of the ten dialogues; unfortunately it was the tenth, the *Philebus*, that Cosimo especially wanted; his son had recently died (in November) and he himself was very ill; he was feeling some urgency about the shortness of his time when he wrote Ficino asking for the *Philebus*:

> Come here as soon as you can, and bring with you the dialogue on the *Summum bonum* from my Plato volume. I assume you have finished translating that dialogue from Greek into Latin, as you promised. There is nothing I want more now than to learn what is the most direct route to earthly bliss.
>
> (Ficino, *Opera*, 1576 ed., p. 1560; tr. mine).

Ficino had to beg off, giving as his excuse the nasty Valdarno weather, he did not actually finish the *Philebus* until the following July. By then Cosimo's uremic poisoning had reached a terminal stage, and he asked Ficino to translate for him Plato's dialogue on death, the *Axiochus*. Before Ficino could finish it, Cosimo died, on August 1, 1464.

Fortunately for Ficino, Cosimo's successor, Piero de' Medici, agreed to continue subsidizing Ficino's work, but only if he moved to Florence, where Piero could keep him under his eye. There, in a small timbered house on the Medici estate at Careggi, in the northwest suburbs of Florence, Ficino worked on the Plato, with minor interruptions, for four more years. Finally, in the autumn of 1468, Ficino closed the book on Plato; after five years of almost continuous work, he had finished the first translation into any language of the complete *Opera* of Plato.

One might have supposed that after completing so heroic an achievement, both Ficino and his then employer, Piero de' Medici, would have been anxious to get the Plato into print as quickly as possible. But the translation was not published for another sixteen years. What caused the delay? For one thing Piero was dying of gout, and may have been pushing Ficino to get the Plotinus done as soon as possible, for Ficino went directly from the Plato into the translation of the Plotinus. The following year, however, Piero died, and Ficino immediately put the Plotinus aside in order to write a little work of his own. This work, the *De amore*, he finished in July, 1469 (the autograph manuscript survives in Rome, Vatican MS lat. 7705).

The *De amore* purports to be an autobiographical report of a party in honor of Plato's birthday, at which seven of Ficino's friends made speeches about love. The first five speeches discuss love in theological terms; the human soul is an emanation from the mystical One, and love is the soul's desire to return to the One. The last two speeches, however, discuss love in different terms altogether: the language of astrology and medicine; here the subject is actually not love but sexual desire, which is shown to be a function of astrological signs and normal human physiology. Although the *De amore* purports to be a commentary on the seven speeches on love in Plato's *Symposium*, Ficino's seven speeches are connected only loosely with Plato's dialogue, as the table overleaf shows.

The *De amore* was written in Latin for members of the Medici court. Ficino's main object was evidently to provide male court aristocrats with arguments to use in justifying their sexual activity, whether heterosexual or homosexual. Lorenzo de' Medici later ordered him to translate it into Italian for two of his friends, Bernardo del Nero and Antonio Manetti (see Kristeller, *Suppl.*, 1937, vol. I, pp. 89–91). The idea for such a treatise Ficino had evidently had with him for a long time, for as early as 1456 he had copied out a collection of passages about love for just such a tract. This collection (which survives today in Florence, Riccardiana MS 92; Gentile, 1984, pp. 58–60) included passages from the *Symposium* and the *Phaedrus*, some quotations of Plato from Diogenes Laertius, bits of the *Argonautica* of Orpheus, scraps of Moschus and Musaeus, and a long passage from Plotinus. In writing the *De amore* Ficino used much of this material, but he also added to it material from the Pseudo-Dionysius, Aquinas, Proclus, Apuleius, Lucretius, several additional dialogues of Plato, and several medieval authorities on medicine (see tr. Jayne, 1985, pp. 5–7).

Ficino was very proud of his *De amore*, and sent copies of it at once to two distinguished members of the clergy, Bishop Joannes Pannonius (1434–1473) in

Table 7. Ficino's *De amore*

Ficino's speaker	Plato's speaker and topics	Sections of Plato and topics actually discussed by Ficino's speaker
I. Giovanni Cavalcanti	Phaedrus: antiquity and nobility of Cupid	definition of terms; *Symp.* 178C–180D
II. Giovanni Cavalcanti	Pausanias: Two kinds of love (heavenly and earthly)	cosmic hypostases
III. Giovanni Cavalcanti	Erixymachus: human love part of a universal natural force	cosmic love; *Symp.* 186B–187D
IV. Cristoforo Landino	Aristophanes; fable of split creatures	fable of Aristophanes, *Symp.* 189C–193D; nature of Man, love as moral force
V. Carlo Marsuppini	Agathon: whether love is beautiful or not	theory of beauty: *Symp.* 195B-E. 197A-B
VI. Tommaso Benci	Socrates: Porus and Penia, ladder of love, immortality, love as daemon	Porus and Penia; *Symp.* 203D-E ladder of love, love; immortality daemons; *Symp.* 207D-208B
VII. Cristoforo Marsuppini	Alcibiades: praise of Socrates	Cavalcanti poem; physiology of love; four madnesses; *Phaedrus* praise of love; of God, and of Socrates; *Apol.*; *Alcibiades* I

Hungary, and to Cardinal Enea Silvio Piccolomini (1439–1503) in Rome. (For the subsequent history of the *De amore* see my tr., 1985, pp. 4–5). Within a month, however, Ficino received from Piccolomini's fellow-Cardinal in Rome, Cardinal Giovanni Bessarion, a copy of the *In calumniatorem Platonis*, and that treatise derailed Ficino from the entire Plato–translation project for fifteen years (Hankins, 1990, pp. 454–459, gives a different interpretation).

It seems likely that the work that gave Ficino his fright was not Bessarion's itself, but the work to which Bessarion's work is a reply, the *Comparationes* of George of Trebizond. As we have seen, in that work Trebizond vilifies Ficino as the new "fourth Plato". It was only after Trebizond was dead (d.1472) that Ficino dared to publish his essay defending the "infamous thing" that Trebizond was trying to *écraser*, the principle of *voluptas*. (Ficino's *De voluptate* was published in 1497, two years before his own death.)

Whether it was Bessarion's tract, or Trebizond's that frightened Ficino, he was sufficiently alarmed to put aside his translation of Plato until such time as he should have improved his standing in the Church. As it turned out, it took him thirteen years to solve this problem, and his solution involved some rather drastic measures:

1. In 1471 he published a translation of Hermes Trismegistus, which he had finished in 1463.
2. In 1473 he entered holy orders (see Kristeller, *Suppl.*, 1937, vol. I, p. lxxvii).
3. In 1474 he published a treatise on Christian theology (*Della religione cristiana*) in Italian.
4. In 1476 he published the same treatise in Latin translation (*De religione christiana*).
5. In 1480 he wrote an essay *De cura valetudinis* on the special health problems of intellectuals.
6. In 1482 he published a scholarly treatise on the immortality of the soul (*Theologia platonica*).

Let us now look at items 4 and 6 on this list. Ficino's *De religione christiana* is an anthology of thirty-six short Latin essays on various subjects, not unlike Ficino's later *Letters*, except that the essays in the *De religione* are all loosely related to one central design, of persuading young men of university age that they should not be seduced away from the faith (as Ficino himself had been) by the attractions of "philosophy". By "philosophy" Ficino here means Paduan Averroism. The work begins with an essay on the importance of the Christian religion, implicitly refuting Pomponazzi's charge that all religions rise and fall, and that Christianity was at that time in the dying phase of its cycle (Allen, 1964, p. 44). In chapter 3, Ficino urges young men to organize their education in the following order: Ethics, Physics, Mathematics, Metaphysics, and Religion, on the ground that this is the order that Plato recommended, and that he followed in his own writings: *Epistles*, *Phaedo*, *Republic I*, *Laws X*.

After three chapters on Christ's disciples, Ficino then devotes chapters 8 through 22 to the subject of Christ himself. Then follow two chapters (23 and 24) on the Sibyls, in which Ficino explains that they correctly prophesied the coming of Christ, and are thus reliable authorities on Christianity, even though they lived before Christ. The remaining eleven chapters of the work (25–36) defend the authority of the Old Testament on various points of Christian doctrine.

The posture of the *De religione* regarding Christianity reflects Ficino's own position except that what he actually feels guilty about is Platonism, whereas what he ostensibly is attacking is Averroism. Even though the subject matter of the *De religione* is mainly religious rather than Platonic, Ficino's knowledge of Plato and Plotinus is amply apparent in the work (e.g. ch. 11, sig. div.^{r}, where he asserts, following Augustine, that Plotinus is the most accurate interpreter of Plato's dialogues).

The other major treatise of Ficino's period of religious reassessment (item 6 above) was the *Theologia platonica*. The subject of this treatise is the immortality of the soul, a subject on which he could again be seen as being on the side of the Church, as opposed to the teaching of the Averroists at the University of Padua. Ficino had available as a source book on this subject, the *Theophrastus* of Aeneas Gazeus, which he had copied in his youth (1456), but Ficino plundered many other authors as well, especially Hermes Trismegistus, Augustine, and Aquinas, whom he quotes in huge, undigested chunks, without any acknowledgment, and without adequate connective tissue (see ed. and tr. Marcel, 1964–1970). The result is that the *Theologia platonica* is nearly unreadable, and it is no wonder that Ficino's later cult–followers preferred his shorter works, the *De amore*, the *De vita*, and the *Epistolae*. After publishing the *Theologia platonica* (1482) Ficino returned to work on his translation of Plotinus. Finally, in 1484, sixteen years after he had finished writing it, Ficino published the first translation into any language of the complete *Works* of Plato (Kristeller, 1978). In the summer of 1489, Ficino wrote a commentary on one section of Plotinus' work, but soon found himself writing instead an entire handbook on Astrology, called "On Bringing One's Life into Harmony with the Heavens" (*De vita coelitus comparanda*, July, 1489). The underlying thesis of this work is that since there is a close correspondence among all the various levels of the hierarchy of being, the key to happiness is to organize every detail of your own personal life according to the pattern of correspondence in the universe. Thus you should take baths and showers only when the moon is in Aries, and be careful not to vomit when the moon is in Leo (Boer tr., 1980, pp. 114–115).

Hardly had Ficino completed this astrological handbook when he plunged into another "How to" book. This one was addressed to old people and was called "How to Prolong your Life" (*De vita producenda*, August, 1489). In this book Ficino has very little to say about Astrology. He does advise old people to consult a good astrologer every seven years (Boer tr., 1980, p. 80), but the gist of his own advice is medical: he wants to help the elderly by explaining what kind of diet, medicine, and regimen is best for people at their stage of life. For example, he says that old people should drink red wine rather than white (Boer tr., 1980, p. 45), eat a lot of lamb (Boer tr., 1980, p. 51), avoid the night air (Boer tr., 1980, p. 51), take laxatives only when the moon is in the right relation to Jupiter (Boer tr., 1980, p. 71), and if they need a tonic, try sucking the milk of girls or the blood of boys (Boer tr., 1980, pp. 65–67).

When Ficino had finished this second book, in the summer of 1489, he decided to publish both books together, and to add to them a similar book that he had written nine years before. This earlier book, called "On Caring for the Health of Intellectuals" (*De cura valetudinis. . .* 1480) was ostensibly a medical handbook for people like himself, who spent most of their time reading books, and thus did not get enough exercise, and tended to fall into depression (the medical term was "to suffer from black bile, or melancholia"). Ficino describes his intended readers variously as "men of letters" or "scholars", but he might better have referred to them as "the leisure class", for it was that class for which he was writing (and which most read the book). We see this everywhere in the work: the reader is advised to comb his hair every morning when he gets up, precisely 40 times, and with an ivory comb, (Boer tr., 1980, p. 17). If you have had a heavy noon meal, you may have to relax for as long as four hours before you can do any serious thinking (Boer tr., 1980, p. 21). You should keep on hand ample supplies of apple juice (Boer tr., 1980, p. 19) and almond-milk (Boer tr., 1980, p. 33), and get as much gold and silver into your diet as possible (Boer tr., 1980, p. 19). Your other activities, of course, should be similarly refined; you could try strumming a lyre, going for a carriage-ride, or going sailing. But whatever activity you select, be sure to do it only in the company of genteel people (Boer tr., 1980, p. 20).

For purposes of publication Ficino revised all three of his "How to books" and arranged them in this order:–
How to stay well as an intellectual
How to stay well in old age
How to get into harmony with the universe

For each of the three books he provided separate dedications, and published the trio in 1489 under the title *On Three Kinds of Life* (*De vita triplici*). It was this book more than any other that made Ficino's reputation in the courts of Europe: it established him as the premier advisor to the leisure-class, the one man who understood their medical and psychological problems, and who realized that they needed a little hocus-pocus (magic-astrology-spiritualism) along with their prescriptions (on Ficino's use of magic see Walker, 1958; Zambelli, 1986; and Copenhaver, 1986). In 1492, as Ficino was preparing to publish his Plotinus translation, his patron, Lorenzo de' Medici, died. Fortunately, Lorenzo's son carried out the family's commitment to this volume (a commitment which dated back to Cosimo), and the Plotinus appeared later that year. In 1493, Ficino published a translation of the *De resurrectione* of Athenagoras, to which Ficino appended his old translation of the *Axiochus*.

One year later (1494), the Medici family was banished from Florence. Ficino, who was by then sixty-one years old, was allowed to remain in the city, and he spent the five remaining years of his life publishing books: his letters, his collected introductions to the dialogues of Plato, an anthology of minor Platonists, and his translations of the *Divine Names* and *Mystical Theology* of Pseudo-Dionysius. I will discuss only the first three of these projects here.

Throughout his life Ficino had been a busy writer of letters. Even during his university years he had kept up an active correspondence with numerous friends. But from the moment he was hired by the Medici, letter-writing became a major part of his routine. The Medici made their living by banking; there were branches of their bank in many major cities. Thus it did not take long for the news that the Medici were sponsoring a new cult of Platonism to spread all over Europe. Correspondence poured in to Ficino. Like all fan mail, it tended to be very repetitive, and he therefore developed form-letter replies, of which he naturally kept copies. He also kept copies of most other letters that he sent out. His copious correspondence quickly established him as a cult–figure in his own right, a combination astrologer-magician-medicine man-spiritualist.

In 1495 Ficino gathered together a large number (about 235) of the letters of which he had kept copies, added to them a number of long unpublished essays, mainly on theological topics, such as "On the Ascent of Paul to the Third Heaven" and "On the Nature of Light", and published them under the title *Epistolae*. (A modern English translation of the collection is in progress at the London School of Economics; it omits Book II, which contains the long essays). Ficino's *Epistolae* enjoyed a wide popularity, and they and the *De vita* were the major vehicles by which the doctrines of Ficino's cult were communicated to the world beyond the walls of Florence. In England, Ficino's *Epistolae* and *De vita* were both widely owned, and one of Ficino's letters (not about Plato) was included, along with ten letters of Poliziano, and many of other Italian authors, as a model of letter-form in William Fulwood's handbook on letter-writing called *The Enimie of Idleness* (1568).

After publishing his *Letters*, Ficino published only two more works: in 1496 a volume containing all of the short introductions that he had composed for the individual dialogues in the *Opera* of Plato, and in 1497 an anthology of minor Platonists. From Ficino's point of view his anthology was a major piece of unfinished business: it presented the completion of the program that Cosimo had originally projected for the translation of all of the Greek authors who could be properly called Platonists. But the anthology was also important to Ficino in other ways as well: it made available to his admirers some of the major authorities behind the demonic magic and dietary medicine that were central elements in his own cult; and in addition the volume gave him a vehicle for publishing one of his own unpublished essays, the *De voluptate*. Ficino did not give his anthology a title, but I shall refer to it as Ficino's *Anthology of Minor Platonists*. The collection, which was published at Venice, contains the following works:

1. Jamblichus, *De mysteriis*
2. Proclus, *In Alcibiadem (primum)*
3. Proclus, *De sacrificio et magia*
4. Porphyry, *De occasionibus*
5. Porphyry, *De abstinentia*
6. Synesius, *De somniis*
7. Psellus, *De operatione daemonum*
8. Priscian, *In Theophrastum, De intellectu et phantasia*
9. Albinus, *De dogmate Platonis*
10. Speusippus, *De definitionibus*
11. Pythagoras, *Aurea verba*
12. Pythagoras, *Symbola*
13. Xenocrates, *De morte* (i.e. *Axiochus*)
14. Ficino, *De voluptate*

Various of the works in Ficino's *Anthology* were subsequently published in other combinations. Ficino himself published one of these the following year (1498). This collection, which was published at Paris, contained his old translation of the *Axiochus* (no. 13 above), together with his translation of a new work, the *De resurrectione* of Athenagoras, and a Latin translation by Ludovicus Odaxius of Cebes' *Tabula*. Ficino died in 1499. The events of his lifetime that bear on the history of Plato may be seen in Table 8 (on Ficino see also Hankins, 1990, pp. 267–359, 454–484).

Table 8. Chronology of the Pletho Revival in Florence (1439–1499)

1439	Council of Florence; 700 Greeks attend
1453	Turks capture Constantinople
1456	Ficino copies Traversari tr. of Aeneas Gazeus
1458	Cosimo hires Ficino for project
1463	Ficino finishes preparations; starts Plato tr.
1464	Ficino finishes ten dialogues;
	Callistos tr. *Letters, Euthyphro* at Studio
	Poliziano tr. *Charmides* for Cosimo; Cosimo dies
1466	Ficino finishes 23 dialogues; Lippi tr. *Ion* for Cosimo
1468	Ficino finishes Plato; starts Plotinus
1469	Ficino writes *De amore* and *Comm. on Phaedrus*; Piero dies
1471	Ficino publishes *Hermetica* tr.
1473	Ficino enters holy orders
c.1473	Filelfo writes *De ideis* for Medici
1474	Ficino publishes *Della religione Cristiana*
	Ficino translates *De amore* into Italian
1475	Chalcondylas replaces Callistos at Studio
1476	Ficino publishes *De religione christiana* and *Axiochus* tr.
1482	Ficino publishes *Theologia platonica*
1484	Ficino publishes Latin *Opera Platonis*, with *De amore*; printed in Dominican Convent (financed by Valori)
1486	Pico writes *Commento* (reply to Ficino's *De amore*)
1489	Ficino publishes *De vita triplici*
1492	Lorenzo dies; Ficino publishes Plotinus tr.
1494	Medici banished from Florence
1495	Ficino publishes his own *Epistolae*
1496	Ficino publishes his *Commentaries* on Plato
1497	Ficino publishes his tr. of *DN* and *MT* of Pseudo-Dionysius
1497	Ficino publishes his Anthol. of Minor Platonists
	(Iamblichus, Proclus, Psellus, Xenocrates, etc.)
1499	Death of Ficino

In the previous section we noticed that none of the repercussions of the Roman phase of the Pletho revival reached England during the pre-Tudor period. Almost the same thing can be said of the Florentine phase of Pletho's influence. The only work of the Florentine phase (see Table 8) that can be placed in England before the Tudor era is a copy of Ficino's translation of the *Pimander* of Hermes Trismegistus which was used by John Doget in writing his *Commentary on the Phaedo* (see p. 25

above). Thus the pre-Tudor revival of Plato in England had almost nothing to do with the Pletho revival in Italy, and must be ascribed almost entirely to the influence of the earlier Chrysoloras revival.

CHAPTER 5

THE EARLY TUDORS (1485–1558)

A. Henry VII (1485–1509)

One would have supposed that since the pipeline that brought new dialogues of Plato from Italy to England had flowed so profusely between 1423 and 1483, it would surely have brought in the complete *Works* of Plato when they were published in 1484, especially since the government expressly opened the border in 1484, for the first time, to foreign books, booksellers and printers (Plomer, 1925). Between 1484 and 1535 the open border provided a rare window of opportunity when England could have caught up rapidly with the revival of classics on the continent. But it did not. Because of the Wars of the Roses and their after-effects, the country instead turned inward.

One symptom of the inward turning that followed the Wars of the Roses was the behavior of the printing industry. Instead of printing new works that would reflect the exciting developments in the revival of classical learning on the continent, English printers limited themselves as much as possible to printing familiar medieval works that were already well established with English readers, works such as the encyclopedias of Honorius and Bartholomaeus Anglicus, the *Ayenbite of Inwyt*, and the poems of Lydgate and Chaucer. As a result, in any book printed in England during the reign of Henry VII, if Plato appears at all, he is seen in his old-fashioned medieval guise as some kind of legendary scientist (see Jayne, 1993, pp. 246–270).

It is true that the study of Greek in England began in this reign (at Oxford), but it began without recourse to Plato. Two of the teachers of Greek, Grocyn and Linacre, were ardent Aristoteleans, and a third, Erasmus, throughout his career used Lucian and Plutarch rather than Plato for his teaching-texts.

There was a near-miss at Oxford in the case of John Colet. While preparing lectures on Genesis and Romans, Colet became interested in the work of Ficino, who had also written a commentary on Romans. Among Ficino's works Colet first used the *Theologia platonica* (1482), and then the *Epistolae* (1495). Colet subsequently corresponded with Ficino, but Colet never had any interest in Ficino's work on Plato, and even though Colet quotes from the *Theologia platonica* in his own commentaries on Genesis and Romans, none of Colet's writings contributed anything to knowledge about Plato in England (see Jayne, 1965; for different interpreta-

83

tions see Gleason, 1989; Trapp, 1986). Colet's copy of Ficino's *Epistolae* is now at All Souls, Oxford. Perhaps coincidentally, it is an All Souls man who gives us our first glimpse of Oxford interest in the Plato of the schools. This was James Goldwell, who owned a copy of Bessarion's introduction to Plato, *In calumniatorem Platonis* (Rome, 1469). Goldwell's copy is still in the All Souls library, with press–mark i.4.4. (Emden, 1957–1959, vol. 2, p. 785).

At Cambridge the pre-Tudor connection with the Chrysoloras revival of Plato was kept alive for a time in the person of John Gunthorpe at Trinity College. By coincidence, shortly after Gunthorpe's death (1498) the Pletho revival finally put in an appearance in England: in 1500–1501 an entering Cambridge student named Thomas Hammond gave the university, as part of his admission fee, a copy of the Venice, 1491 edition of the Latin *Opera* of Plato in the translation of Ficino, (Cambridge Univ. Grace Book B., ed. Bateson, 1903–1905, pp. xi and 140; see also Emden, 1963, p. 284).

Thomas Hammond notwithstanding, however, the reign of Henry VII was a period of doldrums for Plato. The typical view of Plato in England at the end of the reign of Henry VII was still the old medieval view, as may be seen in the numerous but second-hand allusions to Plato in the writings of one of Henry's own manservants, Stephen Hawes (Jayne, *Monographs*, 1994).

B. HENRY VIII (1509–1547)

The decisive event of the reign of Henry VIII for the history of Plato, as for the history of England itself, was the break with Rome in 1535. Henry had been an enthusiastic supporter of Greek learning, but in his struggle with the papacy, in 1535 he closed the border to foreign books, and this action, together with the loss of Reginald Pole (in addition to the earlier loss of Wolsey in 1530) had the effect of snuffing out the flame of a promising revival of Plato.

At the time of his accession Henry was widely admired for his classical scholarship. As a consequence, both of England's universities judged that the time was ripe to strengthen their offerings in that field. At Oxford the teaching of Greek had been inhibited by the traditional *odium theologicum*: the association of Greek studies with heresy. Some teaching of the Greek language had been going on at Magdalen College since 1490, when it was begun by an Italian visitor, Cornelio Vitelli; and the practice had been continued at Magdalen by Grocyn, Linacre, and William Lily, but only as an extra-curricular activity, (Clough, 1977; Tilley, 1938). In 1517, encouraged by the promise of Henry VIII, Bishop Richard Fox founded a new college, Corpus Christi. In his statutes for the new foundation Fox boldly provided for a lectureship in Greek, citing as his authority the mandate of the Council of Vienne (1311). In order to keep his theological skirts clean, Fox spelled out in detail the Greek authors who were to be studied at Corpus; these included mainly literary figures, but Fox suggested that students might be permitted to read Plato in the long vacation (*Statutes of Corpus*. Ward ed., 1843, pp. 99–101). In support of his new program Fox also gave the college 16 Greek manuscripts (Liddell, 1938). None of these included any work of Plato, but that defect was remedied handsomely in 1537 by the first President of the college, John Claymond, who gave the college a Greek manuscript containing the *Republic*, *Timaeus*, *Laws*, and *Philosophus* of Plato, and Proclus' Commentary on *Alcibiades* I as well (Coxe, 1850–1852, vol 2, MS 96).

In spite of Fox's precautions, his new program for the teaching of Greek provoked a violent reaction in Oxford. Conservatives who were opposed to the teaching of Greek organized themselves under the name "the Trojans", and conducted such a strenuous campaign against "the Greeks" that Thomas More, and eventually Henry VIII himself, were forced to intervene. In 1519 Henry put an end to the controversy by issuing injunctions to both universities requiring the teaching of Greek on an official basis. In 1518 Cardinal Wolsey had endowed a Readership of Humanity (i.e. Professorship in Classics). The first holder of the position was John Clement, and he was succeeded in 1520 by Thomas Lupset. Although he was only 25 at the time, Lupset had impressive credentials: he had served as Erasmus' research assistant in editing the New Testament, and he had studied Greek in Paris with Conrad Heresbach (Erasmus *Epist.*, Allen ed., 1906–1965, vol. 5, p. 1316).

Neither Henry's edict of 1519, nor the appointment of Lupset in 1520 did much to improve the status of Plato at Oxford. In 1520 the Oxford bookseller John Dorne did not sell a single copy of any work of Plato; the only books that Dorne sold in which Plato could be read were old medieval florilegia such as the *Dicts or Sayings of the Philosophers* and Walter Burley's *Lives of the Philosophers* (Madan ed. of Dorne's *Daybook*, 1885,1890).

In 1523 Cardinal Wolsey put his shoulder even more firmly to the wheel of Greek studies at Oxford. In the course of establishing a new college of his own, to be called Cardinal College (McConica, 1986, pp. 29–42), Wolsey wrote into the college statutes a provision that there should be lectures on the Greek language every day at 1 P.M., and on Philosophy every day at 7 A.M. The lecturer on Philosophy was directed to make at least occasional use of works of Plato (Cardinal College Statutes; Bond ed., *Statutes of the College of Oxford*, 1853, vol. 11, pp. 122–135; see also Duncan, 1986, pp. 339–341). Wolsey did not at once find a person to give the Philosophy lectures. To give the lectures on Greek he brought from Greece a Greek scholar named Mattheus Calphurnius (Duncan, 1986, p. 341). In addition, Wolsey brought to Oxford with the title Professor of Classics (i.e. Latin), the distinguished Spanish humanist Juan Luis de Vives. Most importantly for Plato, Wolsey made an arrangement with Cardinal Bessarion in Rome to provide Cardinal College with transcriptions of all of Cardinal Bessarion's Greek manuscripts. (Lyte, 1986, pp. 449–450). The significance of this arrangement has not been sufficiently appreciated. If Cardinal Wolsey had actually managed to transplant to an Oxford college the entire corpus of the Greek manuscripts of Cardinal Bessarion, the study of Plato in England would certainly have been advanced dramatically.

From Oxford let us now turn to Cambridge. At Cambridge the climate for Greek studies had from the beginning been very much more hospitable than at Oxford. (Erasmus, *Epistolae*, Allen ed., 1906–1965, vol. 3, p. 407). The teaching of Greek was begun at Cambridge by Erasmus himself, at Queens' College, soon after Henry's accession. Erasmus taught Greek at Queens' for three years (1511–1514), using Lucian and Plutarch as his principal authors. One consequence of Erasmus' teaching was the fact that the first book ever set in Greek type in England was an edition not of Plato but of Lucian, printed at Cambridge in 1521, by John Lair (STC 16896).

Erasmus's method of teaching Greek was continued at Queens' first by Henry Bullock, and then, beginning in 1518, by Richard Croke. Although Croke had studied Greek at Paris with Girolamo Aleandro, he had subsequently taught in Germany, and preferred to use Erasmus' method rather than the Parisian one. Thus the Parisian technique of using Plato as a teaching text in Greek did not get introduced in Cambridge until the arrival of John Redman in 1524. Redman had begun his study of Greek at Corpus Christi College, Oxford, but had soon moved on to Paris. When Redman arrived at St. John's, Plato was not yet being taught there; the founder of St. John's, Bishop John Fisher, was a kindly man, but no Hellenist: he thought that Plato had written a work called the *Georgycke* (*English Works*, Mayor ed., 1876, vol. 1, p. 62). By 1530 Redman had set up a proper Greek course, and his enthusiasm for Plato led a series of Cambridge teachers to use Plato in their teaching, sometimes in tutorials, but also often in lectures. These teachers included Thomas Smith, William Framyngham, John Aylmer, John Cheke, and Nicholas Carr. Roger Ascham, who taught Latin at St. John's, claimed that he once assigned Plato to two students for summer reading *(Works*, Giles ed., 1970, vol. 1.1, p. 74), but Ascham clearly did not teach Plato regularly himself. He did make it a point to mention Plato as often as possible in his letters, and also in a prose treatise on archery that he wrote for Henry VIII in 1545. Ascham's allusions to Plato in this work, called *Toxophilus*, show that Ascham had by then read Plato's *Phaedrus*, but that he otherwise knew Plato mainly through the florilegia of Ricchieri and Tixier (Jayne, *Monographs*).

Meanwhile Henry was encouraging Greek studies in another arena, his own court. Henry's strategy for maintaining social order in his realm was to use as policemen the existing network of gentry established in manor houses all over the country (Dowling, 1986). In order for this policy to work well, however, the gentry needed to be better educated than they were. At the very beginning of his reign, therefore Henry had had a program drawn up for educating the gentry. When the first proposal submitted for this purpose (by Sir Nicholas Bacon) proved useless (Farrington, 1964, p. 12), Henry turned to Thomas Cromwell. Cromwell had spent two extended periods in Italy (1504 and 1510), and believed that training in both the classics and in Italian writers was essential to the education of the aristocracy.

Both aspects of Cromwell's ideas about education quickly became standard enthusiasms at court. One of Henry's older courtiers, Thomas Elyot, threw himself into Cromwell's program with exemplary zeal. In 1531 he produced a handbook of behavior and thought for the governing class called *The Governour*. Two years later (1533) he published another handbook on that subject called *Of the Knowledge that Maketh a Wise Man*; in 1534 he published a commonplace-book, and in 1539 a Latin–English dictionary. All of these works were intended to help educate the aristocracy, and all made a special effort to show the importance of the classics. Allusions to Plato figure importantly in all of these works in Elyot. Although he himself knew Plato only from secondary sources, chiefly Cicero, Erasmus, and Diogenes Laertius, this dependence on secondary sources did not prevent him from boldly casting his tract *Of the Knowledge* in the form of a dialogue between Plato and Speusippus, with the sub-title "A Platonick Disputation" (see Schroeder, 1920; Stob, 1930).

Far more influential than the pseudo-classicism of Elyot was the genuine classicism of two other members of Henry's court, Erasmus and Thomas More. During the early years of Henry's court, Erasmus published a stream of learned books that had the effect of contributing to English knowledge of the Greek classics: these were:

1511 *De ratione studii*
1511 *Moriae encomium*
1513 *Parabolae*
1514 *Opusculae*
1515 *Institutio principis christiani*
1516 *Colloquia*
1518 *Antibarbarorum*
1519 *Paraclesis* (a preface to the New Testament)
1531 *Apophthegmata* (tr. 1539 by Taverner and 1542 by Udall)

(For the allusions to Plato in these works see the Toronto ed., 1974–).

One of Erasmus' most distinguished students in Greek was Thomas More, who also studied Greek with William Lily. With Erasmus, More shared a project of translating some dialogues of Lucian (published in 1506); More contributed only 4 of them. With Lily, More shared a project of translating Greek epigrams (published in 1518). In both of these projects More had ample occasion to learn something about Plato, and he put this knowledge to use in several of his own independent works, chiefly the *Utopia* (1516), in which he shows that he had himself read parts of the *Republic* and *Laws*. (More's life of the elder Pico, 1510, has nothing to do with Plato.) Although More, like Erasmus, was by temperament a Lucianist rather than a Platonist, the *Utopia* gave him sufficient reputation for a knowledge of Plato that in 1532 the Swiss scholar Simon Grynaeus proposed dedicating his new edition of Plato's *Opera* to More. In the end Grynaeus was dissuaded by the argument that it would be embarrassing for More to be endorsed by a Zwinglian. (On Plato in More see Jayne, 1993, pp. 402–422.)

The Italian part of Cromwell's prescription for educating the gentry may be seen in the numerous works by Italian authors that were imported into England before the closing of the ports in 1535. Most of these were not Platonic; some, such as Machiavelli's *Il principe*, reflected Cromwell's interests; others, such as, Marsilio of Padua's *Defensor pacis*, Henry's interest: Henry ordered that Marsilio's work be translated into English for the gentry. But at least one of the Italian books that came into England during this period did contribute to English knowledge about Plato: Castiglione's *Il cortegiano* (1528), which was known in London as early as 1530 (Hogrefe, 1930). In *Il cortegiano* Plato is mentioned 11 times, mainly in connection with political theory; the entire last section of the work is devoted to an exposition of the theory of Platonic love. There was also a wave of interest in Petrarch at Henry's court, but that had nothing to do with Plato. (On the Italian craze in England see Parks, 1963, 1968).

The importance of the Italian connection to Cromwell's policies is even better shown in the fact that before the break with Rome, Henry's regime sent to Italy for training scholars whom it meant to use as propagandists in the campaign to educate the gentry. One of these scholars, Reginald Pole, a 19-year old student at Magdalen College, Oxford, was sent to Italy in 1519. Two years later (1521) the regime sent over a slightly older Magdalen man, Thomas Starkey, to serve as Pole's private secretary. A third trainee was Thomas Lupset, who joined Pole's group in 1523, through an arrangement worked out by Cardinal Wolsey. Wolsey had displaced Lupset from his Readership at Oxford (by bringing in Vives), and had to find something for Lupset to do. His solution was to hire Lupset as tutor to Wolsey's bastard son, Thomas Winter, and attach both men to the already established household of Reginald Pole at Padua. As it turned out, Lupset developed a close friendship with Pole. The two men spent part of the period 1523–1525 in Padua reading Plato together in Greek under the guidance of Niccolò Leonico Tomei. According to Lupset, Pole managed to read through the entire corpus of Plato's *Works* (Letter of 1525 to Erasmus; Gee, 1928, p. 316). Tomei repeats this claim (*Discorsi*, 1525, fol. 1ᵛ; on Pole see Schenk, 1956; on Starkey see Mayer, 1989; on Lupset see Gee, 1928).

In Lupset's case the experience of reading Plato was only moderately influential. When it came time for Lupset to pay for his upkeep in Italy by producing the required pamphlet for Cromwell's educational program, Lupset wrote a straightforward tract called *An Exhortacion to Yonge Men* (1529) urging the aristocracy to recognize its moral obligation of service to the crown. In keeping with Lupset's own bitter experience as a victim of the regime's manipulation, the burden of this tract is Stoic rather than Platonic, but Lupset does cite Plato frequently and accurately, throughout the work, and specifically recommends that young gentlemen read Plato's *Republic* (Gee ed.,1928, p. 245).

In Pole's case, the experience of reading Plato was evidently much more transforming than it was for Lupset. The difference is spelled out clearly in the tract that Starkey later (1529) wrote as his payment to the regime. This work was never finished, and has no title (see ed. Burton, 1948), but it is written as a dialogue between Lupset and Pole on the subject of public service. In the dialogue Pole is shown as a confirmed Platonist throughout, whereas Lupset is shown as taking a more sceptical view. The actual arguments of Starkey's tract are drawn from the treatise that Henry and Cromwell were known to favor, the *Defensor pacis* of Marsilio of Padua, but the portrait of Pole that emerges in the dialogue is that of an admirer of Plato. Pole's enthusiasm for Plato became well enough known at court later to be specifically reproved by Cromwell, who sent Pole a copy of Machiavelli's *Prince*, with the advice that Machiavelli was a much better guide to the real world of politics than Plato (Pole, *Apology*; Lehmberg, 1960, p. 87). That Pole's interest in Plato was more than superficial may be seen in the fact that he made it a point to buy copies of Ficino's Anthology of Minor Platonists and Bessarion's treatise on Plato (Emden, 1974, p. 733; the Venice, 1503 ed. of the *Opera* of Bessarion begins with the treatise on Plato). If Pole had taken up the service for Henry for which he had been selected, trained as he was in the Greek text of Plato, and with full access to the Greek manuscripts of Bessarion, acquired by Wolsey, at his disposal, he might very well have injected a strong strain of Platonic thought into Henry's education program for the gentry.

Thus circumstances were building toward what might have become a major Platonic revival at Oxford. But in 1535 the break from Rome punctured the balloon. The ports were closed to books. Pole refused to take the Oath of Supremacy, and he went into exile on the continent, not to return until the reign of Mary. As for Wolsey, he had already fallen from power, and died (1530) as a consequence of the Divorce problem, and with him had gone any chance of acquiring copies of the manuscripts of Bessarion.

Although the long-term effects of Henry's break with Rome were, as I have suggested, probably negative for Plato, it must be acknowledged that some of Henry's actions actually encouraged the study of Plato. Even the injunctions of 1535 to the universities contained some provisions that had the effect of calling attention to Plato. One of the injunctions of 1535 specified that in place of the Catholic authorities Scotus and Aquinas, students in Theology should now read Melanchthon and Bucer. This injunction actually worked both for and against Plato, for Melanchthon was an enthusiastic advocate of Plato, and Bucer a vehement opponent. Melanchthon was a recognized authority on Plato: in 1518 he had published for school use a group of selections from Lucian, Plutarch, and Plato's *Symposium* (*Werke*, 1963 ed. vol. 1, col. 44); and in 1525 he had published one short selection each from Plato's *Theaetetus* and *Symposium* in another school text called *A Student's Guide to the Greek Language* (*Werke*, 1963 ed. vol. 20, cols. 189–190). In 1537 and 1538 Melanchthon gave lectures on Plato which were subsequently published *(Werke,*

1963 ed. vol. 11 cols., 342–349 and 413–425; on Melanchthon see Hartfelder, 1972. Bucer, too, had read the *Symposium*, and several other dialogues as well, including the *Meno*, but his reaction to Plato was very negative: "Let us beware of the philosophy of Plato" (*Commonplaces*, Wright ed., 1972, p. 114; on Plato in Bucer see Jayne, 1993, pp. 504–509; Hopf, 1946).

Another provision of Henry's Injunction of 1535 that affected Plato was the provision abolishing the teaching of Canon Law (See Charlton, 1965, pp. 187–194; Schoeck, 1962). At Cambridge this provision had the odd effect of making Plato's *Laws* a popular text among students in Arts who expected to go into Civil Law. During the years following Henry's injunction ownership of copies of Plato's *Opera* and *Laws* jumped significantly at Cambridge (Leedham–Green, 1986, vol. 1, pp. 7, 16, 32, 36, 41). By 1545 the Cambridge bookseller Nicholas Pilgrim was stocking on a regular basis copies of the Louvain, 1533 ed. of Plato's *Laws* in Latin (Leedham–Green, 1986, vol. 1, p. 62 # 52).

At Cambridge various initiatives that Henry took regarding the universities during the latter part of his reign actually increased the study of Plato. In 1540, in an attempt to keep up with his rival, Francis I of France, Henry established five Regius Professorships at both universities: in Theology, Greek, Hebrew, Civil Law, and Medicine (Logan, 1977; Duncan, 1986). At Cambridge the first Regius Professor of Greek was John Cheke. Cheke taught Plato only in tutorials (Strype, *Life*, 1974, p. 153), but when Cheke left Cambridge in 1544, his Regius Professorship went to an ardent admirer of Plato at Pembroke Hall, Nicholas Carr, who translated sections of the *Laws*; *Symposium* and *Timaeus*, and wrote commentaries on the *Laws* and *Symposium*. (Demosthenes *Orationes*; Doddington ed., 1571, sig. X2^r).

In 1545 Henry revised the statutes of St. John's College, where Plato was already being taught, to provide that Plato should be included not only in the course in Greek Language but also in the course in Philosophy (*Early Statutes.*, Mayor ed., 1859, vol. 2, p. 107).

Finally, in 1546 Henry established a royal college at each university. At Oxford this college was Christ Church; at Cambridge, it was Trinity. In order to give his new foundations distinguished faculty, Henry raided other colleges mercilessly. For Trinity he commandeered the Regius Professor of Greek, Nicholas Carr, from Pembroke Hall. On his translation to Trinity, Carr instituted public lectures on Plato; these became very popular (Wilson, 1551, sigs. dii^v–diii^r), with the result that Trinity replaced St. John's as the center of Plato studies at Cambridge.

On balance, however, in spite of these belated efforts on Henry's part to repair the damage that he had done to the universities, the opportunity for major progress in advancing knowledge about Plato was lost at the break from Rome. The enthusiasms of Redman and Carr remained isolated: there was no edition or translation of any work of Plato published in England during the reign of Henry VIII. Indeed, apart from tracts that Henry himself commissioned, the English press produced no discussion of Plato that was not based on medieval sources. To cite one example, a collection of quotations from philosophers on the subject of Ethics was printed by William Baldwin in 1547 under the title *A Treatise of Morall Philosophie*. Baldwin includes in his collection a biography of Plato, and 131 quotations attributed to Plato, but this material is drawn entirely from medieval sources, chiefly Walter Burley's *De vita et moribus philosophorum* (1345), and the quotations given are almost all apocryphal. The fact that the English conception of Plato remained stubbornly medieval during the reign of Henry VIII may be seen especially in a work of Robert Greene of Welby (Lincs), written in 1528–1529. In that year Greene translated into English the last 3 books (II–IV) of an alchemical handbook attributed to Plato. The work in question was originally written in Arabic, but is first seen in Europe in a Latin translation of about 1200 A.D. In its Latin version the work was known by several different names, all of which show its attribution to Plato:

Platonis quartorum
Platonis libri tres
Platonis liber quartus
Platonis soliae
Platonis stellicae

Greene's partial translation, under the title *Platonis libri tres*, survives in Cambridge University Library MS Ff.IV.13.fols. 191^r–273^r. (The Latin original is in Zetzner, *Theatrum Chemicum*, 1613–1661; see also Thorndike, 1924–1958, II. 782–783).

C. Edward VI (1547–1553)

One does not ordinarily associate with Plato any of the four men who chiefly ran the country for the boy-king Edward VI: Somerset, Cranmer, Northampton, or Paget. As it happens, however, Sir William Paget, the Royal Secretary, did have an important influence on what was known about Plato in England.

When Edward came to the throne, at the age of ten, in 1547, he had already been under the tutelage of Sir John Cheke for three years. It is thus hardly surprising that in Edward's school-exercises for the years 1548–1552 he occasionally ventures to drop the name of Plato (London, BL MS 4724, fols. 2, 67, 78). All of these allusions are merely passing references, and based entirely on secondary sources. Although Edward's advisors cautiously continued Henry VIII's policy of publishing materials that would help to educate the gentry, the works that they selected for that purpose, such as Francis Seager's commonplace-book, The *scoole of vertue* (1550), mention Plato only in passing, and at second hand. The one exception was a new Latin – English dictionary that the regime published in 1548, almost as soon as Edward was crowned. This dictionary was supposed to be merely a new edition of the old *Bibliothecae Eliotae* of Thomas Elyot (1538), revised by Thomas Cooper with an eye to Protestantizing it wherever necessary. Once into the job, however, Cooper went far beyond his mandate and revised right and left, following his own interests. Thus Cooper's entry for Plato enlarges Elyot's entry considerably, adding new material not only from Augustine's *City of God* (VIII.4–12), but more authoritatively, also from Diogenes Laertius, to whom Cooper refers as "Dionysius" (1548 ed., sig. Eee 2ʳ).

The contributions of Sir William Paget to Plato's reputation began in the same year that Cooper's new dictionary was published (1548), but in connection with an entirely different book, one published on the continent. It had happened that in 1543, while Henry VIII was still on the throne, Paget had befriended a visiting diplomat from Strasbourg named Johann Philippson. In 1548 when Paget was Royal Secretary to Edward VI, Philippson published at Strasbourg a book that was meant to repay Paget. The book contained two works: the first was a Latin translation by Philippson of part of a French treatise on the French system of government, *La Monarchie de France*, by Claude de Seyssel, first published in 1519. The second work in Philippson's book was a Latin précis by Philippson of Plato's *Republic* and *Laws*, with the title *Summa doctrinae Platonis de republica et legibus*. The Seyssel work was dedicated to Edward, and the précis of Plato to Paget. In his dedicatory letter to Paget, Philippson congratulates Paget on his new position, and urges him to read the *Republic* and *Laws* of Plato for guidance (1548 ed., fols. 73ʳ–74ʳ).

A collection of quotations from the *Republic* and *Laws* had been available in France since 1506, when Jacques Le Fèvre d'Étaples compiled one under the title *Hecatonomiae* and appended it to an edition of Aristotle's *Politics* and *Economics*. Philippson's work, however, is not a collection of quotations; it is a précis, in Philippson's own words, of the principal points made, book by book, first in the *Republic* and then in the *Laws*. Although Paget himself was not interested in Plato, he nevertheless became the means by which Philippson's enthusiasm for Plato was transmitted to Cambridge, as I will explain.

At the very beginning of Edward's reign (1549) his advisors, fearing that the universities might become hot-beds of subversion, issued new statutes for the universities, sent agents to confiscate Catholic books found in the college libraries, and hired faculty members to serve as spies (L. Merrill, 1928, pp. 38–50). At Oxford these measures had mixed effects on the status of Plato. On the positive side, the statutes of 1549 encouraged the reading of Plato's *Republic* (Lamb ed., *Documents*, 1838, vol. 1, pp. 124–125); and several colleges and individuals at Oxford acquired copies of printed editions of Plato during Edward's reign. On the negative side, the purging of the libraries at Oxford resulted in the loss of all but one of Duke Humfrey's valuable manuscripts of Plato. (This savaging of the University Library may have been mainly an aberration on the part of the Dean of Christ Church, Richard Cox; see Ker, 1986, p. 466). Only one Oxford scholar of Edward's reign is known to have done any serious work on Plato: this was the greasy government spy Nicholas

Grimald, who made a study of Plato's *Crito* (Bale, *Index*, ed. Poole and Bateson, 1902, p. 303).

At Cambridge during Edward's reign the climate was generally hostile to Plato because during the years 1549–1551 Martin Bucer was in residence at Cambridge, and Bucer as we have seen, was an outspoken foe of Plato. Nevertheless throughout Bucer's time in Cambridge Nicholas Carr continued to give his regular 8:00 A.M. lecture on Plato (Wilson, *De vita et obitu*, 1551, sig. diii^r). After Bucer's death, Carr even managed to push through at Trinity a statute requiring every Trinity student to own a copy of some work of Plato (Trinity Cambridge, *Statutes*, 1552, ch. 18; Mullinger, 1873–1911, vol. 2, p. 616). This requirement was evidently too novel to be enforced, however, for only two Cambridge men are known to have owned copies of Plato's works during Edward's reign, one at Pembroke, and the other at King's (Leedham–Green, 1986, vol. 1, pp. 117, 122; (on Edwardian Cambridge see H.C. Porter, 1958).

Ironically, the Cambridge teacher who did the most to publicize to the world the fact that Englishmen were reading Plato was not the learned Nicholas Carr, who lectured on Plato every weekday, but the petulant Roger Ascham, who never lectured on Plato at all, and who spent nearly the whole of his time at Cambridge trying as hard as he could to escape from the university. The circumstances behind this paradox were as follows. One of the people at court to whom Ascham wrote, in his feverish effort to leave Cambridge, was Sir William Paget. In the Spring of 1548 Paget managed to get Ascham a post as tutor to the Princess Elizabeth. In the course of his correspondence with Ascham about this post Paget evidently informed Ascham about having received from Philippson his précis of Plato's *Republic* and *Laws*, for Ascham acquired a copy of that work himself: his copy still survives in the British Library (press-mark C.45.a.7). During the two years that Ascham served as Elizabeth's tutor (1548–1550) he had no time to pursue the Philippson connection, but in January of 1550 he was abruptly discharged by Elizabeth, and had to return to Cambridge, where he at once began a new campaign of letter-writing, with the purpose of trying to get out again. It was during this period that Ascham followed through with the Philippson connection and began a correspondence with Philippson's colleague at Strasbourg, Johann Sturm.

Sturm, who was then headmaster of the preparatory school at Strasbourg, was a learned student of Plato. He had already published two collections of dialogues of Plato for school use:

1538 *II Alcibiades, Menexenus*
1541 *Apology, Crito, Gorgias*

Ascham's correspondence with Sturm began in April, 1505, and extended over many years. Although the two men never actually met, Ascham named one of his sons after Sturm. Sturm contributed to Ascham's knowledge of Plato only to the extent of getting Ascham to read the *Gorgias*, but he certainly had some hand in encouraging Ascham in his subsequent habit of mentioning Plato in his letters.

In the Spring of 1550 Paget found Ascham another post, as secretary to Sir Richard Morison, who was about to leave for Augsburg, to serve as ambassador to the court of the Emperor Charles V. On his way out of the country Ascham happened to stop at the Leicestershire country house of his friends the Greys. There he noticed 13-year old Jane translating a passage of Plato's *Phaedo* for her tutor, John Aylmer (see Luke, 1986). This episode made a deep impression on Ascham: he mentioned it in no less than six letters to various people, including Sturm. One of these letters, dated April 4, 1550, (Giles ed., 1970, vol. I.1, pp. 181–193) was later published by Sturm, along with a letter of his own (Giles ed., *Works* of Ascham, 1970, vol. I.2, pp. 195–207) as evidence of the new learning of the English nobility (*Epistolae duae de nobilitate anglicana*, published as an appendix to the *De laudibus graecarum literarum* of Conrad Heresbach, 1551). Thus through his influence on Roger Ascham, Sir William Paget accidentally became the means by which scholars on the continent came to realize that there were people in England (women, at least, and perhaps men as well) who knew something about Plato.

Just as during the reigns of Henry VII and Henry VIII a few seeds of the continental court conception of Plato had managed to land on English soil, only to expire, so another such seed landed during the reign of Edward VI, and with similar effect. In 1551, John Dee returned to England after studying for four years on the continent. At the time of his departure from England Dee had held a position as Reader of Greek at Trinity College, Cambridge, but on the continent he had studied primarily with the occultists Johann Trithemius and Cornelius Agrippa. As a consequence of his study of Agrippa's *De occulta philosophia*, and of its sources, Dee became the first Englishman to acquire a thorough understanding of the continental court interpretation of Plato (on Dee see French, 1972; Calder, 1952; Clulee, 1988; Deacon, 1968; Firpo, 1952). Dee brought back with him from the continent an impressive collection of books in the field of Platonic occultism. Among the occultists themselves he owned works of Agrippa, Giorgio, Reuchlin, and Trithemius, and all of the major works of Ficino. As for Plato, Dee owned two copies of the complete *Works*, four of the *Timaeus*, and one each of the *Meno* and *Phaedo*. He also owned, however, two Pseudo-Platonic works: two copies of *Plato's Calf*, and one of *Plato's Fourth Book* (Roberts–Watson, 1990; on *Plato's Fourth Book* see above p. 91). *Plato's Calf* (*Vacca Platonis*) was a popular farmer's handbook showing how to cause rain to fall, how to make cows more intelligent, how to communicate with birds, etc. The work was of Arabic origin, but had been known in Latin translation in England since at least 1170. The work was also known by several other names, but all of these names attribute the work to Plato:

Plato's Ointment	*Plato's Book of Procedures*
Plato's Anequems	*Plato's Active Institutes*
Plato's Laws	*Plato's Liber Nevemich*

(Copies may be seen in Cambridge, Trinity College MS 0.2.48, #9 and Oxford, Jesus College MS 3; for background see Thorndike, 1923–1958; vol. 2, pp. 777–779, 809–810).

D. MARY I (1553–1558)

The violent policies of Mary I did far less damage to the status of Plato in England than one might suppose. Still, the religious preoccupations of the times did prevent the English from developing any special interest in Plato, and at least one valuable opportunity for learning more about Plato was lost.

In the first year of Mary's reign her regime ordered both universities to revert to the statutes that had been in effect under Henry VIII (Cooper, *Athenae*, 1858–1913, vol. 2, pp. 79–80; C. Cross, 1986, pp. 145–148). So far as Plato was concerned, this meant only that instead of being encouraged to read the newly recovered *Republic*, students were sent back to read the old medieval *Timaeus*. In 1556 Cardinal Pole sent agents to Oxford to purge the university libraries of Protestant books; the libraries at Cambridge were purged the following year (1557). For some reason, however, the works of Plato in the Oxford libraries were conspicuously spared (Ker, 1956; 1971; 1986, pp. 458–459, 487–497). I suggest that Pole may very well have specifically exempted Plato, not so much because Plato was regarded as an irrelevant antique as because Pole himself had fond memories of his study of Plato at Padua. (The evidence concerning the purge at Cambridge is less conclusive because only three of the Cambridge inventories of 1557 have survived, and none of the three libraries concerned – University Library, King's College, and Trinity Hall – had owned any Plato before the purge. See Oates–Pink, 1952, pp. 315–337; Thompson, 1954; Malden, 1902; McKitterick, 1978).

Mary herself had no interest in Plato, but her connection with Spain happened to present her subjects with two unusual opportunities to learn something about Plato. One of the leading Plato scholars of the period was a Spanish Catholic, Sebastian Fox Morcillo. In 1554, Morcillo dedicated to Philip II of Spain a book entitled *De consensu Platonis cum Aristotele* (also called *De naturae philosophia*). This book, a comparison between the philosophies of Plato and Aristotle, was the most important work of Platonic scholarship published in Europe during the reign of Mary. Yet even though the book had been dedicated to Mary's husband as a wedding gift on the occasion of his marriage to her, no one in England appears to have paid the slightest attention to it during Mary's reign. There may have been a copy of the work in the Royal Library, but the earliest recorded copies at the English universities are copies at Cambridge in 1558, 1567, and 1581, and at Oxford in 1568 (see Leedham–Green, 1986, vol. 1, pp. 199, 295; Ker, 1986, p. 482; Anderson, 1975, p. 236).

The other relevant Spanish work of Mary's reign did attract some attention, but it was a far less important contribution to knowledge about Plato. This was *Lo relox de principes*, by Antonio Guevara, which was translated into English by Thomas North in 1557 under the title *The Diall of Princes*. In the form in which North translated the work (with the help of a French translation in 1540), *Lo relox de principes* consisted of three books of anecdotal moral advice, and a fourth book on how to be a good courtier. Guevara's work includes 14 allusions to Plato, but all of these references are merely borrowings from commonplace-books, notwithstanding the fact that Guevara twice claims that he used Plato's *Laws* as his source. In any case, Guevara was admired in England only for the practicality of his advice to Catholic courtiers, not for his Platonism.

Toward the end of Mary's reign (1556) a Paris printer published a Latin edition of a collection of quotations from Plato's works called *Divini Platonis gemmae*. This collection became quite well known in England, usually under the title *Gemmae Platonis*, and with no reference to its original editor, Niccolò Liburnio (for details see Jayne, 1993, p. 1864). Copies of the *Gemmae Platonis* were owned by an anonymous scholar at Cambridge, Oxford, in 1558 (Leedham-Green, 1986, vol. 1, p. 200, #6) and by John Dunnet at University College, Oxford, in 1570 (Fehrenbach and Leedham-Green, 1992–1994, vol. 3, p. 225, #85.13).

CHAPTER 6

THE EARLY YEARS OF ELIZABETH I (1558–1578)

Throughout the first four Tudor reigns, as we have seen, the dominant conception of Plato in England was the school conception, adulterated by lingering traces of the apocryphal Plato of the Middle Ages. The only important signs we have seen of English awareness of the new court conception of Plato were Colet's brush with Ficino during the reign of Henry VII, Pole's purchase of Ficino's anthology during the reign of Henry VIII, and Dee's exposure to Agrippa in Paris during the reign of Edward VI. In the third year of the reign of Elizabeth I (1560) the court conception of Plato finally found an English admirer, in Thomas Howell. Between 1560 and 1590 idealized ("Platonic") love gradually became a modish enthusiasm at Elizabeth's court; but by 1595 the fad had waned again, leaving the field once more to the Plato of the schools. With this brief overview in mind, we may now turn to a more detailed examination of the status of Plato during Elizabeth's reign.

Elizabeth I was crowned Queen of England on January 14, 1558. The day before her coronation she made a progress from the City of London to Westminster. At one of her stops, St. Paul's School, a pupil recited a Latin oration in which Plato was invoked in order to flatter Elizabeth:

> That divine philosopher Plato, among many
> wise and famous sayings that he left to
> posterity, said that a common-wealth would
> be happiest if its queen were devoted to
> wisdom and well-endowed with virtues.
> (Nicholas, *Progresses*, I, 1823 ed., vol. 1, p. 52; tr. mine).

The teacher who had written this speech had obviously found in a commonplace-book Plato's aphorism about the philosopher-king, and freely bastardized it for a female ruler. What is interesting about this speech is not so much that it bears so little resemblance to what Plato actually said, but that the teacher assumed that although the Queen was known to speak Latin, and would thus understand what the boy was saying, she would not know enough about Plato to recognize the fraudulence of the allusion. There was nothing especially daring about such an assumption. Elizabeth's own advisors might not have recognized the allusion; even though the philosopher-king aphorism had been one of the two or three best known "famous sayings" of Plato since the time of St. Jerome, (for example, see Whethamstede's way of identifying Plato, p. 23 above), many people in England still thought that Plato was a soothsayer of some kind. I have mentioned that one of the works commonly associated with Plato during the Middle Ages was a fortune-telling device sometimes called *Plato's Sphere*. This device was a paper wheel that supposedly enable its user to solve vexing problems such as finding a lost object, or predicting the prospects for a proposed business venture (for description and illustrations see Singer, 1928, and Gratton and Singer, 1952). This kind of device was still in circulation in England; indeed a copy of it was printed as late as 1560 (STC 20524). In February 1564, a member of the rural gentry in Yorkshire, Sir John Betson, was brought before an Ecclesiastical Commission of the Diocese of York on charges of conjuring; he was ordered

> to bringe in such bookes as he hath
> concernynge the practises of con-
> juracions, and speciallie *Plato Spere*
> and *Pithocoras Spere* and such lyk.
> (Purvis, 1948, p. 198).

The court eventually exonerated Betson of any dealing with the Devil, and ruled that Betson used these devices only, "as he saieth, for thinges lost". Apparently Betson's only misdemeanor was ignorance.

The traditional Tudor technique for remedying such ignorance had been to publish books for the education of the gentry (Stone, 1964; Bennett, 1952, 1970). The early Tudors had usually commissioned original tracts for this purpose. Elizabeth's government, however, proceeded quite differently; it relied mainly on translations of foreign works. Among the many translations published during the first twenty years of the reign, Plato is mentioned frequently in at least 27. (See Table 9 overleaf.)

In almost all of these works it is the school conception of Plato that is represented. The principal exceptions are the *Fior di virtù* of 1565, which is actually a version of the old medieval *Dicts or Sayings*; and works that depict Plato as the philosopher of the courts: Castiglione's *Il cortegiano* (1561), Pasquier's *Le monophile* (1572), and Guicciardini's *Detti e fatti* (1573). The latter two works are particularly interesting for our history, for these two works, published in quick succession, gave English readers a double exposure to Ficino's version of the Platonic theory of love. Both Pasquier and Guicciardini had read Ficino's *De amore*, and both used it prominently (Pasquier in Fenton tr., 1572 ed., Book I, fols. 33^r–35^v, 41^r; Book II, fol. 5^r; Guicciardini, in Sanford tr., 1573 ed., fol. 69^r); of the two, only Guicciardini specifically cites Ficino as his source (Sanford tr., 1573 ed., fol. 36^v; on Castigilone see Schrinner, 1939).

Among the works in Table 9, those that are most notable for the frequency of their allusions to Plato are the works by Manzolli, Calvin, Boiastuau, Agrippa, Pasquier, Aconcio, Guevara, Turler, Aelianus, Daneau, and La Place (for details see Jayne, 1993, pp. 588–649). The works of Calvin and Bullinger I will discuss below.

Table 9. Early Elizabethan Translations

Date	Original author	Original title and date	Translator
1560	Manzolli	*Zodiacus vitae* (1535)	Barnabe Googe
1561	Calvin	*Instit. Christ. religionis* (1536)	Thomas Norton
1561	Castiglione	*Il cortegiano* (1528)	Thomas Hoby
1561	Plutarch	(3 essays; c.120 A.D.)	Thomas Blundeville
1561	Cicero	*Tusculanae* (45 B.C.)	John Dolman
1565	*(Dits moraulx)*	*Fior di virtù* (1491)	John Larke
1566	Boaistuau	*Le théatre du monde* (1558)	John Alday
1568	Guevara	*Lo relox de príncipes*(1529)	Thomas North (new ed.)
1569	Agrippa	*De vanitate scientiarum* (1526)	James Sanford
1570	Sturm	*Nobilitas literata* (1549)	Thomas Browne
1571	Mexia	*Silva de varia lección* (1543)	Thomas Fortescue
1571	Plutarch	*De educatione* (c.120 A.D.)	Edward Grant
1572	Pasquier	*Le monophile* (1554)	Geoffrey Fenton
1573	Paleario	*Del beneficio di Gesu Cristo* (1543)	Arthur Golding
1573	Guicciardini	*Detti e fatti* (1565)	James Sanford
1574	Aconcio	*De methodo* (1558)	Thomas Blundeville
1574	Guevara	*Epistolas familiares* I (1539)	Edward Hellowes
1574	Talpin	*Le policie Chrestienne* (1568)	Geoffrey Fenton
1575	Guevara	*Epistolas familiares* II (1541)	Geoffrey Fenton
1575	Guevara	*Menosprecio de corte* (1539)	Francis Briant and Thomas Tynne
1575	Turler	*De peregrinatione* (1574)	Anon.
1576	Aelianus	*Varia historia* (150 A.D.)	Abraham Fleming
1576	La Place	*Commentaires de l'estat* (1565)	Thomas Tymme
1577	Cartari	*Le imagini de i dei* (1556)	Stephen Bateman
1577	Bullinger	*Sermonum decades* (1552)	H. Middleton
1578	Seneca	*De beneficiis* (c.65 A.D.)	Arthur Golding
1578	Daneau	*Physica Christiana* (1576)	Thomas Twyne

The 1568 version of North's translation of Guevara's *Lo relox de principes* is noteworthy only because in this new edition, which North dedicated to Queen Elizabeth, he thought it appropriate to open his dedication with a long discussion of Plato's theories about maintaining order in society (1568 ed. Dedication). North took his material for this passage entirely from commonplace-books, but it is striking that he thought of citing Plato at all, for this book appeared ten years before anyone in England had any idea that Elizabeth would become the dedicatee of an edition of the *Works* of Plato. In Cartari's work, Plato is referred to only indirectly; he is included among "the Platonists" in identifying Jupiter with the World–Soul (1576 repr., p. 130); and he is included among "some of the Greeks" in distinguishing between two Venuses (1976 repr., p. 540).

To what extent Elizabeth's government actually commissioned and subsidized the translations listed above I cannot say, but the government did try to control very tightly what was and was not printed, and the books that they authorized for publication certainly did affect both the English conception of Plato, and the foreign conception of English knowledge about Plato. An example of the latter is the influence of Roger Ascham. In Elizabeth's bureaucracy Ascham served primarily as a calligrapher, but during the first ten years of her reign Ascham kept up a busy correspondence with friends on the continent, and also wrote a tract on education, entitled *The Scholemaster*. Between the accession of Elizabeth in 1558, and Ascham's own death, in 1568, Ascham managed to mention Plato in his writings at least 45 times. Ascham's own reading of Plato never extended beyond the *Phaedrus*, *Phaedo*, *Gorgias*, and parts of the *Republic* and *Laws*, but his tireless huckstering of English knowledge about Plato in his letters to correspondents abroad, especially Sturm, very likely had some influence on Henri Estienne's decision in 1578 to dedicate part of his new edition of Plato to Elizabeth. (On Ascham see Jayne, *Monographs,* 1994)

In Ascham's case, the only conception of Plato that he wrote about was the school conception, and it was this conception that was fostered, in the early years, by most of the books that Elizabeth's government authorized for publication. But her government's openness to books and refugees from the continent also made it possible for new information about the court conception of Plato to come into the country. One of the earliest examples of this new incursion was the work of an Italian Protestant refugee, Jacopo Aconcio. In a book that he had published on the continent *De methodo* (Basle, 1558) Aconcio compares Plato's own writings with those of the Italian court–Platonist Francesco Patrizi (Radetti ed., pp. 350–355; see also pp. 84, 106; on Aconcio see Dick, 1940, 1941; O'Malley, 1955; on Patrizi see Copenhaver and Schmitt, 1992, pp. 184–195).

In the case of Thomas Howell of Somerset, the source of his knowledge is less clear. But Howell is important because he was one of the very country gentry whom Elizabeth's regime had been trying most assiduously to educate. Though technically a gentleman, Howell was actually only a private secretary in the household of the Earl of Shrewsbury. Heeding the government's message that the gentry was expected to train itself in the classics, Howell chose to study Ovid's *Metamorphoses*. Howell first amused himself by translating into five pages of English couplets Ovid's account of Narcissus. Then, perhaps spurred by the presence in most editions of Ovid, of medieval allegorizations of the story, such as that by Pierre Bersuire, Howell went on to add to his translation a long appendix in 7-line stanzas (1560 ed., sigs. B1^r–E1^v) in which he collected all the allegorizations of the Narcissus story that he could find. By some means Howell learned about the brief allegorization of Narcissus in Ficino's *De amore* (VI.17; Jayne tr., 1985 ed., pp. 140–141), and added this allegorization to his collection (1560 ed., sigs. 3^v–4^v). How Ficino's work came to Howell's attention we do not know, but since he refers to Ficino by his Latin name, "Ficinus", he may have found the passage simply by consulting the Index under "Narcissus" in an edition of Ficino's Latin translation of the *Opera* of Plato that happened to be in his employer's library. By whatever means Howell came by Ficino's *De amore*, Howell appears to have been the first Englishman who actually made use of Ficino's interpretation of the theory of Platonic love, antedating by a dozen years the allusions to Ficino's theory that we have seen in the English translations of Pasquier (1572) and Guicciardini (1573).

Among the writers around Elizabeth during the early years one would have expected that one of those most familiar with Plato, at least with the court conception of his work, would have been John Dee. During the reign of Mary, Dee had been imprisoned. When Elizabeth came to the throne in 1558 and freed Dee from prison, he was still only 31 years old. In spite of his brilliance as a mathematician, the universities tended to ignore him (Feingold, 1984), but in 1570, an unwary member of the gentry, Sir Francis Billingsley, invited Dee to write a Preface to Billingsley's new English translation of Euclid. Seizing the opportunity to be heard, Dee stretched his "Preface" into a full scale treatise, of 156 folio pages. In this treatise Dee mentions Plato several times, but his statements inspire little confidence. For example, Dee says that he regards Plato's *Epinomis*, which is actually only a short appendix to the *Laws*, as "the Threasury of all his doctrine" (Euclid, 1570 ed., sig. al'). In the end Dee contributed very little to either the court conception or the school conception of Plato.

In addition to translations, Elizabeth's government authorized works by English authors as well, some for internal consumption, and some for readers abroad. It is characteristic of these works that those that were intended for English readers do not contain allusions to Plato, whereas those that were intended for foreign consumption do. For example, in none of the numerous histories of England written for English readers is there any reference to Plato, whereas in the histories by John Major and Humphrey Llwyd, which were written in Latin and published abroad, both authors make it a point to refer to Plato. Even though these allusions are purely decorative, they show that the English thought that continental readers would be impressed by allusions to Plato.

Not all English writers, however, were able to drop the name of Plato as freely as the foreign market was thought to require. An interesting comparison may be seen in two works that were commissioned to defend the policies of Elizabeth's government abroad, one by John Jewel in 1562, and the other by Thomas Smith in 1565. Both of these works were defenses of English policy, and both were written in Latin, for continental readers. Jewel's tract, entitled *Apologia ecclesiae anglicorum* was published anonymously in 1562. Jewel knew nothing about Plato, and his work contains no allusion to Plato. Smith, on the other hand, knew a great deal about Plato, and was careful to place decorative allusions to Plato at both the beginning and end of his work, as was the fashion on the continent. Smith, we recall, had been a student of Greek at Cambridge. He had since served as Regius Professor of Civil Law at Cambridge and as Provost of Eton. At the time he wrote his tract for Elizabeth's government, he was serving as Ambassador to France. During his stay in Paris he had met the French scholar Louis Le Roy, and had acquired copies of Le

Roy's French translations of *Timaeus* and *Symposium*, as well as copies of Greek and Latin editions of Plato's *Opera* (Strype, *Life*, 1974, pp. 89, 274–281). Smith's allusions to Plato in the *De republica anglorum* were intended to show continental readers that the English were as well educated in the classics as any continental writer was; the tract was not published until 1583, and by that time it served also to remind English readers that Smith himself had a special reputation as an expert on Plato (e.g. Walter Haddon, *Lucubrationes*, 1567, p. 312; Richard Carew, *A Treatise on. . . the English Tongue*, ed. G.G. Smith, 1967, vol. 2, p. 293: see also Strype, *Life*, 1974, p. 159; Gabriel Harvey, *Marginalia*, ed. Moore-Smith, 1913, p. 197).

Among the secular books that Elizabeth's regime authorized for internal consumption, one would have thought that dictionaries and commonplace-books were the most likely places to find Plato. There is a formal entry for "Plato" (placed at the back) in the revised edition of 1565 of Thomas Cooper's Latin–English dictionary (1565 ed., sigs. 03ᵛ–04ʳ), but Plato rarely appears in other dictionaries, (see Junius' *Nomenclator*, 1555, for example). A significant exception is an allusion to Plato in a dictionary of Italian phrases for English businessmen going abroad, compiled by John Florio and published in 1578 under the title *First Fruites* (1578 ed., fol. 35ᵛ). Plato is mentioned casually in several of the original commonplace-books published early in Elizabeth's regime, but he figures prominently in only two of them, Edmund Elviden's *The closet of counsells* (1569) and John Parinchef's *An extracte of examples* (1572). Elviden's collection includes 47 quotations attributed to Plato; all of these Elviden plundered from other commonplace-books, and most of them are apocryphal.

The full title of the collection by John Parinchef reads: *An extracte of examples, apophthegmes (sic) and histories out of Lycosthenes, Brusonius, and others* (London, 1572). By "Lycosthenes" Parinchef means Lycosthenes' *Apophthegmata* (Basle, 1555); by "Brusonius" Parinchef means Lucio Brusoni's *Facetiarum exemplorumque* (Basle, 1559). By "others" Parinchef means chiefly Diogenes Laertius and Erasmus (*Adagia* and *Apophthegmata*). Parinchef arranges his anecdotes by subject, and gives the source of each in a marginal postilla. Parinchef's subjects are all sternly moralistic, as in the chapter entitled "Of Abstinencie, Continencie and Temperancie". Parinchef himself alludes to Plato in only 5 of his anecdotes, but Parinchef's collection increased knowledge about Plato in another way; it brought Lycosthenes' *Apophthegmata* to the attention of Elizabeth's advisors, who authorized the publication of a London edition of the entire *Apophthegmata* in its original Latin text in 1579. Allusions to Plato in Lycosthenes' work are numerous: the Paris, 1579 edition gives 64. Since Lycosthenes' work is a collection of anecdotes rather than a collection of quotation, his allusions to Plato are mainly apocryphal, and drawn from previous collections such as those of Brusoni and Erasmus. Nevertheless, the frequency of the allusions gave the impression that Plato was a person of some importance, with whom an educated person was expected to be familiar.

I need mention only one other reference work among those that Elizabeth's regime authorized for internal consumption during this period: William Alley's *The Poore Man's Librarie* (1571). Alley's work is not a commonplace-book, but a miniature encyclopedia, containing short articles on various subjects, arranged in no particular order. Sandwiched between an article on "London" and one on "Courtry" [sic] appears a short article on "Plato" (1571 ed. fol. 4ʳ). His comments on Plato Alley twice claims to have taken from St. Augustine, ("as S. Austen sayth"); in fact, however, he took them from John of Salisbury's *Policraticus*.

The fact that Plato happens to be mentioned in so many of the secular books authorized by Elizabeth's regime does not, of course, mean that Elizabeth's advisors had any special interest in advancing knowledge about Plato. They had even less intention of teaching the populace about Plato through their religious publications; yet, as it turned out, more Elizabethan laymen learned about Plato from religious works than from any other kind of book. A case in point is John Calvin's *Institutio Christianae religionis* (Basle, 1536). This work was a foundation stone of Elizabethan policy in religion, and the regime lost no time in making the work available in English to the clergy; an English translation by Sir Thomas Norton was published in Elizabeth's third year on the throne (1561). Through no fault of the regime, or even of Calvin himself, Calvin's *Institutes* became a major source of information about Plato for English readers. Calvin refers to Plato often in the *Institutes:* in 15 places by name, and in 9 other places by epithets such as "Platonic philosophy", or "the philosophers", or "some say". Calvin cites only two dialogues of Plato by name: the *Protagoras* and the *Republic*, but he had obviously read at least 12 other dialogues as well:

Alcibiades II	*Laws*	*Statesman*
Apology	*Meno*	*Symposium*
Cratylus	*Phaedo*	*Theatetus*
Epinomis	*Phaedrus*	*Timaeus*

One of Calvin's allusions to the *Republic* consists of an entire chapter, entitled "Plato's remarks on similar pretense and delusion", which Calvin devotes to a paraphrase of Plato's *Republic* II. 365E–366A. In that passage Plato is ridiculing the naiveté of people who think that by bringing animal sacrifices to the temples they can buy forgiveness of their sins from the gods. Calvin uses this passage to criticize the Roman Catholic practice of buying absolution through masses and pardons, which he had discussed in the previous chapter.

Inevitably, a number of Calvin's comments about Plato elsewhere in the *Institutes* are negative. For example, he criticizes Plato's theory that all sin derives from ignorance (II.2.22; repeated at II.2.25), and Plato's theory that all knowledge is recollection (II.2.14). But on the whole, Calvin's remarks about Plato are laudatory. Calvin specifically commends Plato's belief in immortality (praised at I.15.6) and Plato's statement that man's highest goal should be union with God (praised at I.3.3 and III.25.2). Calvin also quotes approvingly the form of prayer that Plato suggests (in *Alcibiades* II.142E; see Calvin III.30.34). More striking, however, as evidence of Calvin's admiration for Plato, than any of these statements of approval is the spirit of admiration that shines through his other comments about Plato.

For example, in I.5.11 Calvin points out how difficult it is for people to avoid losing all judgment where religion is concerned:

> It is not only the common people and the stupid who are afflicted with this disease. Even the ablest of us, men who in other matters show the keenest discernment, lose their perspective when it comes to religion. Even Plato, the most religious and wisest of all the ancient philosophers, is not exempt from this failing.
>
> (I.5.11; tr. mine).

What one notices in this passage is not that Calvin is criticizing Plato, but that Calvin thinks that Plato was one of the greatest human beings that ever lived. In most medieval and Renaissance theologians (John of Salisbury is a good example) the typical attitude toward Plato is a grudging acknowledgment that even though Plato was a mere pagan, he was accidentally right about some points of doctrine. In Calvin, on the other hand, one gets the feeling that if he had not chosen to go into Theology, he would have gone into Classics. When he speaks about classical authors, he has to grope for words to express the depth of his affection and admiration:

> Read Demosthenes or Cicero; read Plato, Aristotle and others of that kind. They will, I admit, allure you, delight you, move you, even enrapture you, in wonderful measure.
>
> (I.8.1; tr. mine).

One does not ordinarily think of John Calvin as a peddler of Plato, but to an English cleric of Elizabeth's time, Calvin's *Institutes* would certainly have been a revelation in opening up the possibilities that Plato's works might afford to a pious Christian reader.

Many of the allusions to Plato that one finds in the writings of early Elizabethan clerics are merely ornamental references plucked from Erasmus' *Adagia*, or some other commonplace-book. An example is a sermon preached before Queen Elizabeth at Greenwich on March 14, 1573 by Richard Curteys (STC 6135, sig. C4ᵛ). Occasionally one sees a reference to Plato's theory of common property such as Henry Tripp's in his translation of Gerardus' *Regiment of Poverty* (1572, sig. A2ʳ) or John Carpenter's in *A Preparative to Contentation* (1597, sig. I4ʳ⁻ᵛ). But the most influential of the clerical allusions to Plato were those that found their way into the regime's own books of homilies. The original official book of authorized sermons, published by Edward VI in 1547, had given parish priests a mere dozen sermons. In 1562 Elizabeth's chief religious advisers, Archbishop Matthew Parker, Bishop James Pilkington, and Bishop John Jewel, decided to publish a new edition of the *Homilies*, with 21 additional sermons. Two of the new sermons happened to include allusions to Plato.

In the first case the sermon concerned had fallen to Bishop Jewel to provide. Jewel was supposed to produce a sermon that would justify the government's removal from English parish churches of the familiar Catholic paintings, crucifixes, stained glass, statues, candles, incense, and icons. This subject was a particularly touchy one because the Queen herself had insisted on retaining a crucifix and two candles in her own private chapel. Jewel's solution to the problem was to drown the poor congregation in three consecutive sermons on Daniel 11:37–38, all ponderously learned, and all borrowed from the *De origine erroris*, a treatise by Jewel's friend from Zurich days, Heinrich Bullinger (on Bullinger see biography in Parker Society ed. of his *Decades*, vol. 7, pp. xv–xxxii). One of the authorities that Bullinger cites in this treatise is Plato (*De origine erroris*, 1539 ed., fols. 154^v–155^r). Bullinger had borrowed his reference to Plato from Lactantius (*Institutes* II.4), who had based his allusion on *Laws* X. 905D. Jewel uses Bullinger's allusion to Plato in the text of his third sermon "Against. . .the Decking of Churches", but cites as his authority "Dial. de legibus" (*Certain Sermons*, 1968 ed., pp. 70–71).

The second sermon in which Plato was mentioned was a sermon inveighing against "Gluttony and Drunkenness". Plato's association with this subject had actually been known in England for a very long time. A passage in Plato's *Laws* on the subject of drinking is referred to by at least three of the authors who were studied in the Arts course during the Middle Ages.

Aulus Gellius, *Noctes atticae*, XV.2
Macrobius, *Saturnalia*, II.8
Seneca, *De ira*, II.20

From one or more of these sources the allusion had been picked up by John of Salisbury, and had been made familiar through his *Policraticus* (VIII.10; Webb ed., 1965, vol. 2, pp. 291–292).

The citing of Plato on drunkenness in the Elizabethan homily, however, came from a different line of descent. In 1548 the advisers of Edward VI had brought to Oxford, to serve as Regius Professor of Divinity, an Italian Protestant named Pietro Vermigli (Di Gangi, 1973). At the accession of Mary, Vermigli had fled to the continent, and like several other Marian exiles, had settled at Zurich. There he published, in 1556, a *Commentary on Judges* (see J.P. Donnelly, 1990), in which he included a long discussion of the evils of drunkenness, citing among other authorities a passage at the end of Book VII of Plato's *Republic*, VII.573 B–C (*Commentary on Judges*, 1565 ed., fols. 109^r–111^r). At the accession of Elizabeth, Vermigli returned to England, where he became known as Peter Martyr. When Elizabeth's bishops parcelled out the work for the new edition of *Certain Sermons* in 1562, the sermon on drunkenness fell to Bishop James Pilkington. Like Jewel, Pilkington found it more convenient to crib material from someone else than to dig it out for himself: he therefore based his sermon on "Gluttony and Drunkenness" on Vermigli's *Commentary on*

Judges, duly repeating, in the process, Vermigli's two allusions to Plato (*Certain Sermons*, 1968, p. 100). I should point out, however, that if the passage on drunkenness in *Republic* VII had not become familiar in England through Pilkington's sermon, it would in any case have become familiar soon through other channels. It was referred to by the French florilegist Pierre Boiastuau in his popular collection *Theatrum mundi* (1566), and duly appeared in John Alday's translation of that work in 1574 (p. 18).

Improbable though it may seem that the English government's book of official sermons should have been a means by which Plato entered the mainstream of English life, it was not the only Church document that served that purpose. In 1565 John Jewel found himself once again willy–nilly writing about Plato. In 1559 Jewel had issued a challenge (perhaps in imitation of the famous challenge of Pico della Mirandola in 1489) to the entire Catholic Church, to produce any early authority who supported any of the 27 specific tenets of Catholic theology. Five years later this challenge was taken up by John Harding, an English Catholic exile living in Louvain. A tract–duel between Jewel and Harding thereupon ensued (Southern, 1950, pp. 60–67) in the course of which Harding wrote a tract called *An answere to maister Juelles challenge* (1564). In this tract Harding happened to mention that Plato had defined Nature as "the will of God". In his *Replie unto M. Hardinges answear* (1565) Jewel undertook to refute each of Harding's statements, however trivial, and thus found it necessary to deal with the statement about Plato's definition of Nature. Jewel warms up for this challenge by himself voluntarily citing Plato in an earlier passage: "Plato saith 'Robbery is no less in a small matter than in a great'" (*Works*, Parker Society ed., 1968, vol. 1, p. 96). Thus prepared, when Jewel reaches Harding's own reference to Plato, Jewel explodes. He fires his first volley in a marginal note suggesting that Mr. Harding seemed not to have understood "what Plato meant" (*Works*, Parker Society ed., 1968, vol. 1, p. 500). Then Jewel launches into a long essay refuting Plato's supposed definition (*Works*, Parker Society ed., 1968, vol. 1, pp. 500–502).

Unfortunately Jewel knew no better than Mr. Harding "what Plato meant". The definition that Jewel belabors was not written by Plato at all, but by Victorinus (*Explanat. in Ciceronis Rhet.*, Halm ed., 1863, p. 215). There was, however, another Anglican Bishop who knew rather more about Plato than Jewel did. In 1572 the Bishop of Exeter, John Woolton, desperate to publish his way out of the wilderness, launched a series of books dedicated to Sir Francis Walsingham, the Secretary of State (on Woolton see Behm, 1977). The first of these books, *The castell of Christians* (1572), is an attempt to flatter Elizabeth's regime by contrasting the religious stability of England (the *castell* of the title) with the horrors of the recent Massacre of St. Bartholemew's Day in France. In this book Woolton thinks it politic to deprecate classical philosophers in general, but he also takes the trouble to mention Plato's *Phaedo* and *Lysis* by name, in order to serve notice that he is no provincial ignoramus. Four years later (1576) Woolton published a much more scholarly opus, *The Immortalitie of the Soul*. This work carries elaborate documentation in marginal postillae, after the manner of Bishop Jewel. Woolton's references are amazingly wide–ranging, and include many dialogues of Plato, and passages in Ficino and Plotinus as well. But all of this dazzling Platonic learning is second-hand; Woolton took his references from many sources: Agrippa's *De vanitate* ch. 52; the Pseudo-Plutarch's *De placitis philosophorum* IV.7; Morcillo, *De Arist. et Platonis* V.2; and Bullinger's *De origine erroris* I.8, among others. But most of Woolton's Platonic allusions came from a single source, the *De perenni philosophia* (1540) of Agostino Steuco. Woolton's use of Steuco is the more remarkable in that he knew about it even before Steuco's work was introduced in London by Philippe de Mornay in 1577.

Mornay was a Protestant aristocrat who happened also to be a scholar. He and his wife had been invited to England by Philip Sidney, who had met them in Paris in 1572. The Mornays arrived in London in May, 1577 and stayed until June, 1578 (Sinfield, 1979). During that period Mornay completed a treatise in French entitled *De la vérité de la religion chrestienne*. The object of this work was to defend Christian theology against the growing threat posed by French rationalists (Mornay calls them "naturalists") (see also Busson, 1957). Mornay's strategy is to cite against the rationalists, several authorities from among their own ranks, especially "Plato. . . Plotinus. . . and such others", who held beliefs much like Christian doctrines such as the existence of God and the immortality of the soul (sypher ed. Pref., 1976, sig. ***r-v). For each doctrine that Mornay discusses, he lines up his authorities systematically from four major literatures: Hebrew, Egyptian, Greek, and Latin, in order. Such a feat of scholarship was well beyond Mornay's own powers, and in fact he based his book on Steuco's *De perenni philosophia*, using a new edition that had just been published (1577) in Paris. Mornay's book had a slightly different thesis from Steuco's, but Mornay was far more thorough in his use of Steuco than Woolton had been.

In each of the first 19 chapters of his survey of Christian theology Mornay cites Plato as one of his authorities. Altogether he cites 13 different works of Plato: *Axiochus, Cratylus, Epinomis, Epistles, Gorgias, Laws, Parmenides, Phaedo, Phaedrus, Philebus, Republic, Theatetus,* and *Timaeus*. Most of these references he borrowed from Steuco, but Mornay had read a good deal of Plato himself. In a discussion of the theory of Judgment in the next world Mornay confidently asserts that:

> As for Plato, he taketh so greate pleasure in this matter, that he cannot be drawn from it, and he scarsly passeth any one dialog, wherein he hath not some speeche thereof
> (1587 ed., Ch. 19; p. 346).

Mornay also shows intimate first–hand acquaintance with Plato's major followers. Taking his cue from Guillame Budé's *De transitu hellenismi ad christianismum* (1535; Lebel ed., 1973, pp. 15–16), Mornay divides all Platonists into two schools: Pre-Christian and Christian. Among the Christian Platonists, Mornay includes Ficino, but quotes from him only twice (Sypher ed., 1976, ch. 2, p. 350; ch. 34, pp. 630–631).

Among the Pre-Christian Platonists Mornay emphasizes Plotinus. Mornay's familiarity with Plotinus is unique for his time, even in France, let alone England. Mornay quotes from Plotinus at astonishing length in at least 8 places, in one of which his quotation goes on for 8 pages (Sypher ed., 1976, ch. 6, pp. 82–90; see also ch. 17, pp. 307–310).

The significance of Mornay's *De la vérité* for our history is that it was the first wide-ranging account written in England on the theological aspects of Plato's thought. (Woolton's work was slightly earlier, but confined to the subject of immortality). For all its scholarship, Mornay's book derived from the French court conception of Plato, and in England as in France Mornay was an influence at court, not in the schools. Mornay exercised that influence in two other works as well, a French prose treatise on death entitled *Discours de la vie et du mort*, and a French translation of the *Axiochus*.

In the same year that Mornay came to London (1577) but through entirely separate circumstances, Elizabeth's regime happened to give Plato yet another entrée into English religious life. Since the *Certain Sermons* of 1562 had included only 33 sermons, there were still 19 Sundays in the year when a poor local vicar would have to fend for himself. In an effort to provide enough authorized sermons to cover every one of the 52 Sundays in the year, the regime in 1576 commissioned an English translation of Heinrich Bullinger's *Sermonum decades quinque* (1552), a collection of 50 sermons. The translation, made by H. Middleton (referred to on the title-page as "H.I."), was published the following year (1577) under the title *Fiftie godlie and learned sermons*. There are five allusions to Plato and one to "the Platonists" in "Bullinger's Decades", as the book was called:

I.i.   Plato was admired by the gentiles (p. 50)
III.v. Plato wrote a set of laws (p. 219)
III.x. Plato wrote above self-love (*philautia*) (p. 393)
IV.x.   Plato believed in the immortality of the soul (p. 385)
V.x.   Plato travelled in Egypt (p. 480)
IV.x.   The Platonists believed that the soul fell from Heaven (p. 374)
(*Decades*; pages refer to Parker Society ed. by Harding, 1968).

All of these allusions derive from secondary sources; Bullinger cites Plato not to invite attention to Plato's works, but only to give Christian readers a sense of the historical context of their beliefs. In 1586 Elizabeth's advisors ordered copies of Bullinger's *Decades* in the new translation placed in all parish churches as a supplement to *Certain Sermons* (Cardwell, *Synodalia*, 1966, vol. 2, p. 562). Thus the Anglican hierarchy itself once more inadvertently exposed the English population to Plato.

We turn now to the universities. Elizabeth's Prime Minister, Burghley, did not regard the universities as much of a threat to the Queen's security; he therefore did not get around to issuing new statutes for the universities until the sixth year of her reign (1564). In these statutes the government restored the Edwardian provision that Plato might be read in the *Republic* as well as in the *Timaeus* (Gibson, *Statuta*, 1931, p. 390; Lamb ed., *Documents*, 1838, vol. 1., pp. 315–354, 454–457; Dyer, *Privileges*, 1824, vol. 1, pp. 161–162), but the new statutes had virtually no effect on the actual reading of Plato at either university.

At Oxford a new interest in Plato developed accidentally as an adjunct to the new vogue of writing epigrams. The writing of epigrams had been used in English schools as a technique for teaching Latin since at least the twelfth century (Hudson, 1966, p. 145). In 1499 Erasmus had shown at Oxford that epigrams could also be used to teach Greek, but the first good printed collection of Greek epigrams, the Venice 1503 edition of the *Greek Anthology*, was too unwieldy for student use, and the technique lapsed when Erasmus left Oxford. In London, however, Erasmus had also introduced the technique to his friends Thomas More and William Lily, who engaged in a friendly competition to see which of them could translate the same Greek epigram into Latin more elegantly. In this way they translated 18 epigrams from the *Greek Anthology*, of which 5 related to Plato.

About the time of Elizabeth's accession a new edition of the *Greek Anthology* became available in England, and the technique of teaching Greek by means of writing epigrams revived, first at Winchester and Eton, and then at New College and Merton College, Oxford. The new edition of the *Greek Anthology* that sparked this revival was specifically designed as a teaching text for schools, by a German physician, Janus Cornarius. Cornarius pared down the 3700 epigrams of the original *Greek Anthology* to a mere 785, and for each Greek epigram he provided one or more Latin translations by various authors, including himself. (For a few pieces he even provided Greek paraphrases as well). For some reason, perhaps related to the fact that Cornarius himself had visited England, his edition of the *Greek Anthology*, entitled *Selecta epigrammata graeca* (Basle, 1529), became the standard text in English schools. More importantly, it also established in England the connection between the epigram and Plato, not only because Cornarius had produced a new Latin translation (Basle, 1561) of the *Works* of Plato, but because Plato figured importantly in the text of the *Greek Anthology* itself.

In the edition of the *Greek Anthology* used by Erasmus (the so-called Planudean version), there were 27 epigrams attributed to Plato, and 14 that were about Plato; one of the latter even included a line–drawing portrait of Plato. In the Cornarius edition of the *Anthology* there were 17 epigrams attributed to Plato as author, and 10 about him. The epigrams related to Plato caught the attention of one of the principal teachers of epigrams at Oxford, John Parkhurst of Merton. In the preface to his own collection of epigrams, Parkhurst says:

Even Plato, who was both a very great philosopher and a very virtuous man, sometimes set aside his stern philosophical seriousness, and in lighter vein, wrote epigrams addressed to his "Stella".

(Parkhurst, *Ludicra*; 1573 ed., sig. Aiv^r; tr. mine); the entire preface, which was written in 1558, is translated by Hudson, 1966, pp. 140–144).

Parkhurst's allusion refers to the fact that in Cornarius' *Selecta* from the *Greek Anthology*, two of the poems attributed to Plato are addressed to "My Star" (*aster emou* in Greek, *Mea Stella* in the Latin of Guarino de Verona, which Cornarius prints; Cornarius, Book III, 1529 ed., pp. 261–262; in the Loeb ed. of the *Greek Anthology*, ed. by Paton, 1916–1918, the poems are #669 and #670, vol. 2, pp. 356–357). The young Philip Sidney was a student at Christ Church, Oxford between 1568 and 1571, at the height of the epigram fad (Osborn, 1972, pp. 16–24). Ten years later (1581), when Penelope Devereaux rebuffed Sidney, and he set out to express his hurt feelings in a collection of poems, he chose as his name for Penelope, "Stella". I suggest that he borrowed this name from Plato's poems lamenting his dead "Stella". Like Plato, Sidney would henceforth be able to love his "Stella" only as a distant star, and he therefore entitled his collection *Astrophil and Stella* (see p. 117 below).

The title of Parkhurst's collection of epigrams, *Ludicra*, like the preface that I have just quoted, shows that among adults the writing of epigrams was regarded as a recreative rather than as a serious pastime. Thus the stigma of print that inhibited many gentlemen from publishing their writings (Saunders, 1967), did not apply to the epigrams that they had written as school exercises. One result, therefore, of the vogue of writing epigrams in the university was that it became fashionable for gentlemen to publish collections of their epigrams (Lathrop, 1928). Parkhurst's collection of 1573 was only one of at least seven such collections published during the early reign of Elizabeth:

1565 Thomas Drant (Latin)
1567 George Turberville (English)
1570 George Gascoigne (English)
1571 Lawrence Humphrey (Latin)
1573 Richard Wills (Latin)
1573 John Parkhurst (Latin)
1577 Timothy Kendall (English)

In two of these collections there are allusions to Plato: Turberville's (1567 ed., fols. 45^r–55^r) and Kendall's (1874 ed., pp. 119 and 149; there was another burst of such collections in the 1590's).

Apart from the epigram fad, Plato was little read at Oxford. Copies of Plato's works were rarely acquired there during the period 1558–1578. It is true that the Oxford bookseller Nicholas Clifton stocked the *Laws*, just as his counterpart at Cambridge, Nicholas Pilgrim, had done (McConica, 1986, p. 706), but I know of only two copies of Plato's *Works* that were acquired by Oxford colleges during this period: a copy given to St. John's College in 1559 (Emden 1974, p. 717) and one given to Sidney's College, Christ Church, in 1562 (Ker, 1986, p. 503).

Among Oxford authors who wrote during Elizabeth's early years, only Lawrence Humphrey of Magdalen College showed any significant interest in Plato. In his influential Latin treatise on the art of translation (*Interpretatio linguarum*, 1559) Humphrey urges his fellow Englishmen to translate Plato into English (1559 ed., sig. L6^v). In his even more influential treatise on the Nobility as a class, *Optimates, sive de nobilitate*, published in Latin in 1560, and translated into English in 1563, Humphrey cites Plato 7 times (1563 ed., sigs. Aiii^v, d6^v, e6^v–7^r, g4^r, g8^r, h4^v, y6^v). Humphrey's references, however, even those to the *Republic* and *Laws* by name, are all taken from Diogenes Laertius rather than directly from the text of Plato.

The only Oxford book of the period that I know of in which Plato is referred to in terms of the court conception of Plato is a commonplace-book, misleadingly entitled *A Philosophical Discourse*, compiled by Thomas Rogers of Christ Church in 1576. Rogers cites Plato in 21 of his selections. Most of these are apocryphal anecdotes of the type familiar from the *Dicts or Sayings*; all three of Rogers' references to specific dialogues by name (*Laws*, *Republic*, and *Symposium*) are incorrect. But in one long selection Rogers does give a reasonably accurate account of Plato's distinction among the four kinds of madness, in the *Phaedrus*. Rogers took this account not directly from the *Phaedrus*, but from Ficino's *De amore* (VII.4; Jayne tr., 1985, pp. 170–171), which he presumably found, just as Howell had found it, in one of the several available editions of Ficino's Latin translations of Plato's *Opera*, perhaps the copy of the Basle 1534 edition that I have just mentioned, that had been given to Rogers' own college in 1562 (but also see Clements, 1954).

At Cambridge the teaching of Plato had declined sharply from the time of Nicholas Carr, when St. John's and Trinity had vied for preeminence in the teaching of Greek. In 1560 Trinity revoked the statute of 1552 requiring that each student own a copy of Plato. A few tutors continued to use works of Plato in tutorials: for example, John Whitgift at Trinity (Gaskell, 1979, p. 289), and Samuel Fleming at King's (Harington tr., Ariosto *Orlando Furioso*, ed. McNulty, 1972, pp. 14–15).

In the absence of statutory requirements for the reading of Plato, neither the college libraries nor the University Library at Cambridge made any special effort to acquire editions of works of Plato. There were several Cambridge men who were interested in Plato, but each for an entirely different reason. John Caius, for example, who was a physician, gave a copy of Plato's *Works* to his College, Gonville, in 1569 (Leedham-Green, 1981, p. 351; a gift which another Fellow of the college matched in 1573; Grierson, 1978, p. 74), but only because Caius had edited a medical work of Galen in which Plato figured prominently, *De placitis Hippocratis et Platonis* (Basle, 1544; see O'Malley, DSB, vol. 3, pp. 12–13: Grierson, 1978). Similarly, a nearly anonymous Cambridge scholar named Henry Dethick cites several dialogues of Plato by name in a Latin treatise on poetics, *Oratio in laudem poeseos* (1572; edited as a work of Rainolds by Ringler, 1940, but see Binns, 1975). Dethick took all of his references to Plato from one florilegium, the *Polyanthea* of Nani-Mirabelli (1512 ed., p. 804).

Perhaps the most revealing glimpses that we get of the status of Plato at Cambridge are those given us by Gabriel Harvey. In a letter of 1579, reporting to his friend Edmund Spenser on current conditions at the university, Harvey says that Lucian is no longer being read very much; in his place people are reading Plato and Xenophon, who are thought to be better models of style (*Three proper. . .letters*; 1580 ed., p. 27). In another letter, however, Harvey also makes clear that it is not Plato's dialogues that are being read: Plato is being read mainly in "epigrams and emblems" (*Letterbook*, Scott ed., 1884, p. 81). By "epigrams" Harvey presumably means that epigrams were being read at Cambridge, just as they were at Oxford. Harvey also mentions "emblems". This may be only a case of doubling, for Plato is mentioned by name in only two Renaissance emblem books, both of which are continental. One, in which Plato is also represented in the woodcut, is an emblem "On Plato" in Pierre Cousteau's *Pegma* (Lyons, 1555, p. 187). The other is emblem #69 on Narcissus, in Andreas Alciati's *Emblemata* (Antwerp, 1577). Even in the latter work the allusions to Plato occur only in a commentary by Claude Mignault, who is discussing the concept of *philautia* (self-love). It seems likely that what Harvey means by "emblems" is *imprese*. A popular handbook for devising *imprese* was Paolo Giovio's *Dialogo dell' imprese* (1555), translated by Daniel in 1585. Giovio's work nowhere mentions Plato, but there is an allusion to Plato in Abraham Fraunce's handbook on *imprese, Insignium armorum. . .* (1588, sig. L4^r). (On *imprese* see Orgel ed. of Giovio, 1979; Daly, 1985, 1988; Hoeltgen, 1986; Skretkowicz, 1986, 1988; Tung, 1988).

Harvey's own opinion of Plato changed as he grew older. During his Cambridge years he admired Plato for the breadth of his learning (Harvey calls it "incredible"; *Letterbook*, Scott ed., 1884, p. 133). But by 1593, when Harvey was jousting with Nashe, he had come to think of Plato's writings as mere "enthusiastical ravishment", "marvelous eggs in moonshine" (*Pierce's Supererogation*; Scholar repr., 1970, p. 24; for the allusions to Plato in the marginalia of Harvey's books see Stern, 1979; and Moore–Smith ed. of *Marginalia*, 1913).

Harvey's growing conviction that Plato was an irrationalist is an indirect measure of the growth in England of the court conception of Plato. That conception was already beginning to be heard at Cambridge in Harvey's time. A minor example is an allusion in a commonplace-book compiled about 1572 by Hugh Platt of St. John's College (on Platt see Mullett, 1946). Platt's collection, called *The Floures of philosophie*, contains 885 quotations; of these only one mentions Plato by name, (unnumbered; Panofsky ed., 1982, p. 172). But in one of his other "quotations" Platt defines love as the loss of self; a continental reader would have recognized this definition as having come from the *Symposium*, by way of Ficino's *De amore* (Platt #75; Panofsky ed., 1982, p. 7; from *De amore* II.8; Jayne tr., 1985, pp. 54–57).

A more substantial example of the court conception of Plato occurs in the *Poematum liber* (1573) by Richard Wills. Wills had attended Winchester and New College, Oxford, but had later studied on the continent (Prescott, 1978, pp. 96–98). The *Poematum liber* is an anthology of model poems in Latin; appended to it is a treatise on the theory of poetic inspiration. Wills took some of the material for this appendix from Nani–Mirabelli's *Polyanthea*, and Vives' *De causis corruptarum artium*; but Wills also took some of his material directly from Ficino's *Commentary on the Ion* (Fowler ed. of Wills, 1958, p. 125; see also p. 28), which is a document in the court–conception line of writings about Plato.

The most important example of the growing awareness of the court conception of Plato at Cambridge was a Latin treatise called *Theoria analytica*, by Everard Digby, of St. John's College, written in 1578 and published early in 1579 (on Digby see Butters, 1980; Jardine, 1974, pp. 50–65; Schmitt, 1983, pp. 47–52). Digby's work is a scholarly exposition of the theory of universal religion that was familiar on the continent in works by Ficino and Steuco. The work that Digby used, however, was the *De comparatione Platonis et Aristotelis* (1573), by the French Platonist Jacques Charpentier. The title of Charpentier's work is misleading: the book is actually a commentary on the *Introduction to Plato* by Albinus. Digby cites 8 different dialogues of Plato by name (*Cratylus, Phaedo, Phaedrus, Philebus, Republic, Symposium, Theaetetus,* and *Timaeus*), but Digby takes all of these references from Charpentier; it is unlikely that Digby had read any of these dialogues himself except for the *Timaeus*, which he had read in the old medieval translation of Calcidius (Digby, 1579 ed., pp. 223, 407). Digby's treatise was finished in 1578, and shows that the English academic establishment was already paying serious attention to the court conception of Plato even before the Stephanus Plato arrived in England.

To conclude, we may say that during the first twenty years of Elizabeth's reign, everywhere in England, among the gentry and among the clergy, as among academics, it was the school conception of Plato that dominated. A useful reminder of this fact is an incident that occurred during the summer of 1578, when Elizabeth paid a visit to Norwich in order to endow a new hospital. At the end of her visit the Queen was required to suffer through a farewell oration in Latin delivered by a local schoolmaster, Stephen Limbert. In this oration Limbert chose to flatter the Queen by reporting that she was said to have read in Plato's *Laws* the principle that mendicancy should be illegal:

> You are said, in your great wisdom and learning, to have read that noble rule which the most wise Plato stated in the eleventh book of *Laws*: "There shall be no beggars in our state."
> (Nichols, *Progresses*; 1823 ed., vol. 2; Latin on p. 155; tr. in part on p. 157; this tr. mine)

Plato's *Laws* had been commonly available in Latin translation in bookstores at nearby Cambridge since 1535. The passage referred to is *Laws* XI. 936C. Limbert quotes the passage in Greek, but he probably borrowed the allusion from a commonplace-book. The important thing to notice about his allusion is that even before the Stephanus Plato arrived in England, it was thought appropriate to mention Plato in connection with Queen Elizabeth; familiarity with Plato was already accepted in England as a sign of classical learning.

But awareness of the court conception of Plato had also begun to grow, especially during the last five years of the period, as is seen in the following chronology:

1560 Howell (love theory)
1572 Fenton (i.e. Pasquier) (love theory)
1573 Sanford (i.e. Guicciardini) (love theory)
1573 Wills (theory of poetry)
1576 Woolton (theology)
1576 Rogers (love theory)
1577 Mornay (theology)
1578 Digby (theology)

Of the three theological writers in this sequence (Woolton, Mornay, and Digby), Digby was an aberration; his interest in Charpentier proved to be sterile. The line represented by Woolton and Mornay, on the other hand, deriving from Steuco's *De perenni philosophia*, proved to be the line of the future: it led on to both the Oxford Platonism of Thomas Jackson, and the Cambridge Platonism of Henry More.

CHAPTER 7

THE LATER YEARS OF ELIZABETH I (1579–1603)

In 1578 two French Protestant exiles, Henri Estienne II and Jean de Serres, dedicated to Queen Elizabeth I the first volume of a new three-volume edition of the *Opera* of Plato, in gratitude for the succor that she had extended to Huguenot exiles ever since the Massacre of St. Bartholomew's Day in 1572 (1578 ed., vol. 1, fol. *111ᵛ). The new edition was intended for scholars; indeed Estienne's Greek text is still used today as the standard text by which scholars refer to passages in Plato's works. In England, however, because the first copies of the work were sent to the Queen and to Philip Sidney (Languet, *Epistolae*, Dalrymple ed., 1776, p. 238), the new edition had the paradoxical effect of stimulating interest in the court conception of Plato rather than in the school conception. Like Malvolio, who imagined that Olivia admired yellow stockings (*Twelfth Night*, III.ii, iv), the subjects of Elizabeth imagined that because the new Plato had been dedicated to her, she must admire Plato, and they promptly bestirred themselves to mention the name of Plato as often as possible for her benefit.

The new Plato arrived in London in February or March, 1579. At that time Sidney was living at Leicester House, with his uncle, the Earl of Leicester. Also living at Leicester House was Edmund Spenser, the Earl's secretary. Sidney and Spenser were friends, and Sidney undoubtedly told Spenser about the new Plato soon after it arrived. Spenser's reaction was to try to incorporate some allusions to Plato into a collection of poems that he was about to publish, dedicated to Sidney. This collection was a set of 12 virtuoso eclogues, in 38 different verse forms, gathered under the title *The Shepheardes Calender*. The eclogues themselves had apparently already been finished by the time the new Plato arrived at Leicester House, and Spenser was in the process of composing a prose gloss for each poem. Thinking that allusions to Plato would now be impressive to both Sidney and Elizabeth, Spenser set about adding such allusions to the prose glosses of the *Calender*. To the gloss on "January" he added an allusion to Plato's "*Alcibiades*" (Dodge ed., Spenser's *Poetical Works*, 1936, p. 11). To the gloss on "October" Spenser managed to add two mentions of Plato, one of which was a reference to Plato's "first book de *Legibus*" (Dodge ed., 1936, p. 46). And to the gloss on "November" Spenser added a reference to "Plato in *Phaedone*" (Dodge ed., 1936, p. 52). In his haste to collect these allusions Spenser relied on secondary sources. As a result, his references to *Alcibiades* and the *Laws* are both incorrect. His allusion to the *Phaedo* is partially correct, but his spelling of the title shows that he took the reference from the opening paragraph of Guillame Budé's *De transitu hellenismi* (Lebel ed., 1973, p. 1), not from the *Phaedo* itself.

Another early effort to capitalize on a possible royal interest in Plato was one made by John Lyly. In the late Spring of 1579 Lyly was writing a new play to be presented before the Queen at Blackfriars (Hunter, 1962, p. 74). This play, called *Alexander and Campaspe*, was about Alexander the Great, but apparently when Lyly heard about the new Plato edition, in his eagerness to please the Queen, he added an irrelevant sub–plot, in which Plato appears as a character (I.ii.30–45; I.iii).

Sidney's own reactions to the new Plato edition were far subtler than those of Spenser and Lyly, perhaps because, as Leicester's nephew, he did not have to work as hard as they to get the Queen's attention (Heninger, 1983). About three months after the new Plato arrived, Sidney was asked by Leicester to write an entertainment for the Queen, to be presented during her visit to Leicester's country house, Wanstead Manor, in Surrey, during the first week in May (Martin, 1986). The short skit that Sidney wrote, called *The Lady of May*, has been thought by some scholars (e.g. Pickett, 1976) to incorporate Plato's theory of the two major passions (appetitive and aversive). Sidney must at least have intended some kind of allusion to Plato, for he took the trouble to reread Pico's *Commento* before writing the skit (see Jayne, *Studies*, 1994). Three months later, in August, 1579, Sidney quarreled with the Earl of Oxford, and left the court. He did not return until October 1580.

The following Spring (April 1581; see Read, 1960, p. 258) Sidney was once again asked to write an entertainment for Elizabeth; on this occasion he was given the difficult assignment of tactfully conveying to a visiting French legation of at least 200 members that the Queen had decided against the marriage to the Duc d'Alençon which it was their mission to negotiate (see Fogel, 1960). Knowing that Platonic love was a faddish subject at the French court, Sidney consulted the latest French work on the subject, Guy Lefèvre de la Boderie's translation of Ficino's *De amore* (1578), and with its help constructed an entertainment called *The Fortress of Perfect Beauty*, in which he tactfully announced to the French that Elizabeth was not available for marriage to d'Alençon, for the reason that she represented Heavenly Beauty, whereas he was seeking marriage with Earthly Beauty. The Platonic origin of the distinction between Heavenly and Earthly Beauty would probably have been familiar to the French visitors, even though Sidney nowhere mentions the name of Plato. And it was evidently recognized by some of the English spectators as well, for two months later one of the Queen's secretaries, Thomas, Lord Paget, made it a point to buy himself two introductions to Plato's philosophy, one by Morcillo (1554), and the other by Albinus (1567) (bookbill ed., A. Anderson, 1975, p. 236).

One of Sidney's colleagues in the tilt part of *The Fortress of Perfect Beauty* was Fulke Greville. At the same time that Sidney and Greville were making themselves familiar with the French fad of Platonic love, for the purposes of *The Fortress*, they were also experimenting with the fad in their own verse. As one of their experiments they agreed to match wits by each writing a poem opposing Platonic love. Sidney's effort was a sonnet, beginning "Leave me, O Love. . ." (CS#32; Ringler ed., 1962, pp. 161–162). Greville's effort was a longer poem, beginning "Loue, of mans wandring thoughts. . ." (*Caelica* #10; Bullough ed., *Works*, 1945, vol. 1, p. 78). Both men subsequently wrote other poems on the same theme. Greville's may be seen in *Caelica* #3 and #16 (Bullough ed., 1945, vol. 1, pp. 74, 81; on Greville see Rees, 1971; Maclean, 1964; Rebholz, 1971; Waswo, 1977). Sidney wrote his Platonic poems in connection with his unhappy love for Penelope Devereux.

Penelope had arrived at court at the age of eighteen in January, 1581. Sidney seems to have become infatuated with her only after the departure of the French legation in May. Penelope apparently reciprocated Sidney's feelings, but her aunt intended her to marry Robert, Lord Rich. That marriage took place in November, 1581. The following March, 1582, Sidney withdrew to Wales, and for six months poured out his hurt feelings in a series of 119 poems, in which he refers to Penelope as "Stella". As I have said (p. 110 above), I think that the name "Stella" Sidney derived from his reading of the epigrams of Plato, at Oxford. Sidney mentions Plato twice in *Astrophil and* Stella, once by name (*AS* #21) and once by epithet: "The wisest scholler of the wight most wise" (*AS* #25). The theme of Platonic love appears in several other poems in *Astrophil and Stella*, but usually as something that Sidney rejects, as in *AS* #5.

In 1581 Sidney published his translation of the *De la Vérité* of Mornay. Among Sidney's other writings Plato figures prominently only in the *Defense of Poesie* (see Partee, 1970, 1971; Samuel, 1940). In both versions of Sidney's *Arcadia* there are allusions to specific theories of Plato, especially the theory of the two major passions and the theory of idealized love, but never to Plato himself. (For detailed analysis of Plato in Sidney see Partee, 1970; McCabe, 1984; Roe, 1994; see also Jayne, *Studies*, 1994.)

Queen Elizabeth herself had in her youth twice been exposed to French Platonism (Jayne, 1993, pp. 508–581), but had never had any interest in it. Her ambitious courtiers, nevertheless, supposed that she did, and taking their cue from Sidney, began to write poems about Platonic love on the French model. An example is Sir Arthur Gorges, who tried the theme of Platonic love in two poems that he wrote in 1584, one in imitation of Desportes, and the other in imitation of Ronsard (#70 and #75; Sandison ed. of Gorges, 1953, pp. 70, 73–74). It is possible that John Lyly may also have continued to try to work Platonic themes into his court plays of the period (see Bryant, 1956; Long, 1909; Huppé 1947; Swift, 1976; and Meyer, 1981). But it must be acknowledged that in none of the plays concerned (*Gallathea*, 1585;

Endimion, 1588; and *Midas*, 1589) is there any allusion to Plato by name, and in every case the motifs that modern critics have regarded as Platonic could well have been interpreted differently by an Elizabethan audience.

Meanwhile Elizabeth's advisors were inadvertently making Plato better known in England through their program of encouraging the publication of books for the education of the gentry. During the years 1579–1590 the regime continued to encourage translations. Among these Plato figures significantly in at least the following:

Table 10. Late Elizabethan Translations

1579 Lopez de Mendoza	*Los proverbios* (1494)	Barnabe Googe
1581 Guazzo	*La civil conversatione* (I-III) (1574)	George Pettie
1581 Lycosthenes	*Prodigiorum* (1557)	Stephen Bateman
1582 Barth. Anglicus	*De proprietatibus* (c. 1296)	Stephen Bateman
1582 Giraldi Cinthio	*Tre dialoghi* (1584)	Lodowick Bryskett
1583 Montemayor	*Diana* (1564)	Bartholomew Yonge
1584 Du Bartas	*La Seconde Sepmaine* (1584)	Joshua Sylvester
1586 Guazzo	*La civil conversatione* (IV) (1574)	Bartholomew Yonge
1586 Coignet	*Instruction aux Princes* (1584)	Edward Hoby
1586 Primaudaye	*Academie françoise* (1581)	Thomas Bowes and Richard Dolman
1588 Tasso	*Il padre di famiglia* (c. 1587)	Thomas Kyd

Among these authors Lopez de Mendoza and Bartholomaeus Anglicus reflect a medieval conception of Plato; the Renaissance school conception of Plato appears prominently only in Coignet. In all of the other authors on the list the court conception of Plato prevails. Indeed, in Montemayor's *Diana* there is no actual allusion to Plato by name at all, but the work is based on the court theory of Platonic love as formulated by Pico in the *Commento*, and from him borrowed by Leo Hebreus (see Solé–Leris, 1959; Melczer, 1975; Damiens, 1971; Ivanoff, 1936; Perry, 1980).

By far the most important translations on my list for the history of Plato are those of Lycosthenes, Coignet, and Cinthio. The Lycosthenes translation is interesting because it provides an unusual example of the impact of the arrival of the Stephanus Plato in England. In the original text of Lycosthenes' *Prodigiorum ac ostensorum* (1557) there is no allusion to Plato. Nor is there any allusion to Plato in Bateman's translation. But the translation was published in 1581, shortly after the arrival of the Stephanus Plato, and the printer, Henry Bynneman, took it upon himself to acknowledge that fact by tacking on at the end of the preliminaries of the 1581 edition a one-line "quotation" from Plato, given in three different languages: Greek, Latin, and English:

Mono theum geras ezin einai tetragounon. – Plato
Solus Dei honor est esse quadratum, id est perfectum.

The honor of God alone is to be four-cornerd (sic),

that is to say, perfect.

(1581 ed., sig. #2ʳ; the Greek line is in Greek type).

Bynneman's initial reason for adding this quotation to the book was no doubt only that he disliked blank space, and needed something to fill up the page. He could easily, however, have selected some other kind of filler, and the fact that he chose to "quote" from Plato may indicate that he wanted to show that he kept abreast of events at court, and was ready with a font of Greek type, in case it should be wanted. That Bynneman's motives were far from scholarly may be seen in the fact that the line that he quotes is not actually from Plato; Bynneman found it in some commonplace-book and merely attached the name of Plato to it for effect.

Coignet is important because, by citing actual dialogues of Plato in 20 of his 50 chapters he gave English readers a model for matter-of-fact dependence upon Plato as a familiar authority; the fact that Coignet took his material on Plato entirely from intermediate sources such as Nani–Mirabelli and Steuco would not have been apparent to an English reader (on Coignet see Jayne, 1993, pp. 1147–1166). Bryskett is important for an entirely different reason. He embedded his translation of Cinthio in a work of his own called *A Discourse of Civill Life*. Though not published until 1606, the *Discourse* was written in 1582, and describes a meeting the previous year (1581) at Bryskett's house, involving Bryskett, Spenser, and eight of their friends. Bryskett's account of this meeting gives us the only picture we have of Tudor Englishmen actually discussing the philosophy of Plato (as opposed to merely quoting or citing him) (see Jayne, 1993, pp. 1247–1262).

There is one other point that needs to be made regarding the translations that I have listed above: the work of Du Bartas that I have listed was only the last of three that Sylvester translated. He had also translated *La Muse chrétienne* in 1574, and *La Sepmaine* in 1578 (see Jayne, 1993, pp. 1054–1064 on Plato in Du Bartas).

Among the florilegia encouraged by Elizabeth's regime between 1579 and 1590, almost all included some reference to Plato, at least in the dedication, and usually among the selections as well. Examples are:

1580 Gifford	1585 Robson
1581 Marbecke	1586 Paulet
1583 Peacham	1586 Whetstone
1584 Whetstone	1590 Greene
1584 Fiston	

The collection of Peacham is of particular interest in that it provides still another bit of evidence showing the impact of the arrival in England of the Stephanus Plato in 1579. Peacham had published the first edition of his *Garden of Eloquence* in 1577 (STC 19497), before the arrival of the Stephanus Plato; in that edition he had made no reference to Plato at all. In the second edition, however, in 1583 (STC 19498), Peacham added two allusions to Plato, in one of which he invented the verb "to

Platonize" (Crane ed., 1954 pp. 15, 19).

In the 1580's Elizabeth's regime authorized publication of English editions of several new works in languages other than English. Some of these editions were printed with the academic market in mind, including several epitomes and commentaries on Aristotle: Scribonius (1581), Verro (1581), Gerardus (1583), the anonymous medieval *Problemata* (1583), and Velcurio (1588). Of these, only Gerardus and Velcurio contained significant discussions of Plato (Jayne, 1993, pp. 807–836).

Some of the other new editions were intended for laymen. Among these, the one containing the most material about Plato (64 quotations) was Lycosthenes' *Apophthegmata* (1579; see Jayne, 1993, pp. 644–648). There were also a few references to Plato in the new English edition by Richard Hutton of the Latin dictionary of Guillame Morel, *Verborum latinorum* (1583). By far the most influential of the new foreign language editions were six works of Giordano Bruno which were not printed for English readers, but for continental readers, and were accordingly given spurious continental imprints, even though they were all printed in London. Bruno rarely mentions Plato by name in any of these works, but three of them were very influential in promulgating the court conception of Plato, especially as it was used to give allegorical interpretations of classical myths; the three important works were *Degli eroici furori*, *De umbris idearum*, and *Lo spaccio de la bestia trionfante* (see Jayne, 1993, pp. 1019–1041).

At both universities during this period the dominant authority was still Aristotle. The two universities differed greatly in their attitude toward Plato. At Oxford the attitude was stiffly conservative. Only one college, Corpus Christi, owned significant holdings in Plato, and academic publishing was dominated by the steady steam of Aristotelean commentaries produced by John Case (Schmitt, 1983). It is no wonder that Giordano Bruno received such a hostile reception when he tried to lecture at Oxford in 1583 (Gatti, 1989; Massa, 1977; McNulty, 1960).

At Cambridge, on the other hand, the period 1579–1590 saw at least one sign of a new openness toward Plato. It is true that only six Cambridge men are known to have owned copies of works of Plato during these years (Leedham-Green, 1986, vol. 1, pp. 375, 415, 429, 444, 481, 482). Moreover, the Cambridge cleric, Andrew Willett, consistently criticizes Plato in the three relevant sections (3, 5, and 6) of his *De animae natura* (1585): "if we may judge by Plato", Willett sneers (1585 ed., p. 91). Nevertheless it is also true that it was at Cambridge during this period that the first printed edition of any work of Plato ever published in England appeared. This was a Greek–Latin edition of the *Menexenus*, printed by Thomas Thomas in 1587 (Morris, 1968). The copy–text that Thomas used for the Greek text of the dialogue was the Stephanus edition, a copy of which Thomas conveniently happened to have in his shop at the time, brought there for binding by a Cambridge student, James Smith. (Smith's copy is still in the Cambridge University Library, with the press-mark P* I.2–4). Thomas printed 200 copies of the *Menexenus*, apparently hoping that its subject, patriotism, would be attractive to students who were being drafted for military service, in anticipation of the war with Spain. The book did not, however, sell very well: at Thomas' death a year later (1588) the appraisers found 147 copies of the *Menexenus* still unsold in his shop (Leedham–Green, 1986, vol. 1, p. 393; see also Gray and Palmer, 1915, pp. 64–72). In 1592 Robert Gardner, of Cambridge, still owned a copy of the work (Leedham–Green, 1986, vol. 1, p. 524), but only one of Thomas' original 200 copies survives today: it is in the British Library, with press-mark C.132.i.55.

Encouraged by the presence of allusions to Plato in so many of the continental works being published with Elizabeth's blessing, English hack writers now began to hang ornamental allusions to Plato onto works that they published for the mass market. Among the hacks, those who used decorative allusions to Plato most often were George Whetstone and Robert Greene. Whetstone mentions Plato in 5 of his works; the last two are of special interest, because they show the difference in English attention to Plato before and after the arrival of the Stephanus Plato. In Whetstone's play *Promos and Cassandra*, written in 1578, immediately before the arrival of the new Plato, there is only one perfunctory reference to Plato (1578 ed., sig. Aii'). In Whetstone's *Heptameron*, on the other hand, dedicated to Sir Christopher Hatton in 1582, a quotation from Plato forms the chief unifying motif of the narrative (Jayne, 1993, pp. 1124–1138). Whetstone's 13 allusions to Plato in the *Heptameron* (Shklanka ed., 1977) are all taken from secondary sources, chiefly Mexia's *Silva* (on Whetstone see Izard, 1942).

The pathetic London pampleteer Robert Greene is an even more egregious example of an effort to capitalize on a supposed current enthusiasm for Plato. Among the numerous works that Greene produced to support himself between 1579 and 1590, only one, a commonplace–book called *The Royal Exchange* (1590), gave him the slightest reason for mentioning Plato; yet in almost all of his writings, especially the romances, Greene makes it a point to sprinkle the name Plato liberally across his pages. Occasionally these allusions come near the truth; for example, Greene mentions that Plato wrote a work called "*Timaeo*" (*Farewell to Folly*; Grosart ed., 1964, vol. 9, pp. 245–246). More often, however, Greene's allusions to Plato are entirely fictional; for example, he repeatedly refers to a dialogue of Plato called the *Androgyna* (*Penelope's Web*, Grosart ed., 1964, vol. 5, p. 163; *Morando*, Grosart ed., 1964, vol. 3, pp. 115–116; *Royal Exchange*, Grosart ed., 1964, vol. 7, p. 259). It seems likely that Greene derived this title from a French translation by Héroet of a small section of Ficino's *De amore* that Héroet published under the title *L'Androgyne* in *Opuscules d'amour* (1547). (For allusions to Plato in Greene's works see Jayne, 1993, pp. 1186–1200; on Greene himself see Crupi, 1986.)

In 1576–1577, James Burbage constructed two large public theatres in London, with the result that public theater soon became a thriving industry. The playwrights who wrote for the public theater naturally felt no great compulsion to refer to Plato.

One of the few dramatists who actually put a reference to Plato into a play for the public theater during the period 1579–1590 was Christopher Marlowe, who ventured to do it in his first play, *I Tamburlaine*, in 1587 (IV.ii. 95–96). Marlowe also mentioned Plato in his last play, *Edward II* (1592; IV.vii. 17–19).

But if Plato was not being discussed onstage, he was certainly being discussed offstage. Burbage had deliberately located his two theaters, The Theatre and The Curtain, on the south bank of the Thames, in order to avoid the jurisdiction of the London authorities. But that did not prevent the London clergy from raising loud objections to the theaters, on moral grounds. Beginning in 1577 pamphlets began to appear, attacking not only the theaters themselves, but all of the arts associated with the theater, including drama, music, and poetry.

To these attacks other pamphlets were promptly published in reply, and for nine years, between 1577 and 1586, tracts for and against the arts flew back and forth. Among the works related to this episode at least eight contained allusions to Plato, namely the tracts by:

1577 Northbrooke
1579 Gosson
1579 Lodge
1580 Munday
1580 Sidney
1580 Puttenham
1582 Gosson
1586 Webbe

(Analyzed in Jayne, 1993, pp. 1049–1054, 1072–1106). In addition there were two related works in which Plato did not appear, those of Thomas Watson (*Hekatompathia*, 1582) and Philip Stubbes (*The Anatomie of Abuses*, 1583).

In the works that do cite Plato, the Platonic references usually have to do either with Plato's contention that poets should be banned from an ideal society (*Republic* X. 595A–608B) or with Plato's theory that poets are inspired by one of four kinds of madness (*Phaedrus*). Except for Sidney, who had read both the *Republic* and *Phaedrus*, as well as the *Ion* and the *Symposium*, none of the writers who refer to these opinions of Plato had actually read Plato: they knew about him only from some other source. In the case of Lodge this source was Jodocus Badius (Ringler, 1939). In the cases of the others, the source was usually a commonplace-book, ordinarily Aelianus, Erasmus, or Nani-Mirabelli. Among the authors that I have listed above, Puttenham is unusual in making a deliberate attempt to impress Elizabeth. His book is dedicated to her, and he carefully places references to Plato or the Platonists at both the beginning and end of the book (Willcock ed., 1936, pp. 3, 307–308).

There remain to be mentioned four other writers of the period 1579–1590. Two of these mention Plato only briefly: Robert Bostocke in *The Differences between the auncient phisicke and the latter phisicke* (1585) and William Fulbecke in *A booke of*

Christian ethicks (1587). But two other authors deserve fuller comment.

Richard Mulcaster was the Headmaster of the Merchant Taylor's School, (on his life see Barker ed., *Positions*, 1982, pp. 1–55). In 1581 Mulcaster published a major treatise on the theory of education, entitled *Positions*. The thesis of this work ran directly counter to the educational policy that Elizabeth's advisors had been pursuing; whereas the regime had been promoting the use of continental works in English education, Mulcaster took the nationalistic view that English schools should teach English matters. Nor was Mulcaster's hostility to continental authors limited to contemporary writers; he boldly attacked the classics as well:

> it is no proufe bycause Plato praiseth it. . .
> that therefore it is for vs to vse.
> (Ch. 3; 1581 ed., pp. 11–12).

Mulcaster's argument is the stronger for the fact that he himself had been thoroughly trained in the classics. He had been educated at Eton and Corpus Christi College, Oxford, and could read Greek as well as Latin. Indeed, he makes it a point to call attention to his prowess in the field. He cites Plato 22 times in the course of his treatise. In eleven of these passages he documents his statement with a correct reference to the *Republic*, the *Laws*, or the *Laches*. The *Republic* and *Laws* he had seen at first hand; the *Laches* he knew only through other sources. Mulcaster's sources for allusions to Plato include Mercuriale, Proclus, Plutarch, Diogenes Laertius, and Quintilian (sources identified by Barker; see his ed. of *Positions*, 1982). In two places Mulcaster quotes brief words or phrases of Plato in Greek (1581 ed., pp. 216, 247); and in one place he gives a long quotation in Greek from *Laws* VII. 794D–E (1581 ed., ch. 19, p. 80).

The last author of this period whom we need to consider is Abraham Fraunce. Fraunce was a typical example of the Elizabethan "aspiring mind", a man whose ambitions far over-reached his abilities. He attended Shrewsbury School and St. John's College, Cambridge, and then took the usual next step toward preferment by entering the Inns of Court. After five years at Gray's Inn (1583–1588) he eventually became a lawyer on the staff of the Court of the Marches in Wales (on his life see Moore–Smith ed., *Victoria*, 1906, pp. xiv–xl). Throughout his early career Fraunce wrote prolifically. Even at Cambridge he produced five different works, none of which he published in their original form. He did eventually publish seven books, four of them during the period when he was at Gray's Inn. Of these four, two contain allusions to Plato. One, entitled *Insignium armorum. . .* (1588), is a book of *imprese*, in imitation of the popular work of Giovio in the genre, recently translated by Daniel (1585). Fraunce's *Insignium* includes only one allusion to Plato, a commonplace-book reference to Plato's *Alcibiades* II and *Euthydemus* (*Insignium*, sig. L4^r).

Fraunce's *The Lawier's Logike* (1588) is a textbook of Logic designed specifically for lawyers, in which the examples are taken from legal cases and codes rather than from literary works. Fraunce modelled this work on a similar work by François

Hotman entitled *Dialecticae institutiones* (1573); see Blocaille, 1970), but he also used the standard Logic taught at Cambridge, that of Ramus and Talon. There are 29 allusions to Plato in Fraunce's handbook, including references to 8 different dialogues by name. Most of these references are accurate because he has taken them all from Hotman or Ramus–Talon (for analysis see Jayne, 1993, pp. 1212–1238). Fraunce's book must be supposed to have contributed a good deal to English familiarity with Plato's views on ethical and political subjects, at least among members of the legal profession.

During the years 1590–1596 interest in Plato fell to almost nothing at the universities, while at the same time rising slightly among poets. Which is to say that the school conception of Plato declined in importance, while the court conception rose, for the conception of Plato that the poets drew on, though they rarely mentioned Plato by name, was the theory of love and beauty described by Ficino in the *De amore*, and by the French court poets who professed to be Ficino's followers. (The demand for Ficino's work among French writers is shown by the fact that in 1588 Guy Fefèvre de la Boderie published a new edition of his French translation of the *De amore*, with a French translation of Pico's *Commento* appended.) The most important of the English poets who wrote about Platonic love and beauty were Spenser and Chapman. Both of these poets have been thoroughly studied (on Spenser see especially Taylor, 1924; Ellrodt, 1960; Bieman, 1988; Bulger, 1994; on Chapman see especially Schoell, 1926; Maclure, 1966; Waddington, 1974; Snare, 1989; Gorsch, 1990). Spenser mentions Plato by name only in *H.H.B.*, 1.83 (Dodge ed., 1936, p. 755) and in the three prose glosses in *The Shepheardes Calender* (January, October, and November) already noticed. Chapman mentions Plato by name only in marginalia or in prefatory material to his poems and translations, never in the text of the poem itself. (For a full statement of my own observations on Spenser see Jayne, 1993, pp. 957–964 and 1239–1390; Chapman's work before 1603 I have discussed in Jayne, 1993, pp. 1391–1467; for Chapman's work after 1603 see Jayne, *Studies*, 1994.)

In the previous chapter I mentioned that there were two other works of Philippe de Mornay besides his *De la vérité* that proved to be influential in England, his *Discours de la vie et du mort*, and his French translation of the *Axiochus* of Xenocrates. There is no allusion to Plato in either of these two works, but the second of them, the *Axiochus*, nevertheless requires our attention, for until 1484, when Ficino identified its true author as Xenocrates, the *Axiochus* had been commonly attributed to Plato. Through circumstances that are not entirely clear, Philip Sidney's sister (Mary, Countess of Pembroke; on Mary see Hannay, 1990) and Edmund Spenser both produced English translations of the *Axiochus*, she from Mornay's French version, and Spenser from a Latin translation by Herman Rayan (Cologne, 1568). Spenser's translation was published in 1592 (STC 19974.6) at the same time that Mary Sidney published a translation of Mornay's *Discours* (STC 18138), but Mary's translation of the

Axiochus was not published until 1607 (STC 18155). Mornay himself did not regard the *Axiochus* as a work of Plato, and the Sidneys probably did not either; they were interested in the work only because they had undertaken to translate three of Mornay's works into English. Spenser may have been interested in the work because he wanted to participate in the Sidneys' Mornay–project or because he wanted to compose a tribute to his friend Philip Sidney after his death in 1586 (for further discussion see Jayne, 1993, pp. 1349–1356).

Apart from Spenser and Chapman, only a few of the many English poets who wrote about Platonic love and beauty bothered to consult Ficino or Pico for authority. Michael Drayton, Sir Robert Sidney, and Sir John Davies may have seen Ficino's *De amore*, but almost all of the other English poets of the period borrowed their allusions to Platonic love and beauty from commonplace-books, from French poets such as Ronsard, Du Bellay, and Desportes, or merely from each other. Examples are Barnabe Barnes, Henry Constable, Samuel Daniel, Sir Arthur Gorges, Henry Lok, and Sir Walter Ralegh (on the first five of these see Jayne, 1993, pp. 1468–1528; on Ralegh see Jayne, *Studies*, 1994).

One minor negative point that needs to be made regarding the vogue is that the poem called "The Phoenix and Turtle", which is usually attributed to Shakespeare, and has sometimes been interpreted as a "Platonic" poem (e.g. Fairchild, 1904), was actually written by Ben Jonson, and has nothing to do with Plato (Jayne, *Shakespeare's Phoenix and Jonson*, 1991; but see Medcalf, 1994).

Among prose writers of the period 1590–1596, as among poets, allusions to Plato tend to derive from Renaissance reference books rather than from Plato himself. Examples are the sermons of Henry Smith, (Jayne, 1993, pp. 1549–1554) and a commentary on Daniel by Hugh Broughton (1592; sigs. C3^v, C4^r, D2^{r-v}). Another example is a mythography put together by Abraham Fraunce in 1592, under the title *Amintas Dale*. Fraunce assembled this work chiefly from materials that he found in Conti, Alciati, Agrippa, and Nani-Mirabelli; by virtue of his borrowings from these authors, Fraunce mentions Plato in 8 places in the work (Jayne, 1993, pp. 1233–1238).

As had been the case during the early years of Elizabeth's reign, her advisors continued in the nineties to encourage the publication of translations and commonplace-books, but at a much slower pace. During the years 1590–1596 I know of only four important translations that involved allusions to Plato:

1590	Sansovino	*Concetti politici* (1578)	Robert Hitchcock
1591	Ariosto	*Orlando Furioso* (1516)	Sir John Harington
1593	Landi	*I Paradossi* (1543)	Anthony Munday
1594	Le Roy	*De la vicissitude* (1575)	Robert Ashley

Among the commonplace-books published during these years, allusions to Plato appear in the following:

1590	Fenne	*Fennes frutes*
1594	Platt	*Manuale sententias. . .complectens* (in Latin)

At the universities interest in Plato was at a very low ebb. At Oxford in 1594 a physician named Robert Barnes donated to his former college, Merton, a copy of the Basle, 1534 edition of the *Works* of Plato in Greek, (Emden, 1974, p. 715; the book is still in the college library, with press-mark A9/B46), but no one at Oxford was actually teaching Plato, and individual students had no reason to buy copies of his works. The only Oxford don of the time who wrote anything about Plato, so far as I know, was the Regius Professor of Law, Alberico Gentili, who incorporated a long and interesting discussion of Plato into one of his commentaries on Justinian's Code, published at Oxford in 1593 (on Gentili see Panizza, 1981; the passage on Plato is translated by Binns, 1972, pp. 260–263; on the neglect of Plato at Oxford see McConica, 1986, pp. 704–706, 712–713).

At Cambridge the dropping off of interest in Plato may be seen in the fact that whereas in earlier years numerous Cambridge men had owned copies of the complete *Works* of Plato, during the years 1590–1596 men tended to own only a single dialogue. Thus the Professor of Physics, Thomas Lorkin, in 1591 owned a copy of the *Laws*, and one of the *Timaeus* (Leedham–Green, 1986, vol. 1, p. 503); and Robert Gardner in 1592 owned a copy of Thomas' ill-fated *Menexenus* (Leedham–Green, 1986, vol. 1, p. 524). Only one man, John Cocke of Emmanuel, in 1593, owned a copy of the complete *Works* (Leedham–Green, 1986, vol. 1, p. 528). The only book of this period containing significant material about Plato that is remotely related to Cambridge is a reprint that was printed at Cambridge in 1594, of the Strasbourg 1589 edition of Johann Hawenreuther's Latin epitome of Aristotle's *Physics (Compendium. . .Aristotelis)*. Even in Hawenreuther's book the material about Plato is of secondary importance; in the preliminaries Hawenreuther ostentatiously refers to Plato and to specific dialogues on almost every page, and even quotes a passage of Plato in Greek (1594 ed., sig. B1^{r-v}), but there is no allusion to Plato at all in the text of the work (on Cambridge see especially Kearney, 1970).

By 1597 Burghley was gravely ill. At his death the following year Elizabeth's regime went into a defensive mode, trying to hold things together until the ageing Queen herself should die. Gone were the activist days when the government had tried aggressively to educate the gentry by encouraging the publication of translation and commonplace–books. During Elizabeth's last years only two translations were published that involved any allusion to Plato: Romei's *Discorsi* (1586) translated in 1598 by John Kepers, and Cartari's *Le imagini* (1556), re-translated in 1599 by Richard Linche (a translation by Stephen Bateman had already been published in 1577). In neither Romei nor Cartari does Plato figure importantly. Elizabeth herself made two translations in her old age, one from Greek and one from Latin. Neither translation was intended for publication; she was merely seeking diversion from her own depression. The translation that she attempted from Greek was not a work of Plato, but a light-hearted essay of Plutarch, "On Being a Busybody" (*Moralia*; Loeb ed., 1962 vol. 6, pp. 471–517). Elizabeth's Latin translation was a rendering of

Boethius *De consolatione philosophiae*; in this work she did encounter several allusions to Plato (Pemberton, *Elizabeth's Englishings*, 1899).

As for commonplace-books, in 1597 John Bodenham launched a series of four new handbooks intended to elevate English poetry above the plateau of tired cliché on which it had been lodged for several years. Bodenham's handbooks for poets, whom he calls "wits", were the following:

1597 *Wits Commonwealth* (a collection of quotations)
        edited by Nicholas Ling
1598 *Wits Treasury* (a collection of similes)
        edited by Francis Meres
1599 *Wits Theatre* (a collection of anecdotes)
        edited by Robert Allott
1600 *Bel-vedere* (a selection of examples from the same three genres as those in the
        other volumes)
        edited by Anthony Munday

In all of these volumes Plato figures prominently, but not always instructively. In *Wits Commonwealth* there are many quotations attributed to Plato, but they were all taken from the old Baldwin–Palfreyman *Treatise of Morall Philosophie* (1547), and all are apocryphal. In *Wits Treasury* there are 11 selections involving Plato; in *Wits Theatre*, 36; and in *Bel-vedere*, 13 (for details see Jayne, 1993, pp. 1639–1651).

Bodenham was not the only one who was publishing reference works during Elizabeth's last years. Two knights of the realm also undertook such ventures. Sir Richard Barckley's effort, published in 1598, consisted of 717 pages of apocryphal "quotations" from famous people, under the title *The Felicitie of Man*. The three statements that Barckley attributes to Plato in this work are all figments of someone's imagination. Sir William Vaughan, on the other hand, published a quite respectable commonplace–book entitled *The Golden Grove* (1600). Vaughan's collection includes 5 selections from Plato, some including citations of Plato's *Gorgias*, *Republic*, and *Laws*. Vaughan took all of these references from commonplace–books, but at least they are accurate.

In the realm of popular literature Plato appeared most often in the work of Thomas Lodge. From 1597 onward, Lodge was a physician, but during the years 1587–1597 he tried to make a living by writing for the mass market, especially romances and satires (Paradise, 1971; Rae, 1987). In keeping with what he regarded as being "commercial" at the time, he makes it a point to mention Plato frequently. The most striking example is a prose satire called *Wits Miserie* (1596) on his favorite subject, devils. In this work alone Lodge cites Plato 9 times, usually with the name of a dialogue attached. Lodge did not feel obliged, however, to make these allusions accurate; he borrowed them from commonplace-books, and altered them freely to suit his own convenience (for Plato in Lodge see Jayne, 1993, pp. 1654–1667 and 1701–1703).

There are more interesting references to Plato in two other London prose writers who were publishing during these years. A single observation about Plato appeared in a work patriotically called *St. George for England*, by Gerard de Malynes (1601). Malynes was a London merchant; he was worried about what was going to happen to the English economy after the death of Elizabeth, and he wrote this tract as a blue–print for a national economic policy. One of his recommendations is that the country avoid the trap of trying to achieve economic equality among all its citizens, as advocated by

> Plato the Philosopher. . .whom sir Thomas More in his Utopian common weale seemeth to imitate. . .this equality cannot be established.
> (1601 ed. sig. B1^{r-v}).

The greatest of the writers at court during Elizabeth's last years was her own Lord Chancellor, Sir Francis Bacon. Bacon had been educated at Trinity College, Cambridge. His tutor there, John Whitgift, had bought a copy of Plato's *Works* in Latin for him (Gaskell, 1979, p. 289). Bacon had dipped into the *Republic, Laws*, and *Gorgias*, and knew of the existence of the *Timaeus, Protagoras*, and *Critias* (which he calls *Atlanticus*). Between 1587 and 1589 Bacon bought a copy of the new Stephanus edition of Plato for the Grammar School at St. Albans (*Victoria History of Hertfordshire*, 1971, vol. 2, p. 61), but Bacon himself never had any serious interest in Plato, and never quotes Plato verbatim. Bacon did acknowledge that

> Anyone who did not concede that. . .Plato and Aristotle were among the greatest of all mortals in genius would be either stupid or unjust.
> (*Redargutio philosophorum* (1608); Spedding and Ellis ed., *Works*, 1857–1874, vol. 3, pp. 565–566; tr. mine).

But Bacon thought that Plato's main contribution lay in the field of political theory:

> My opinion of Plato is as follows. . .He was by nature and inclination a political creature, and devoted most of his energies to political theory. He really cared nothing about science. . .As a result nothing that Plato wrote about science has any substance. He habitually contaminated and infected science with religion. . .
> (*Redargutio philosophorum* (1608); Spedding and Ellis ed., *Works*, 1857–1874, vol. 3, p. 569; tr. mine).

Beneath this cool rationalization about Plato lay a much more emotional antipathy on Bacon's part. He actually despised Plato as being an irrationalist. Bacon's inner distaste for Plato comes out in a Latin satire that he wrote in the year of Elizabeth's death (1603):

> Now call to the stand that nit–picking logic–chopper, poetical windbag, and religious fanatic, Plato.
> (*Temporis partus masculus*. Ch. 2; Spedding and Ellis ed., Works, 1857–1874, vol. 3, p. 530; tr. mine).

Having pretended to call Plato to the stand, Bacon then addresses Plato directly:

Your philosophy, Plato, consisted of fragments of other people's ideas, polished up, and strung together. By pretending to be humbly ignorant, you tried to make your reader think that you were wise. By stating your ideas in poetic terms you tried to divert your reader's attention and prevent him from thinking clearly. I concede that your works do sometimes provide topics for meal-time discussion among the literate and cultivated, and in this way add a little grace and charm to some otherwise ordinary conversations. But you committed an unforgivable crime against Mankind when you falsely claimed that knowledge is innate in the human mind and does not enter the mind from outside. By this theory you diverted Mankind from the habit of observation, from paying attention to external nature, which we can never sufficiently study and respect. Instead you taught us to look inward and worship our own vague and invisible ideas, in the name of "contemplation". You committed a second and equally heinous crime when you tried to apotheosize Irrationality by brazenly defending irrational thinking in the name of religion. A third and only marginally less serious crime of yours is that you spawned an endless progeny of imitators, writers who, like you, were so seduced by the desire for quick literary fame, that they settled for a superficial, folk-loristic conception of nature, and thus obstructed Man's efforts to find a more rigorous and thorough way of seeking Truth. Among these were Cicero, Seneca, and Plutarch, and many lesser writers.

(*Temporis partus masculus.*, ch. 2; Spedding and Ellis ed., Works, 1857–1874, vol. 3, pp. 530–531; tr. mine; Farrington, 1964, tr. p. 64).

I have quoted this passage at length not because it tells us that Elizabeth's courtiers occasionally discussed Plato at the dinner table, but because it tells us that the conception of Plato that they discussed was what I have called the "court" conception, inherited from Ficino, namely that Plato was primarily an irrationalist theologian, not a rationalist philosopher. (On Plato in Bacon's other works see Jayne, 1993, pp. 1705–1714).

In 1598 English poets, bored with the unnaturally epideictic posture that they had been forced into, by the accident of having a maiden lady for a ruler, began gleefully slashing at each other in satirical verse. Between 1598 and 1599 a torrent of vicious personal satires spewed from the pens of Barnfield, Breton, Carew, Corbet, Davies, Dekker, Donne, Guilpin, Hall, Harvey, Lodge, Marston, Middleton, Nashe, Rankins, and Weever. With each successive round of charge and counter–charge, the rhetoric became more and more venomous until finally, on June 2, 1599, Archbishop Whitgift stepped in, and banned the publication of satires (*Stationers Register*, Arber ed., 1875–1894, vol. 3, p. 677).

In the highly personal, vitriolic verse produced by these satirists there are naturally very few allusions to Plato (Jayne, 1993, pp. 1652–1691). What is more surprising is that there are almost no allusions to Plato in either of the two major anthologies of the period, John Bodenham's *England's Helicon* (1600) or Francis

Davison's *Poetical Rhapsody* (1603). Nor does Nicholas Breton, Robert Parry, John Davies of Hereford, or John Donne mention Plato in any poem written during the reign of Elizabeth. It is true that in many poems of the period 1597–1603 there are still allusions to the familiar clichés of the nineties, such as the theory of Ideas, the theory of transmigration, and the theory of idealized love and beauty (for example 12 of the 194 poems of Donne refer to Platonic love in some way; on Donne see especially Smith, 1958, Roe, 1944). But it was no longer fashionable to mention Plato himself. The old–fashioned Welsh cleric Robert Chester mentions Plato in *Loues Martyr* (1601), but Chester lived in the hills of North Wales, and was out of touch with what was happening in London.

The change in attitude toward Plato that had taken place among the London gentry since the early nineties was recognized very swiftly by George Chapman. Chapman sensed that the winds had changed as early as 1597, and in the first play that he wrote for the public theater, a comedy of that year called *An Humerous Days Mirth*, Chapman took the bold step of ridiculing Platonic love (Sc. vii.211–216, Parrott ed., 1914, p. 72; the passage anticipates Donne's "Aire and Angels" of 1600). Marston, too recognized the change, and derided several Platonic commonplaces, such as the theory of transmigration, both in his *Antonio's Revenge* (1599; III.ii., H. Wood ed., 1934–1939, vol. 1, p. 101) and in his *Jack Drum's Entertainment* (1600; III, H. Wood ed., 1934–1939, vol. 3, p. 214). Ben Jonson caught the change as well, and in *Everyman out of his Humour*, (1600; III.iv.21–31) made fun of Plato by attributing to him a dialogue called *Histriomastix*, a work actually written by Marston the previous year. Chapman went even further in his next play for the public theater, *Sir Giles Goosecap* (1601). In this play he devoted a whole plot–line to Plato: a "Platonic" pander, Momford, arranges a "Platonic" assignation for a "Platonic" lover, Clarence, with a female intellectual, Eugenia (I.i, III.ii, IV.i, IV.iii, and V.ii).

The court conception of Plato had obviously gone into steep decline among the gentry, and the school Plato was not faring very much better at the universities (Curtis, 1958; Feingold, 1984). At Oxford the works of Plato were still most easily available at Corpus Christi College. Not only did the college itself still own several copies of the *Works* of Plato, both in Latin and in Greek (inventory of 1598; Liddell, 1938, p. 404) but the President of the college, John Rainolds, also owned several copies in his own personal library of almost 1500 volumes (Feingold, 1984, p. 58; a catalogue is in Oxford, Bodl. MS Wood D.10, being edited by Feingold). The mere availability of texts, however, did not mean that Plato was actually being read at Oxford, as is shown amusingly in the case of Rainolds himself. In 1599 Rainolds belatedly decided to contribute a tract to the campaign to shut down the London theaters. In this tract, *The overthrow of stage playes* Rainolds includes several allusions to Plato, but he took them not from any of the several copies of Plato's *Works* that he had at his elbow, but from a commonplace-book by Jean Tixier, the *Officina*. For this lapse

Rainolds was immediately scolded by his colleague, the Regius Professor of Law, Alberico Gentili (1600 ed. of Rainolds' tract, p. 165).

The Oxford publisher James Barnes reprinted in 1598 and again in 1599 the old medieval essay on book–collecting, *Philobiblon* (1345), by the Bishop of Durham, Richard d'Aungerville (Richard de Bury). In these reprints readers were once more reminded that Plato held approved views on the Creation, the philosopher–king, and *contempus mundi*. But many Elizabethan readers would have noticed that d'Aungerville's knowledge of Plato was very old–fashioned: he cites the *Timaeus*, but only from Gellius, and the *Phaedo*, only from Augustine (*Philobiblon*, Maclagan ed., 1970, pp. 17, 18, respectively).

The one modern scholarly reference to Plato at Oxford during this period was written by a Balliol man, Robert Mason. In 1602, Mason published a work called *Reasons Monarchie*. He tells us that he intended this to be a systematic treatise on the human faculty of the Reason, but it is in fact little more than an undergraduate term paper, synthesizing quotations from various authorities under various topics. Among the authorities whom Mason cites is Plato: he refers to Plato in three different passages (1602 ed., pp. 7, 8, and 99). In the first two of these passages he cites in quick succession no less than seven specific works of Plato: *Laws II*, *Timaeus*, *Republic III*, *Phaedo*, *Republic X*, *Alcibiades*, and *Laws I*. This battery of references comes, however, from a commonplace-book, not from Mason's own personal reading of Plato's *Works*.

At Cambridge during this period there was still no copy of the *Works* of Plato in the University Library (Oates and Pink, 1952), and the only individual Cambridge man whom we know to have owned any Plato was Robert Ball of Trinity College, who owned a copy of the *Laws* in 1601 (Leedham–Green, 1986, vol. 1, p. 545). It was still possible to flatter the eloquence of an old preacher by comparing him to Plato, as John Weever flatters both William Covel of Queens' College (*Epigrammes* #22 of 3rd Week, McKerrow ed., p. 60), and "mellifluous" Dr. John Plaifer, the Lady Margaret Professor of Divinity (Epigrammes #13 of 4th Week, McKerrow ed., 1911, p. 69). But among undergraduates the new rage for satire was taking hold, and most of the allusions to Plato in Cambridge writing of this period are satirical. Examples may be seen in Joseph Hall's *Virgidemiarum* in the first edition (1597; III.iii. 17–25; Davenport ed., 1949, p. 37) and twice more in the second (1598; V.ii.61–66, Davenport ed., 1949, p. 80; and V.iii.24–33, Davenport ed., 1949, p. 84). Hall's wit is also seen at work in the three famous satirical Cambridge plays of this period, called the *Parnassus Plays* (1598–1600; for Hall's part see F. Huntley, 1979, pp. 29–45; questioned by McCabe, 1982, p. 368, n.21). In the first and last of the three *Parnassus Plays* there is no specific allusion to Plato, but in the middle play, called *The First Return to Parnassus*, there is an allusion to "the Platonicall diaeresis" (*First Return* I.i.415–520, Leisham ed., 1949, p. 150). I have explained this allusion at some length elsewhere (Jayne, 1993, pp. 1675–1677; on late Elizabethan Cambridge see especially Kearney, 1970).

During Elizabeth's last year, 1603, England was stricken by a serious epidemic of the plague. The anxieties of the epidemic spawned numerous pamphlets (Wilson, 1927). One of these was written by the physician Thomas Lodge in a conscientious effort to help people understand the nature of the disease. In this tract, called *A Treatise of. . .the Plague* (1603), Lodge lapsed back into the old habits that he had employed as a hack writer in the early nineties, including his habit of citing Plato as often as possible. Using materials borrowed from intermediate sources such as Elyot's *Gouernour* and Pico's *Commento*, Lodge cites Plato at some length, and in several places (Gosse ed., *Works*, 1966, vol. 4, pp. 3, 5–6, 9, 16–18, 42–43; on Plato in Lodge see Jayne, 1993, pp. 1654–1667; 1689–1702).

One of the other pamphlets that resulted from the plague of 1603 was one by Thomas Dekker called *The Wonderful Year*. In this tract Dekker identifies the expression, "the wonderful year" with Plato's theory of the recurring "great year" (*Timaeus* 39D):

> Platoes *Mirabilis Annus* (whether it be past alreadie or to come within these foure yeares) may throwe Platoes cap at *Mirabilis*, for that title of wonderfull is bestowed vpon 1603.
> (1603, 2nd ed. sigs. B4ᵛ–C1ʳ).

Dekker's allusion is especially interesting in that he refers to Plato's cap. The expression "to throw one's cap at" meant to despair of catching someone who was being chased (see Ray, 1847, p. 181). In Dekker's statement the allusion therefore may be paraphrased: Plato may speak of "wonderful years" all he wishes, but he is talking of something beyond his comprehension, for the truly wonderful year was 1603. The following year some unknown author picked up Dekker's phrase and made it the title of a satirical pamphlet called *Platoes Cap Cast at the Yeare 1604*. This work is a satirical comment on the events of 1604, as Dekker's had been of those in 1603. The author merely means by the title, just as Dekker had said, that events of 1604 were amazing beyond Plato's conception of a wonderful year.

At the death of Elizabeth in 1603 her old courtier, John Lyly, who had been one of the first to pay attention to the Queen's receiving the Stephanus Plato in 1579, now thought it appropriate to mention Plato in an exequy that he wrote on her death. After stating that Elizabeth's subjects, like "the Platonists", believe that Elizabeth's soul will live eternally (Bond ed., *Works*, 1902, vol. 1, p. 512), Lyly goes on to say that although "Plato in his lawe" forbade lamentation at funerals, if Plato could have seen what a great ruler Elizabeth had been, he would undoubtedly have made an exception in her case, and would have written an elegy for her funeral (Bond, ed., *Works*, 1902, vol. 1, pp. 513–514).

Lyly's allusion to "Plato in his lawe" is correct (the reference is to *Laws* XII. 949), but Lyly did not take it directly from Plato; he is merely quoting Plutarch's *Consolation to Apollonius*, ch. 22, which was Lyly's source for the entire oration.

Still, Lyly could easily have omitted the allusion to Plato altogether; perhaps he was moved to keep it, in remembrance of his own youthful effort to impress the young Queen 24 years earlier by writing a sub–plot about Plato into his play *Alexander and Campaspe*.

At any rate, thanks to Lyly, the great Queen who herself had nothing but scorn for Plato, was attended by Plato at her death, just as she had been at St. Paul's School on the eve of her coronation.

THE STUART PHASE (1603–1700)

In my remarks "To the General Reader" I suggested that the Renaissance revival of Plato in England appears to have gone through three phases:

1423–1485 Enthusiasm for the school Plato
1485–1603 Tudor interlude
1603–1700 Enthusiasm for the court Plato

As we have now seen, what I have politely referred to as the "Tudor interlude" might almost be called the "Tudor blackout", for the English attitude toward Plato throughout the Tudor era was cold, if not hostile. When the Tudors came to power in 1485, the school conception of Plato had become the dominant conception, and it remained so throughout the Tudor period: much the most commonly owned and most often quoted dialogue of Plato was the *Laws*, not, as is often supposed, the *Symposium*. But even the school Plato generated very little enthusiasm in Tudor England. Plato was never widely taught, and only one edition of one authentic dialogue was ever published in England during the whole of the Tudor era: a school text of the *Menexenus*, published at Cambridge in 1587. One symptom of the general ignorance about Plato is that Tudor writers felt so free to attribute to Plato works that he did not write, or wrote under some other title:

Androgyna (i.e. *Symposium*)	*Histriomastix*
Atlanticus (i.e. *Critias*)	*Libri tres*
Axiochus	*Naturalis phisica* (i.e. Timaeus)
Calf	*Politia* (i.e. Republic)
De virtute	*Socrates in exortacionibus*
Fourth Book	(i.e. *Timaeus*)
Georgycke (i.e. *Gorgias*)	*Sphere*

The court conception of Plato was apparently first brought to England by John Dee in 1551, during the reign of Edward VI; but there was no serious interest in Plato of any kind during Edward's reign or Mary's. During the reign of Elizabeth the school conception of Plato continued to dominate. The court conception gradually became better known, through Howell (1560), Wills and Fenton (1572), Woolton and Rogers (1576), and Digby (1578), but it did not acquire any vogue in England until Sir Philip Sidney, after the arrival of the Stephanus Plato in 1579, popularized at court the practice of alluding to the French court theory of Platonic love.

Even Sidney's initiative, however enjoyed only limited success. Elizabeth herself never acknowledge receiving Estienne's Plato (Languet, *Epistolae*, Dalrymple ed., 1776, p. 238; moreover, all three of the writers of her time who made the most serious effort to introduce court Platonism to English readers were stiffly rebuked: Sidney by the Queen herself, Spenser by Burghley, and Chapman by his peers, Marston and Jonson. Loyal admirers of Sidney and Spenser, such as Sidney's brother Robert, Henry Lok, and Michael Drayton, tried for a time to imitate the topoi and vocabulary of the theory of Platonic love, but by 1596 the tentative English experiment in court Platonism had collapsed, and was being openly ridiculed not only by cynics like Hall, Jonson, and Bacon, but even by one of its own former champions, George Chapman.

One of the best ways to appreciate how little interest in Plato there was in England is to contrast England with France. During the same 1485–1603 period when the English published only one edition of one authentic dialogue of Plato, the French, only 25 miles away, published well over 100 editions of Plato, including many editions of the complete *Works*.

Why was there so little interest in Plato in England during the Tudor era? The most reasonable explanation is that the Tudor monarchs controlled what was thought in England, and they themselves were not interested in Plato. The tightness of the Tudor grip on the thought of the English population is often underestimated. During the Tudor era the population of England was about 4 million. (Germany had 20 million, France 16 million, and Italy, 9 million; for these estimates see Emery, 1976, Glass, 1945, Hollingsworth, 1967, King, 1936, Laslett, 1971, Mandell, 1970, Rich, 1950, Russell, 1948, Wrigley, 1966). Because England was an island, the Tudors were able to mold their small population into an extraordinarily homogeneous society. They did this primarily by religious education, catechizing from infancy every soul at every level of the social hierarchy, to accept the authority of the regime:

> Question: What is thy duty toward thy neighbour?
> Answer: . . .To order myself lowly and reverently toward my betters
>   . . . to do my duty in that state of life into which it shall please God to call
>   me. (*First Book of Common Prayer* (1549), Catechism, 1876, ed., p. 324).

But the Tudors did not rely on religious education alone. They also used their control of the printing press and import licenses to dictate what books the English people were allowed to read. Nor was that all. Whenever an unruly citizen stepped out of line, the regime swiftly whipped him back into position, using any method that seemed appropriate: confiscation of property, imprisonment, exile, torture, public maiming (hands and ears were the favorite body parts), and public execution (usually beheading, burning, or hanging).

By these means the Tudors were able to control what their subjects thought, even in matters of religion. Thus when Henry VIII decided to break away from the Bishop of Rome, the entire country was expected en bloc to become Protestant. When Mary

I came to the throne, with the mission to returning the country to the Roman Church, the entire country was expected en bloc to become Catholic. When Elizabeth I came to power, because she wished to revert to Protestantism, the entire country was expected en bloc to become Protestant again. This extraordinary shifting of the entire country as a unit, back and forth between Protestant and Catholic religion was not the way things were handled in France, nor was it the way things had been handled in England before the Tudor era. Nor have the English behaved in this way at any time since the Tudor era. The Tudors were exceptional in being able to dictate what their people thought, and it was because none of the five Tudor monarchs ever had any interest in Plato that there was no general interest in Plato in England during the Tudor period.

The proof that it was the regime itself that was primarily responsible for the "blackout" of Plato during the Tudor era is that during the Stuart dynasty that followed, English interest in Plato immediately burgeoned. The change began with the marriage of James I to Princess Anne of Denmark. Anne took an active interest in the French practice of court entertainments on the theme of Platonic love, and court entertainments involving allusions to Platonic love were soon being written by Ben Jonson (*Masque of Blackness*, 1605, *Masque of Beauty*, 1608, *Haddington Masque*, 1608, *Masque of Queens*, 1609, *Oberon*, 1611; and *Pleasure Reconciled to Virtue*, 1618); by Daniel (*The Queen's Arcadia*, 1605; and *Hymen's Triumph*, 1614); and by John Fletcher (*The Faithfull Shepherdess*, 1609). Jonson, who owned a copy of the Stephanus Plato (Jonson, *Works*, ed. Herford and Simpson, 1925–1952, vol. 1, pp. 266–267), refers to Plato by name in one of the poems in *Forest* (1616; poem 10). Daniel's *Hymen's Triumph* was written for the marriage of one of Queen Anne's court ladies, Jean Drummond. A relative of hers, William Drummond of Hawthornden, later wrote several poems on the theme of idealized love (Harrison, 1980; Fogel, 1952). Platonic love also appears in the Jacobean poems of Donne (Doggett, 1934; Jayne, *Studies*, 1994). (For Plato in Ralegh see Lefranc, 1968; Jayne, *Studies*, 1994.)

In the schools Plato was still being taught primarily as a text for practice in learning the Greek language: in 1612 John Brinsley complained that there was no English translation of any of Plato's works in print for students to use in translation exercises (*Ludus literarum*, 1612, p. 239). By the middle of James' reign the court's interest in continental court Platonism had metastasized to Oxford. Beginning in 1613 the Oxford theologian Thomas Jackson wrote a series of *Commentaries* upon the Apostles' Creed (STC 14308–14319; see Hutton, 1979). Jackson's *Commentaries*, which eventually extended to 12 volumes, published over the years 1613 to 1657, were based on Platonic theology.

Queen Anne died in 1619, but under Charles I (1625–1649) the fad of Platonic love at court revived because Charles' wife, the French Princess, Henrietta Maria, had acted in court entertainments on the theme of Platonic love in France, and brought the practice with her to England. At least eleven of Charles' subjects wrote entertainments and plays to feed Henrietta's appetite for such works:

Carew	Kynaston
Davenant	Montagu
Goffe	Rutter
Heywood	Suckling
Jonson	Townshend
Killigrew	

(see Reyher, 1909; Sensabaugh, 1938, 1940, 1944; Cope, 1973).

In addition, Milton wrote a masque in the Platonic mode for presentation at Ludlow Castle in 1634 (Jayne, 1968), and Ben Jonson even attempted a play on Platonic love for the public theater (the ill-fated *New Inn,* 1629). Jonson also alluded to Plato several times in his miscellany, *Timber* (1641; 11. 849–851, 1832–1839, 2416–2417, 2638–2640, Herford and Simpson ed., 1925–1952, vol. 8, pp. 555–649).

In 1632 a friend of Michael Drayton, Henry Reynolds, published a treatise entitled *Mythomystes* expounding the Platonic theory of poetry (Cinquemani, 1970). Reynold's conception of this theory was essentially the French court conception, in which poets were thought to write entirely from inspiration, and to prefer the esoteric style and the syncretic view of authority (Levi, 1970; R. Merrill, 1957). The Caroline court was awash with poems for and against Platonic love. There were poems on the "for" side by William Habington, John Hoskins, Thomas Randolph, and Thomas Stanley, among others; and poems on the "anti-platonique" side by Robert Ayton, Ben Jonson, John Fletcher, Abraham Cowley, Alexander Brome, Francis Beaumont, William Cartwright, John Cleveland, and George Daniel of Beswick.

In 1649 Charles I was executed, Queen Henrietta was exiled, and the country was declared a "Commonwealth". (The name was subsequently changed to "Protectorate".) During the Commonwealth period, writers who were interested in the court conception of Plato no longer had a court to write for; with some exceptions (the Vaughans, for example; see Durr, 1962; Hamilton, 1974) they wrote for the universities instead. At Oxford an academic treatise on Platonic love was written by Robert Waring in 1657. At Cambridge there were treatises or poems on Platonic theology by John Smith, Ralph Cudworth, Benjamin Whichcote, and above all Henry More (see Cassirer, 1932; Hutin, 1966; Lichtenstein, 1962; Saveson, 1955, 1958; Staudenbauer, 1974). For the first time the status of Plato as a subject for instruction was openly debated at the universities, in treatises by Seth Ward (1654) and John Webster (1654). In both the "Oxford Platonism" and the "Cambridge Platonism" of this period it was the court Plato (that is, the Plato of love-theory and Theology) rather than the school Plato that was involved. Thus when Thomas Stanley, perhaps acting on a suggestion made by Francis Bacon (*De augmentis scientiarum*, Book III, Spedding and Ellis ed., 1857–1874, *Works*, vol. 1, p. 563), wrote the first English *History of Philosophy* (1655–1660), he devoted his section on the philosophy of Plato to a translation of the treatise on Platonic love by Giovanni Pico della Mirandola, *Commento* (1519).

In 1660 the Stuart dynasty was restored to the throne. But Charles II had been tutored in France (1646–1649) by the materialist philosopher Thomas Hobbes, and Charles' wife, Catherine of Braganza, was a Catholic from Portugal; it is therefore not surprising that there was no resumption at their court of the Platonic entertainments that Charles' mother, Henrietta Maria, had favored. Nevertheless, some poets, especially Traherne (see Cox, 1971; Day, 1968; Guffey, 1969; Sicherman, 1966a) continued to be interested in some aspects of court Platonism. By 1666 there had been so much discussion of the court conception of Plato at both universities that it alarmed a minor vicar in Kent named Samuel Parker, who published a tract warning against this trend: *A Censvre of Platonick Philosophy* (London, 1666; Wing P463). Parker was sufficiently impartial to publish a warning against Hobbes as well, and for these efforts he was made Bishop of Oxford in 1668. Parker notwithstanding, however, interest in Plato at Oxford continued unabated. In 1667 Dr. John Fell published the first English translation of the *Introduction to Plato* by the ancient authority Albinus. For good measure, Fell added, as an appendix to his edition, a bibliography of works by and about Plato in Oxford libraries; this bibliography had been compiled mainly by the librarian of the Bodleian, Gerard Langbaine. In Fell's position as Vice–Chancellor (and censor) of the university, he also approved for publication a massive treatise by a private tutor, Theophilus Gale, comparing Platonic doctrine point by point with Jewish doctrine (*The Court of the Gentiles*, 1669–1678, 4 volumes). At Cambridge there was continued writing about the court Plato in both prose and verse, by Joseph Glanvill, George Rust, Peter Sterry, and Edward Benlowes.

Interest in both the school and court conceptions of Plato remained active in England until at least 1700. In 1673 appeared the first English edition of a selection of Plato's dialogues for school use: a collection of nine complete dialogues and one book of the *Laws,* printed in Greek, with Ficino's Latin translation, edited by John North, and published in Cambridge. Two years later (1675) appeared the first English translations ever printed of authentic dialogues of Plato: the *Apology* and *Phaedo*, translated by an anonymous hand and published in London. In 1688 the rector of George Herbert's church at Bemerton, John Norris, published the last significant English work on the court conception of Plato, a prose tract entitled *The Theory and Regulation of Love* (Wing N1272; on Norris see Mackinnon, 1910). It was not until 1700 that a reaction against Plato finally closed the door on the Platonic revival. This reaction is reflected in a book entitled *Platonisme unveil'd*, an English translation published in London of a French work, *Le Platonisme dévoilé*, by Mattieu Souverain (French version Paris, 1700. BN: English version BL). During the eighteenth century interest in Plato died down (but see Evans, 1943), not to revive again until the time of Thomas Taylor and Benjamin Jowett in the nineteenth century (for these later periods see Baldwin, 1994).

By dint of very long searching I have found allusions to Plato in a number of Tudor books, but by comparison with the interest of Plato at the same time in France, and during the Stuart era in England, these few allusions of the Tudor period constitute little more than a quiescent interlude; the main advances of the Renaissance revival of Plato in England occurred during the sixty years that immediately preceded the Tudor era, and during the Stuart era that followed it.

APPENDICES

Appendix 1a. Works attributed to Plato and in England (1423–1485)

No.	Date	Title	Owner	Pres. Location	Reference
1	1423	Platonis Phaedon (tr. Aristippus)	John Whethamstede (given to Duke Humfrey, and by him to Oxford University)	Oxford, Corpus Christi, 243, fol. 115ᵛ ff.	Coxe, II, pp. 100–101; Hunt, 1970, p. 8, #14
		Super thimeum Platonis (tr. Calcidius)		fol. 135ʳ ff.	
		Platonis Menon (tr. Aristippus)		fol. 184ᵛ ff.	
2	1439	Novam traductionem totius politiae Platonicae (1st half only); tr. P.C. Decembrio	Duke Humfrey	London, BL Harley 1705	Hunt, 1970, p. 5, #9; London, BL, Harley cat. vol. 1 (1759) #1705
3	1441	Platonis politia (entire); tr. P.C. Decembrio	Duke Humfrey; then Richard Nix, Bishop of Norwich	Durham D+C C.IV.3	Rud, Cat. Durham MSS p. 294; Pers. comm. from Durham; On Nix see Emden: 'Nykke'
4	1441	Republic (tr. P.C. Decembrio)	Duke Humfrey	Vatican, lat. 10669	Codices Vaticani lat. IV (1914), pp. 638–639; Hunt, 1970, pp. 5–6, 10; Zaccaria, 1959, p. 180
5	1442	Platonis Socrates sive dialogus de morte (ie. Axiochus; tr. Cencio)	William Grey	Oxford, Balliol 315, fols. 62ᵛ–67ʳ	Mynors, 1963, pp. xxvii and 332–333; Hunt, 1970, p. 25, #40
6	1444	Novam traduccionem tocius policie Platonice	Oxford Univ.		Anstey, 1868, I, p. 237
7	1445	liber Platonis in Phedone (i.e. Phaedo)	Oxford Univ.	lent to Duke Humfrey	Anstey, 1868, I, p. 246; Vickers, p. 415, n.1, says Phaedrus
8	1447	Socrates de morte contempnenda (frag. of Axiochus; tr. Cencio)	Henry Cranebrook (Cant. College, Oxford)	London, BL, Royal 10.B.ix, fols. 70ᵛ–71ᵛ	Warner, I, p. 318; Hunt, 1970, p. 11–12, #22
9	1447	De morte Socratis (i.e. Phaedo, tr. Bruni)	Thomas Francis (London M.D.)	Florence, Riccard. 952, fols. 30–34ᵛ; see also fol. 77ʳ	Biagiarelli, p. 240 (corrects Weiss, 1967, p. 188); Pers. comm. from Riccardiana

Appendix 1 (cont.)

No.	Date	Title	Owner	Pres. Location	Reference
10	1448	Timeum Platonis	St. Albans Abbey	borrowed Wm. Dolte	Hunt in Parkes, p. 275
11	1451	In Timeo	Henry Caldey (Cookfield)		Anstey, 1868, II, p. 611
12	1451	Socrates de morte contempnenda (i.e. Axiochus, tr. Cencio)	John Manyngham (Oxford)	Dublin, Trinity 438, fols. 122^r–132^v	O'Sullivan, 28–39 Colker, vol. 2, p. 867 Hunt, 1970, p. 11, #21
13	1452	Phaedo (tr. Bruni)	Camb. Kings (formerly Duke Humfrey)		Munby, 1951, p. 282 (James, 1895, p. 75, and Weiss, 1967, p. 64, say Phaedrus)
14	1452	Novam traductionem totius politiae Platonicae (tr. P.C. Decembrio; 1st half only)	Camb. Kings (formerly Duke Humfrey)	London, BL, Harley 1705	Munby, 1951, p. 282 Hunt, 1970, p. 5, #9
15	1452	Epistolae (tr. Bruni)	Thomas Wodeford (later Thomas Hynde, John Dee, Thomas Bodley)	Oxford, Bodl. Auct. F.6.2, fols. 6^v–62^r	Oxford, Bodl. SC,II, #21457 Bertalot, II, p. 271 (Possibly MS noted by Leland, Collect. III, pp. 58–62; see Mynors, 1963, p. 387)
		Apology (tr. Bruni; 2nd version)		fols. 63^c–92^t	Mynors, 1963, pp. xxxv, 110–111; see also p. 387
16	1453	Platonis Axiochus (tr. Rinuccio)	William Grey	Oxford, Balliol 131, fols. 20–30^v	
		Euthyphro (tr. Rinuccio)		fols. 31^r–37^r	
		Crito		lost	
17	1453	Apology (tr. Bruni; 2nd version)	Oxford, Balliol (gift of Grey?)	Oxford, New College 286, fols. 136–149^r	Coxe, vol. 1, pp. 100–102 Bertalot, II, p. 270 Leland, vol. 4, p. 66
		Crito (tr. Bruni; 2nd version)			Leland, vol. 4, p. 61
18	1459	Socrates de morte contemnenda (i.e. Axiochus; tr. Cencio)	Reginald Boulers	Aberystwyth, Nat'l Lib. Wales, MS Peniarth 336A (Hengwrt 220), pp. 208–227	Handlist Nat'l Lib. Wales I (1940), p. 2 Hankins, 1984, p. 201

Appendix 1 (cont.)

#	Date	Work	Owner	Location	Reference
19	1465	Calcidius (i.e. Timaeus)	John Gunthorpe (Dean of Wells)	Camb. Trinity 824, (R.9.23)	James, 1901, vol. 2, pp. 265–266
20	1468	(Timaeus; Gk text by Emman. of Const.)	George Neville (Archb. York)	Durham D + C C.IV2, item 1	James, 1927, p. 351
		(Letters; Gk text by Emman. of Const.)		Leyden Univ. Voss Gr. #56	Weiss, 1967, p. 145
21	c1472	Phaedo (tr. Bruni)	Thomas S (Oxford scribe)	Oxf. Magd. Lat. 39 fols. 35r–77r	Hunt, 1970, p. 33, #57; Coxe, vol. II, pp. 23–24; Bertalot, II, p. 266
22	1473	Axiochus (tr. Cencio)	John Gunthorpe (Dean of Wells)	Paris, BN lat. 6729A, fols. 55v–60r	Paris, Cat. MSS Bibl. Reg. IV (1744), p. 527
		Apology (tr. Bruni; 2nd version)		fols. 62r–73r	(Bertalot, II, p. 271 omits)
		Crito (tr. Bruni, 2nd version)		fols. 73v–79r	Bertalot, II, p. 270
23	1475	Policie Platonis (tr. P.C. Decembrio)	Camb. St. Catherine's		Corrie, 1846, p. 3
24	1478	Platonis Axiochus (tr. Rinuccio)	Oxford, Balliol (gift of Grey)	Oxford, Balliol 131, fols. 14r–19v	Leland, vol. 4, p. 61 (= #16 above; see also Mynors. 1963, pp. xxxv, 110–111, 387)
		Euthyphro (tr. Rinuccio)			Leland, vol. 4, p. 61
		Republic (tr. P.C. Decembrio)		fols. 20–30v	Mynors, 1963, p. 387
		Epistles (tr. Bruni)			Leland, vol. 4, p. 61; Mynors, 1963, p. 387
25	1482	Naturalis phisica Platonis	Leicester Abbey		James, TLAS, vol. 19, p. 29, #761 (also p. 135)
26	1481	Socrotes in exortacionibus (sic)	Leicester Abbey		James, TLAS, vol. 21, p. 14, #589 (also vol. 19, p. 134)
27	1482	Liber Platonis (i.e. Timaeus)	Leicester Abbey		James, TLAS, vol. 21, p. 14, #590
28	1482	Plato in Thimeo	Leicester Abbey		James, TLAS, vol. 21, p. 15, #608 (also vol. 19, p. 135)
29	1483	Phaedrus (tr. Bruni)	Unknown	Glasgow, Hunterian MS U.1.10, fols. 1r–8v	J. Young et al., # 206
		Phaedo (tr. Bruni)		fols. 8v–32v	

Appendix 1b. Dubia: works attributed to Plato but only possibly in England before 1485

No.	Date	Title	Owner	Pres. Location	Reference
1	15th c	Axiochus (tr. Cencio)	Unknown	Camb. Corp. Chr. Coll. MS 472, pp. 265–293	James, 1912, vol. 2, pp. 408–411
		Apology (tr. Bruni; 2nd version)		pp. 491–537	Bertalot, II, p. 134 (Bertalot, II, p. 271 omits)
		Crito (tr. Bruni; 2nd version)		pp. 538–566	Bertalot, II, p. 270
2	15th c	Phaedrus (tr. Bruni)	Unknown	Dublin, Trinity K.4.20	Colker, vol. 2, pp. 1192–1193; MS 923
		Axiochus (tr. Cencio)			
		Gorgias (tr. Bruni)			
		Apology (tr. Bruni; 2nd version)			
		Crito (tr. Bruni; 2nd version)			
		Phaedo (tr. Bruni)			
		Epistolae (tr. Bruni)			
3	15th c	Phaedrus (tr. Bruni)	Unknown	London, BL, Addit. 11, 274, fols. 2^r–13^r	London, BL, Cat. (1837), p. 46 Bertalot, II, p. 270
		Apology (tr. Bruni; 2nd version)		fols. 13^v–30^r	
		Crito (tr. Bruni; 2nd version)		fols. 31^r–38^v	
		Phaedo (tr. Bruni)		fols. 40^r–86^v	
		Epistolae 1–6, 8–12, 7 (tr. Bruni)		fols. 87^r–121^v	
4	15th c	De virtute (tr. Cencio)	Unknown	London, BL, Addit. 11, 760, fols. 137^r–140^v	London, BL, Cat. (1850) Bertalot. II, p. 134
5	15th c	Phaedrus (tr. Bruni)	Unknown	London, BL, Addit. 11, 898; fols. 1^r–12^r	London, BL, Cat. (1841), p. 16
		Apology (tr. Bruni; 2nd version)		fols. 16^r–35^v	
		Crito (tr. Bruni; 2nd version)		fols. 36^v–45^r	
		Gorgias (tr. Bruni)		fols. 45^v–78^r	
6	1467	Phaedo (tr. Bruni)	Unknown	London, BL, Addit. 19, 744; fols. 46^r–94^v	Hankins, 1984, p. 220
		Gorgias (tr. Bruni)		fols. 95^v–148^v	
7	15th c	Axiochus (tr. Rinuccio)	Unknown	London, BL, Arundel 277, fols. 116^r–125^v	London, BL, Cat. (1834), pp. 81–82
8	15th c	Epistolae (tr. Bruni)	Unknown	London, BL, Burney 74, fols. 103^r–129^v	London, BL, Cat. (1834), pp. 24–25 possibly MS seen by Leland, *Collect.* III, pp. 58–62; Mynors, 1963, p. 387

Appendix 1 (cont.)

9	15th c	Epistolae (tr. Bruni)	Unknown	London, BL, Harley 4.923, fols. 293r–310r	London, BL, Harley 1808 vol. 3, p. 221
		Axiochus (tr. Rinuccio)		fols. 310r–314r	
		Crito (tr. Bruni; 2nd version)		fols. 314r–322	
10	15th c	Axiochus (tr. Cencio)	Unknown	Oxford, Bodl. 881, fols. 39v–44v	Oxford, Bodl, SC, V, p. 334 #27707
11	15th c	Axiochus (tr. Cencio)	Unknown	Oxford, Bodl. Hatton 105, fols. 78r–87v	Oxford, Bodl. SC, II. pp. 814–815 (wrongly ident. as Ital.) Hankins, 1984, p. 233
12	15th c	Republic (tr. P.C. Decembrio; fragments only)	1. Unknown	Oxford, Merton E.3.21	Ker, Pastedowns #1091
			2. John Bolderne in 1577	Oxford, Magdalen MS lat. 182	Ker, Pastedowns #1219
			3. Unknown	Oxford, Bodleian Savile R. 6	Ker, Pastedowns #1698

Appendix 2. The Social Status of Tudor Writers

Peers:	Lord Brooke (F. Greville)*	Earl of Oxford (Ed. de Vere)*
	Earl of Dorset (T. Sackville)*	Earl of Surrey (H. Howard)
	Lord Herbert (of Cherbury)*	Lord Verulam (F. Bacon)*
Knights:	Sir William Alexander*	Sir Thomas More*
	Sir Lodowick Bryskett*	Sir Walter Ralegh*
	Sir John Davies*	Sir Philip Sidney*
	Sir Edward Dyer*	Sir Thomas Wyatt*
	Sir John Harington*	
Country gentlemen:	B. Barnes*	N. Breton*
	R. Barnfield*	W. Drummond*
	F. Beaumont*	A. Golding*
	E. Benlowes*	W. Habington*
	R. Brathwaite*	W. Percy*
Court gentlemen:	W. Baldwin*	G. Gascoigne*
	W. Basse	B. Googe*
	W. Browne*	W. Hunnis
	G. Chapman*	J. Lyly*
	T. Churchyard	G. Turberville*
	S. Daniel*	T. Tusser*
	M. Drayton	
Professionals:	T. Campion* physician	J. Marston* clergyman
	J. Davies teacher	T. Nashe* (clergyman)
	J. Fletcher (clergyman)	J. Skelton* clergyman
	J. Ford* lawyer	R. Southwell priest
	A. Fraunce* lawyer	N. Udall* teacher
	N. Grimald* clergyman	G. Wither* lawyer
	J. Hall* clergyman	

Merchants:	J. Donne* (ironmonger)	G. Peele* (salter)
	T. Lodge* (grocer)	J. Sylvester (clothier)
	H. Lok* (mercer)	R. Tofte (fishmonger)
	A. Munday (draper)	G. Whetstone (haberdasher)
Artisans:	H. Chettle (dyer)	C. Marlowe* (cobbler)
	T. Dekker tailor	W. Shakespeare (glover)
	T. Deloney silk-weaver	J. Speed* (tailor)
	S. Gosson* (carpenter)	E. Spenser* (clothmaker)
	R. Greene* (saddler)	J. Stow (tailor)
	G. Harvey* (ropemaker)	J. Webster (tailor)
	B. Jonson (bricklayer)	
Servants:	Stephen Hawes groom	Roger Ascham (steward)
	Isabella Whitney maid	

Note: Asterisk indicates attendance at a university. Occupation in parentheses is that of writer's father. Classes above the double line are 'gentlemen'.

BIBLIOGRAPHY

Aconcio, Jacopo, *De methodo* (1558), ed. and transl. (Ital.) Giorgio Radetti (Florence, 1944)

Aconcio, Jacopo, *De methodo* transl. Thomas Blundeville as *The true order and methode of wryting and reading hystories* (London, 1574) STC 3161

Adelard of Bath, *De eodem et diverso*, ed. Hans Willner (Münster, 1903) BGPM 4.1

Aelianus, Claudius, *Varia historia*, ed. M. Dilts (Leipzig, 1974)

Aelianus, Claudius, *Varia historia,* transl. Abraham Fleming as *A Registre of Hystories*, (London, 1576) STC 164

Aggas, Edward, see La Place; Mornay

Agrippa von Nettesheim, Henricus Cornelius, *Opera* (Lyons, c. 1600); repr. Hildesheim, 1970, 2 vols)

Agrippa von Nettesheim, Henricus Cornelius, *De incertitudine et vanitate scientiarum et artium*, transl. James Sanford (London, 1569) STC 204

Agrippa von Nettesheim, Henricus Cornelius, *De incertitudine et vanitate scientiarum et artium,* ed. Catherine M. Dunn (Northridge, 1974)

Albinus, *De dogmate Platonis*, ed. P. Louis (Paris, 1945)

Albinus, *De dogmate Platonis,* ed. and transl. John Fell as *In platonicam philosophiam* (Oxford, 1667) Wing A886, pp. 95–111 contain bibliography of works on Plato in Oxford, begun by Gerard Langbaine, in Oxford, Bodleian MS Wood donat. 5, and finished by Fell

Albinus, *De dogmate Platonis*, transl. George Burges in Plato, *Works* (London, 1854) vol. 6, pp. 241–314 (Bohn)

Alciati, Andrea, *Omnia emblemata*, ed. Claude Mignault (Antwerp, 1577)

Alciati, Andrea, *The Latin Emblems*, ed. Peter M. Daly *et al.* (Toronto, 1985)

Alday, John, see Boaistuau

Alexander the Great, see *Wars of Alexander*

Allen, Don Cameron, *Doubt's Boundless Sea* (Baltimore, 1964)

Allen, Michael J. B., "Cosmogony and Love", *JMRS*, 10 (1980), pp. 131–153

Allen, Percy S., "Bishop Shirwood of Durham and his Library", *EHR*, 25 (1910), pp. 445–456

Alley, William, *Ptochomuseion: The poore mans librarie* (London, 1565) STC 374 (2nd ed. London, 1571)

Allott, Robert, *Wits Theatre of the Little World* (London, 1599) STC 381 (repr. Amsterdam, 1971)

Anderson, Andrew H., "The Books of Thomas, Lord Paget", *TCBS*, 6 (1975), pp. 226–242

Anstey, Henry ed., *Epistolae Academicae Oxonienses* (Oxford, 1898)

Anstey, Henry ed., *Munimenta Academica* (London, 1868) 2 vols (Rolls)

Anthologia graeca, see *Greek Anthology*

Antonio dalla Paglia, see Paleario

Apuleius of Madaura, *Opera*, ed. Paul Thomas (Stuttgart, 1970) 3 vols

Apuleius of Madaura, *De deo Socratis*, in *Opuscules philosophiques*, ed. and transl. (Fr.) Jean Beaujeu (Paris, 1973) pp. 20–45

Apuleius of Madaura, *De deo Socratis*, transl. (anon.) in Apuleius, *Works* (London, 1853) pp. 350–373 (Bohn)

Apuleius of Madaura, *De Platone et eius dogmate* (Greek) (Paris, 1521)

Apuleius of Madaura, *De Platone et eius dogmate*, transl. (Lat.) by Petrus Balbus (Rome, 1469; repr. Venice, 1512) BL

Apuleius of Madaura, *De Platone et eius dogmate*, Gk. and transl. (Lat.) by Denys Lambin (Paris, 1567) BN

Apuleius of Madaura, *De Platone et eius dogmate*, transl. George Burges in Plato, *Works* (London, 1854) vol. 6, pp. 323–403 (Bohn)

Apuleius of Madaura, *De Platone et eius dogmate*, ed. and transl. (Fr.) by Jean Beaujeu in *Opuscules philosophiques* (Paris, 1973) pp. 49–107

Aquinas, Thomas, *Summa contra gentiles*, transl. Charles J. O'Neal (Notre Dame, 1975) 5 vols.

Arber, Edward, see London

Ariosto, Lodovico, *Orlando Furioso*, transl. Sir John Harington (London, 1591) STC 746

Ariosto, Lodovico, *Orlando Furioso*, transl. Sir John Harington, ed. Robert McNulty (Oxford, 1972)

Aristotle, *Complete Works*, transl. Jonathan Barnes (Princeton, 1984) 2 vols.

Aristotle, *Aristoteles Latinus*, ed. Lorenzo Minio–Paluello (London, 1951–1961)

Aristotle, *De anima*, ed. and tr. W. S. Hett (Cambridge, Mass., 1957) (Loeb).

Aristotle, *Nicomachean Ethics*, ed. and transl. Horace Rackham (Cambridge, Mass., 1956) (Loeb)

Aristotle, *Nicomachean Ethics*, transl. (Lat.) Leonardo Bruni (Oxford, 1479) STC 752

Aristotle, *Politics and Economics*, transl. (Lat.) Leonardo Bruni with Commentary by Jacques Lefèvre d'Étaples (Paris, 1506; Appendix, by Lefèvre d'Étaples, is *Hecatonomiae*, a florilegium of Plato's *Republic* and *Laws*)

Ascham, Roger, *Works*, ed. J. A. Giles (London, 1864) 3 vols. in 4 (repr. New York, 1970)

Ascham, Roger, *English Works*, ed. W. A. Wright (Cambridge, 1904; repr. Cambridge, 1970)

Ascham, Roger, *Epistolarum familiarum*, ed. Edward Grant (London, 1576) STC 826 (later eds. STC 827–829)

Ascham, Roger, *Letters*, (selection) transl. M. A. Hatch (Lexington, 1958)

Ascham, Roger, *The Scholemaster* (London, 1570) STC 832

Ascham, Roger, *The Scholemaster*, ed. Lawrence Ryan (Ithaca, 1967)

Ascham, Roger, *Toxophilus* (London, 1545) STC 837 (repr. London, 1965)

Ashby, George, see Mubashshir ibn Fatik

Aston, T. H. gen. ed., *The History of the University of Oxford* (Oxford, 1984–date) 8 vols.

Augustine, Aurelius, *Confessiones*, ed. Lucas Verheijen (Turnhout, 1981) (CC 27= *PL* 32: 659–868)

Augustine, Aurelius, *Confessiones*, transl. F. J. Sheed (New York, 1943)

Augustine, Aurelius, *De civitate dei*, ed. Bernardus Dombaert et al. (Turnholt, 1965) (CC 47, 48 = *PL* 41)

Augustine, Aurelius, *De civitate dei*, transl. Henry Bettenson (London, 1972)

Augustine, Aurelius, *De civitate dei*, (Strasbourg, 1473) HD (contains Commentaries of Trivet and Waleys)

Augustine, Aurelius, *De civitate dei*, transl. John Healy (London, 1610) STC 916, see also Barroll

Augustine, Aurelius, *De doctrina Christiana*, ed. William M. Green (Vienna, 1963) *(PL* 34:15–122)

Augustine, Aurelius, *De doctrina Christiana*, transl. John J. Gavigan (New York, 1947)

Aungerville, Richard d' (Richard de Bury), *Philobiblon*, ed. Thomas James (Oxford, 1598) STC 958.5

Aungerville, Richard d' (Richard de Bury), *Philobiblon*, ed. and transl. Ernest C. Thomas, ed. Michael Maclagan (Oxford, 1970)

Axiochus, see Xenocrates

Ayenbite of Inwyt, see Lorens d'Orleans

Ayton, Sir Robert, *English and Latin Poems*, ed. Charles B. Gullans (Edinburgh, 1963)

Bacon, Francis, *Works*, ed. James Spedding, R. L. Ellis, and D.D. Heath (London, 1857–1874) 14 vols.

Baines, Barbara, *Thomas Heywood* (Boston, 1984)

Baker–Smith, Dominic, "Uses of Plato by Erasmus and More" in A. Baldwin, pp. 86–99

Baldwin, Anna and Sarah Hutton, eds., *Platonism and the English Imagination* (Cambridge, 1994)

Baldwin, William, *A Treatise of Morall Phylosophie* (London, 1547) STC 1253

Baldwin, William, *A Treatise of Morall Phylosophie*, enlarged ed. Thomas Palfreyman (London, 1557) STC 1257, repr. Robert H. Bowers (Gainesville, 1967)

Bale, John, *Index Britanniae scriptorum*, ed. Reginald L. Poole and Mary Bateson (Oxford, 1902)

Barckley, Sir Richard, *A Discourse of the Felicitie of Man* (London, 1598) STC 1381

Barnes, Barnabe, *Poems*, ed. Alexander B. Grosart (London, 1875)

Barnfield, Richard, *Poems*, ed. Edward Arber (Birmingham, 1882)

Baron, Hans, *The Crisis of the Early Italian Renaissance* (Princeton, 1966)

Baron, Hans, *From Petrarch to Leonardo Bruni* (Chicago, 1968)

Baron, Hans, see also Bruni

Barroll, Leeds, "Some Versions of Plato in the English Renaissance", *Shakespeare Studies*, 2 (1966) pp. 228–295, repr. the following: Augustine, *City of God*, VIII.1–16, Healey transl. of 1610; Plutarch, *Platonic Questions*, from Holland transl. of *Moralia*, 1603; Plutarch, Creation of Soul in *Timaeus*, from Holland transl. of *Moralia*, 1603; Seneca, *Epistle* 58, from Lodge transl. of *Works*, 1614

Bartholomaeus Anglicus, *De proprietatibus rerum* (c.1296) transl. Stephen Bateman (London, 1582) STC 1538

Bartholomaeus Anglicus, *De proprietatibus rerum*, transl. John of Trevisa (1399), ed. M. C. Seymour *et al.* (Oxford, 1975–1988) 2 vols.

Bateman, Stephen, see Bartholomaeus Anglicus; Cartari; Lycosthenes

Beard, Thomas, *The theatre of gods judgement* (London, 1597) STC 659

Beaumont, Francis, *Poems* (London, 1640) STC 1665

Bede, Venerable, *De natura rerum*, ed. Charles W. Jones (Turnhout, 1975) (CC 123A, Part I, pp. 174–234=*PL* 90: 187–278, with gloss attributed by Byrhferth)

Behm, Vicki, *The Life and Writings of John Woolton* (Univ. of London diss., 1977)

Bekynton, Thomas, *Memorials of the Reign of King Henry VI: the Official Correspondence* (London, 1872) 2 vols. (Rolls) (repr. New York, 1964)

Bembo, Cardinal Pietro, *Gli Asolani* (Venice, 1505) BL

Benlowes, Edward, *Lusus poeticus poesis* (London, 1634) STC 1878

Benlowes, Edward, *Theophila* (London, 1652) Wing B1879

Bennett, Henry S, *English Books and Readers* (Cambridge, 1952–1970) 3 vols.

Bennett, Josephine W., "Andrew Holes", *Speculum*, 19 (1944) pp. 314–335

Bersuire, Pierre, see Ovid

Bertalot, Ludwig, *Studien zum italienischen und deutschen Humanismus*, ed. P. O. Kristeller (Rome, 1975) 2 vols.

Berti, Ernesto and Antonella Carosini, eds. Plato, *Crito*, transl. (Lat.) Leonardo Bruni and Rinuccio Aretino (Florence, 1983)

Bessarion, Giovanni, Cardinal, *In calumniatorem Platonis* (Rome, 1469) BL

Bessarion, Giovanni, Cardinal, *In calumniatorem Platonis* (Venice, 1516) Bodl.

Bessarion, Giovanni, Cardinal, *In calumniatorem Platonis*, ed. Ludwig Mohler in his *Kardinal Bessarion* (Paderborn, 1923–1942) 3 vols. (vol. 2 contains *In calumniatorem Platonis*)

Biagiarelli, Berta, "Manoscritti della raccolta dell' umanista Nicodemo Tranchedini nella Biblioteca Riccardiana di Firenze" in *Miscellanea di studi in memoria di Anna Saitta Revignas* (Florence, 1978)

Bieman, Elizabeth, *Plato Baptized* (Toronto, 1988; on Spenser)

Bigi, Emilio, "Giovanni Aurispa", *DBI*, vol. 4, pp. 593–595

Bigi, Emilio, see also Petrarca

Binns, James W., "Alberico Gentili in Defense of Poetry and Acting", *SRen.* 19 (1972), 224–272

Binns, James W., "Henry Dethick in Praise of Poetry", *Library*, 5th Ser. 30 (1975), 199–216

Binns, James W., *Intellectual Culture in Elizabethan and Jacobean England* (Leeds, 1990)

Bishop, Morris, *Petrarch and his World* (Bloomington, 1963)

Bisticci, Vespasiano da, *Vite di uomini illustri del secolo XV* (Florence, 1938)

Blades, William, see Mubashshir ibn Fatik

Blake, Norman F., *Caxton and His World* (London, 1969)

Blake, Norman F., ed., *Caxton's Own Prose* (London, 1973)

Blocaille, Etienne, *Étude sur François Hotman* (Dijon, 1902; repr. Geneva, 1970)

Boaistuau, Pierre, *Theatrum mundi* (London, 1587) STC 3166

Boaistuau, Pierre, *Theatrum mundi*, transl. John Alday as *Theatrum mundi* (London, 1566) STC 3168

Bocados de Oro, see Mubashshir ibn Fatik

Boccaccio, Giovanni, *De casibus virorum illustrium*, ed. Henry Bergen (London, 1924–1927) 4 vols. (EETS: es 121–124)

Boccaccio, Giovanni, *De casibus virorum illustrium* (Strasbourg, 1475) BL

Boccaccio, Giovanni, *De casibus virorum illustrium*, transl. John Lydgate as *The Falle of Princis* (London, 1494) STC 3175

Bodenham, John ed., *England's Helicon* (London, 1600) STC 3191

Bodenham, John, see also Allott; Ling; Meres; Munday

Boethius, A. M. S., *De consolatione philosophiae*, ed. Ludwig Bieler (Turnholt, 1957) (CC 94)

Boethius, A. M. S., *De consolatione philosophiae*, ed. and transl. H. F. Stewart (London, 1918) (Loeb)

Boethius, A. M. S., *De consolatione philosophiae*, transl. (ME) Geoffrey Chaucer (Westminster, 1478) STC 3199

Boethius, A. M. S., *De consolatione philosophiae*, transl. (ME) Geoffrey Chaucer ed. Larry Benson in Chaucer, *Works* (Boston, 1987) pp. 395–469

Boethius, A. M. S., *De consolatione philosophiae*, transl. Queen Elizabeth I, ed. Caroline Pemberton in *Englishings of Elizabeth* (London, 1899) pp. 1–120 (EETS:os 113)

Bolgar, Richard R., *The Classical Heritage and its Beneficiaries* (Cambridge, 1963)

Bond, Edward A., see Oxford, University of, *Statutes of the Colleges*

Bonilla y San Martin, Adolfo, *Fernando da Cordoba* (Madrid, 1911)

Borsa, Mario, "Correspondence of Humphrey, Duke of Gloucester and Pier Candido Decembrio", *EHR*, 19 (1904), pp. 509–526

Bostocke, Robert, *The difference betwene the auncient phisicke the latter phisicke* (London, 1585) STC 1064

Boston, John (of Bury), *Gladius Salomonis* (excerpts), ed. Churchill Babington in his ed. of Reginald Pecock, *The Repressor of over much blaming of the Clergy* (London, 1860) vol. 2 (Rolls)

Bowes, Thomas, see Primaudaye

Breton, Nicholas, *Works*, ed. Alexander B. Grosart (Edinburgh, 1879–1880) 2 vols.

Bridges, Shirley F., *Thomas Chaundler* (Univ. of Oxford diss., 1949)

Bright, Timothy, *In physicam Gulielmi Adolphi Scribonii* (Cambridge, 1584) STC 3745

Brinsley, John, *Ludus literarius* (London, 1612) STC 3768

Brinsley, John, *Ludus literarius*, ed. E. T. Compagnac (Liverpool, 1917)

Brome, Alexander, *Poems*, ed. Alexander Chalmers (London, 1810)

Broughton, Hugh, *An Apologie* (London, 1592) STC 3845 (a commentary on Daniel)

Bruni, Leonardo, *Works* (selection in Eng. transl.) ed. Gordon Griffith *et al.* as *The Humanism of Leonardo Bruni* (Binghamton, 1987)

Bruni, Leonardo, *Humanistische und philosophische Schriften*, ed. Hans Baron (Leipzig, 1928; repr. Wiesbaden, 1969) (includes "Life of Aristotle", pp. 41–49)

Bruni, Leonardo, *Epistolae*, ed. Lorenzio Mehus (Florence, 1741) 2 vols.

Bruni, Leonardo, see also Aristotle; Berti; Lefèvre d'Étaples

Bruno, Giordano, *Dialoghi italiani*, ed. Giovanni Gentile rev. Givanni Aquilecchia (Florence, 1958, 3rd ed.)

Brusoni, Lucio, *Facetiarum exemplorumque* (Basle, 1559) HD

Bryant, Joseph, "The Nature of the Allegory in Lyly's *Endimion*", *Renaissance Papers* (Columbia, S.C. 1956) pp. 4–11

Bryskett, Lodowick, see Giraldi Cinthio

Bucer, Martin, *Opera* (Basle, 1838; repr. Farnborough, 1969)

Bucer, Martin, *Commonplaces*, ed. and transl. David P. Wright (Appleford, 1972)

Budé, Guillaume, *Opera* (Basle, 1557) 4 vols. (facs. repr. Farnborough, 1969)

Budé, Guillaume, *De transitu hellenismi ad Christianismum*, transl. (Fr.) Maurice Lebel (Sherbrooke, 1973)

Bulger, Thomas, "Platonism in Spenser's *Mutabilitie Cantos*" in A. Baldwin, pp. 126–138

Bullinger, Heinrich, *De origine erroris* (Zurich, 1539) BN

Bullinger, Heinrich, *Fiftie godlie and learned sermons*, transl. H. I. (i.e. H. Middleton) (London, 1577) STC 4056. (Also called *Decades*.)

Bullinger, Heinrich, *Fiftie godlie and learned sermons*, repr. of 1587, ed. Thomas Harding (Cambridge, 1849–1852) 4 vols. (Parker Society, vols. 7–10, repr. New York, 1968). (Also called *Decades*.)

Burley, Walter, *De vita et moribus philosophorum*, ed. Hermann Knust (Tübingen, 1886)

Burton, Robert, *The Anatomy of melancholy* (Oxford, 1621) STC 4159

Burton, Robert, *The Anatomy of melancholy*, ed. Floyd Dell and Paul Jordan–Smith (New York, 1927) 2 vols.

Bush, Douglas, *Mythology and the Renaissance Tradition in English Poetry* (Minneapolis, 1932; repr. New York, 1963)

Busson, Henri, *Le rationalisme dans la littérature française de la renaissance (1533–1601)* (Paris, 1957, 2nd ed.)

Butters, S. A., *Life and Works of Everard Digby* (Univ. of Oxford diss., 1980)

Calder, Ian R. F., *John Dee Studied as an English Neoplatonist* (Univ. of London diss. 1952) 2 vols.

Calderini, Aristide, "Ricerche intorno alla biblioteca e alla cultura greca di Francesco Filelfo", *Studi italiani di filologia classica*, 20 (1913) pp. 204–424

Calecas, Manuel, *Correspondance*, ed. R. Loenertz (Vatican, 1950)

Calvin, Jean, *Christianae religionis institutio* (Basle, 1536) BL

Calvin, Jean, *Christianae religionis institutio*, transl. Sir Thomas North as *The institution of christian religion* (London, 1561) STC 4415

Cambridge University Grace Book B, ed. Mary Bateson (Cambridge, 1903–1905) 2 vols.

Cammelli, Guiseppe, *I dotti bizantini...* (Florence, 1941–1954) 3 vols.: 1. Manuele Crisolora; 2. Giovanni Argiropulo; 3. Demetrio Calcondilo

Capgrave, John, *The Chronicle of England*, ed. Francis C. Hingston (London, 1858)

Caponetto, Salvatore, *Aonio Paleario* (Turin, 1979)

Cardwell, Edward, *Synodalia* (Oxford, 1842) 2 vols. (repr. Farnborough, 1966)

Carew, Richard, *The Poems...with...Coelum Britannicum*, ed. Rhodes Dunlap (Oxford, 1949)

Carew, Richard, *Poems* (London, 1640) STC 4620

Carew, Richard, *Coelum Britannicum* (London, 1634) STC 4618.2

Carreras y Artau, Tomas *et al.*, *Historia de la filosofia espanola: Filosofia cristiana de los siglos XIII al XV* (Madrid, 1939–1943) 2 vols.

Cartari, Vincenzo, *Le imagini de i dei* (Venice, 1556) BL Venice, 1571 ed. repr. Stephen Orgel (New York, 1976)

Cartari, Vincenzo, *Le imagini de i dei*, transl. Stephen Batemas as *The golden booke of the leaden goddes* (London, 1577) STC 1583

Cartari, Vincenzo, *Le imagini de i dei*, transl. Richard Linche as *The fountaine of ancient fiction* (London, 1599) STC 4691

Cartwright, William, *Comedies, tragicomedies, with other poems* (London, 1651) Wing C709

Casa, Giovanni della, *Il Galateo* (Milan, 1559) BL

Casa, Giovanni della, *Il Galateo*, transl. Robert Peterson (London, 1576) STC 4738

Casa, Giovanni della, *Il Galateo*, ed. Joel E. Spingarn (London, 1914)

Casady, Edwin, "The Neo-Platonic Ladder in Spenser's *Amoretti*", *PQ*, 20 (1941), 284–295

Cassirer, Ernst, *Die platonische Renaissance in England* (Leipzig, 1932)

Cassirer, Ernst, *Die platonische Renaissance in England*, transl. James Pettigrove (New York, 1953)

Castiglione, Baldassare, *Il cortegiano* (Venice, 1528) BL

Castiglione, Baldassare, *Il cortegiano*, transl. Sir Thomas Hoby (London, 1561) STC 4778

Cato, Marcus Porcius, *Disticha*, transl. William Caxton as *Caton* (Westminster, c.1483) STC 4853

Caxton, William, *Prose*, ed. Nicholas Blake (London, 1973)

Caxton, William, *Prologues and Epilogues*, ed. W. J. B. Crotch (London, 1928) (EETS: os 176)

Caxton, William, *Mirrour of the World* (Westminster, 1481) STC 24762

Caxton, William, *Mirrour of the World*, ed. Oliver M. Prior (London, 1912; repr. London, 1966) (EETS: es 110) (=ME transl. of Gossuin's *L'Image du monde)*

Caxton, William, see also Blake, N.F.; Boethius; Cato; Chaucer; Gossuin; Guilleville; Honorius, Laurent; Mubashshir ibn Fatik

Cely Letters 1472–1488, ed. Alison Hanham (Oxford, 1975)

Certain Sermons, see Church of England

Champier, Symphorien, *La nef des dames vertueuses* (Lyons, c. 1503) HD; Book IV, entitled *Le livre de Vraye amour*, ed. separately James B. Wadsworth (Hague, 1962)

Champier, Symphorien, *Libelli duo* (Lyons, c.1506) HD

Champier, Symphorien, *Symphonia Platonis cum Aristotele* (Paris, 1516) BL

Chapman, George, *Plays*, ed. Thomas M. Parrott (London, 1914)

Chapman, George, *Comedies*, ed. Allan Holaday *et al.* (Urbana, 1970)

Chapman, George, *Poems.*, ed. Phyllis Bartlett (New York, 1941)

Chapman, George, see also Homer

Charlton, Kenneth, *Education in Renaissance England* (London, 1965)

Charpentier, Jacques, *Platonis cum Aristotele in universa philosophia comparatio* (Paris, 1573) HD (a commentary on *Isagogue* of Albinus)

Chaucer, Geoffrey, *Works*, ed. Larry D. Benson (Boston, 1987, 3rd ed.)

Chaucer, Geoffrey, *Canterbury Tales* (Westminster, 1477) STC 5082

Chaucer, Geoffrey, *Hous of Fame* (Westminster, 1483) STC 5087

Chaucer, Geoffrey, See also Boethius

Chester, Robert, see *Loues Martyr*

Chrimes, S. B., *Henry VII* (London, 1972)

Church of England, *The booke of the common prayer* (London, 1549) STC 16267

Church of England, *The booke of the common prayer*, ed. anon. (London, 1883)

Church of England, *Certain Sermons* (London, 1547) STC 13638.5

Church of England, *Certain Sermons*, repr. of 1623, ed. Mary E. Rickey and Thomas B. Stroup (Gainesville, 1968)

Church of England, *Certain Sermons*, ed. G. E. Corrie (Cambridge, 1850) (includes 1st and 2nd *Book of Homilies*

Cicero, Marcus T., *Opera* (London, 1573) STC 5265.7 (repr. 1574, 1579, 1584, 1585) STC 5265.8, 5266, 5266.2, 5266.4

Cicero, Marcus T., *De academicis*, ed. and transl. Horace Rackham (London, 1956) (Loeb)

Cicero, Marcus T., *De amicitia*, transl. John Tiptoft (London, c. 1530) STC 5275

Cicero, Marcus T., *De officiis*, transl. Richard Whittington (London, 1534) STC 5278

Cicero, Marcus T., *Tusculan Disputations*, transl. John Dolman as *Those fyve questions* (London, 1561) STC 5317

Cinquemani, A. M., "Henry Reynolds' *Mythomystes...*" *PMLA*, 85 (1970), pp. 1041–1049

Claudianus Mamertus, *Opera*, ed. Augustus Engelbrecht (Vienna, 1885) (CSEL, 11)

Clements, Robert J., "Ronsard and Ficino on the Four Furies", *Romanic Review*, 45 (1954), pp. 161–169

Cleveland, John, *Poems*, ed. Brian Morris and Eleanor Withington (Oxford, 1967)

Clough, Cecil H., "Thomas Linacre, Cornelio Vitelli, and Humanistic Studies at Oxford" in Francis Maddison *et al.* eds., *Linacre Studies* (Oxford, 1977) pp. 1–23

Clulee, Nicholas H., *John's Dee's Natural Philosophy...* (London, 1988)

Coignet, Matthieu, *Instruction aux princes* (Paris, 1585) BN

Coignet, Matthieu, *Instruction aux princes*, transl. Edward Hoby as *Politique discourses vpon trueth and lying* (London, 1586) STC 5846

Colet, John, *Opuscula*, ed. and transl. J. H. Lupton (London, 1876; repr. Ridgewood, 1966)

Colker, Marvin, *Trinity College Library, Dublin, Medieval, and Renaissance Latin Manuscripts* (Aldershot, 1991) 2 vols.

Compendium of Alchemy, in Oxford, Bodleian MS Ashmole 1416, item 36

Cooper, C. H. and T., *Athenae Cantabrigienses, 1500–1611* (Cambridge, 1858–1913) 3 vols.

Cooper, Thomas, *Thesaurus linguae romanae et britannicae* (London, 1565) STC 5686, see also Elyot

Cope, Jackson, *The Theatre and the Dream* (Baltimore, 1973)

Copenhaver, Brian, *Symphorien Champier* (Hague, 1978)

Copenhaver, Brian, see also Hermes Trismegistus

Copenhaver, Brian and Charles B. Schmitt, *Renaissance Philosophy* (Oxford, 1992) (Platonism pp. 127–195)

Cornarius, Janus, *De conviviorum...ritibus* (Basle, 1518) HD (includes transl. and comm. Plato's *Symposium)*

Cornarius, Janus, *Eclogae decem in dialogos Platonis omnes* in his *Opera* (Basle, 1561) BL

Cornarius, Janus, see also *Greek Anthology*; Plato, *Works*

Corrie, George E., "A Catalogue of the Books...given to St. Catherine's Hall, Cambridge", *CAS* Quarto Ser. vol. 1 (1846), pp. 1–11

Corrie, George E., see also Church of England

Court of Sapience (Westminster, 1480) STC 17015

Court of Sapience, ed. E. Ruth Harvey (Toronto, 1984)

Cousteau, Pierre, *Pegma* (Lyons, 1555) HD

Cox, Gerard, "Traherne's Centuries...", *MP*, 69 (1971), pp. 10–24

Coxe, Henry O., *Catalogus codicum...in collegiis...Oxoniensibus* (Oxford, 1850–1852) 2 vols.

Craster, H. H. E., "Index to Duke Humphrey's Gifts to the Old Library of the University in 1439, 1441, and 1444", *BQR*, 1 (1915) pp. 131–135

Crupi, Charles W., *Robert Greene* (Boston, 1986)

Cuffe, Henry, *The differences of the ages of mans life* (London, 1607) STC 6103

Curry, Walter Clyde , *Chaucer and the Medieval Sciences*. New York, 1960. 2nd ed.

Curteys, Richard, *A Sermon preached before the queenes maiestie...at Grenewiche* (London, 1573) STC 6135

Curtis, Mark H., *Oxford and Cambridge in Transition 1558–1642* (Oxford, 1959)

Cusanus, Nicholas, *Opera* ed. Ernst Hoffman (Heidelberg, 1929–1977) 7 vols.

Cusanus, Nicholas, *Selections*, (n.p., 1490) BL (includes *De docta ignorantia*)

Cusanus, Nicholas, *De docta ignorantia*, transl. Jasper Hopkins (Minneapolis, 1981)

Daly, Peter M. *et al.* eds., *The English Emblem and the Continental Tradition* (New York, 1985)

Daly, Peter M., *The English Emblem Tradition* (Toronto, 1988)

Damiens, Suzanne, *Amour et intellect chez Léon Hébreu* (Toulouse, 1971)

Daneau, Lambert, *Physica christiana* (Geneva, 1576) BL

Daneau, Lambert, *Physica christiana,* transl. Thomas Twyne as *The Wonderfull Woorkmanship of the World* (London, 1578) STC 6231

Daniel, George (of Beswick), *Poems*, ed. Alexander B. Grosart (Boston, 1878) 4 vols.

Daniel, Samuel, *Works* (London, 1601) STC 6236, see also Giovio

Dannenberg, Friedrich, *Das Erbe Platons in England* (Berlin, 1932)

Davenant, Sir William, *Works* (London, 1673) Wing D320

Davies, John (of Hereford), *Complete Works*, ed. Alexander B. Grosart (London, 1878) 2 vols. (repr. Hildesheim, 1968)

Davies, Sir John, *Poems*, ed. Robert Krueger (Oxford, 1975)

Davison, Francis, *A poetical rapsody*, (sic) (London, 1602) STC 6373

Davison, Francis, *A poetical rapsody*, ed. Hyder Rollins (Cambridge, Mass., 1931–1932) 2 vols.

Day, Malcolm M., "Traherne and the Doctrine of Pre–Existence", *SP*, 65 (1968), pp. 81–97

Deacon, Richard, *John Dee* (London, 1968)

Dee, John, *Diary*, ed. James O. Halliwell (London, 1842; repr. New York, 1968) (Camden Society ser. 1, vol. 19)

Dee, John, *Library Catalogue*, ed. Julian Roberts and Andrew G. Watson (London, 1990)

Dee, John, see also Euclid

Dekker, Thomas, *Dramatic Works*, ed. Fredson Bowers (Cambridge, 1953–1961) 4 vols.

Dekker, Thomas, *Satiromastix* (London, 1601) STC 6520.7

Dekker, Thomas, *The wonderfull yeare* (London, 1603) STC 6535a

Dekker, Thomas, *The wonderfull yeare*, ed. G. B. Harrison (London, 1924)

Della Torre, Arnaldo, *Storia dell' Accademia Platonica di Firenze* (Florence, 1902)

Demosthenes, *Orationes*, transl. (Lat.) Nicholas Carr, ed. with biographical "Epistola" by Bartholomew Dodington (London, 1571) STC 6577

Des Periers, Bonaventure, *Oeuvres*, ed. Louis Lacour (Paris, 1856)

Desportes, Philippe, *Les Premières Oeuvres* (Paris, 1573) BN

Desportes, Philippe, *Les amours de Diane* (1587), ed. Victor E. Graham (Geneva, 1959)

Dethick, Henry, *Oratio in laudem poeseos* (London, c. 1575) STC 6787.4

Dethick, Henry, *Oratio in laudem poeseos*, ed. William Ringler and transl. Walter Allen (Princeton,

1940) (attributed by them to John Rainolds)

Dick, Hugh G., "Giacomo Concio: a Renaissance Exile", *Modern Language Forum*, 26 (1941), pp. 12–18

Dick, Hugh G., "Thomas Blundeville's *The true order and Methode of wryting and reading Hystories* (1574)", *HLQ*, 3 (1940), pp. 149–170

Dicts or Sayings of the Philosophers, see Mubashshir ibn Fatik

Di Gangi, Mariano, *Peter Martyr Vermigli* (New York, 1973)

Digby, Everard, *Opera*, ed. Jean Le Clerc (Leiden, 1706) 10 vols.

Digby, Everard, *Theoria analytica* (London, 1579) STC 6843

Diogenes Laertius, *De vitis philosophorum*, ed. and transl. Robert D. Hicks (Cambridge, Mass., 1972, 2nd ed.) (Loeb)

Dodington, Bartholomew, see Demosthenes (London, 1473)

Doget, John, *Examinatorium in Phedonem Platonis* (London) BL MS Addit. 10.344

Doggett, Frank A., "Donne's Platonism", *Sewanee Review*, 42 (1934), pp. 274–292

Dolet, Etienne, *Le second enfer* (Lyons, 1544; BN (includes his Fr. transl. of *Axiochus* of Xenocrates and *Hipparchus* of Plato)

Dolet, Etienne, *Le second enfer*, ed. Claude Longeon (Geneva, 1978)

Dolman, John, see Cicero

Dolman, Richard, see Primaudaye

Donatus, Aelius, *Ars minor*, ed. and transl. Wayland J. Chase (Madison, 1926)

Donne, John, *Complete Poetry*, ed. John Shawcross (Garden City, 1967)

Donne, John, *Poems*, ed. Herbert J. C. Grierson (Oxford, 1912) 2 vols.

Donne, John, *Divine Poems*, ed. Helen Gardner (Oxford, 1978)

Donne, John, *Elegies and Songs and Sonnets*, ed. Helen Gardner (Oxford, 1965)

Donne, John, *Epithalamions, Anniversaries, and Epicedes*, ed. W. Milgate (Oxford, 1978)

Donne, John, *Satires, Epigrams, and Verse Letters*, ed. W. Milgate (Oxford, 1967)

Donne, John, *Biathanatos*, facs. ed. J. W. Hebel (New York, 1930)

Donne, John, *Catalogus librorum aulicorum*, ed. Evelyn M. Simpson and transl. Percy Simpson as *The Courtier's Library* (London, 1930)

Donne, John, *Devotions upon emergent occasions*, ed. Anthony Raspa (Montreal, 1975)

Donne, John, *Ignatius his conclave*, ed. T. S. Healy (Oxford, 1969)

Donne, John, *Letters to Several Persons*, ed. Charles E. Merrill (New York, 1910)

Donne, John, *Paradoxes and Problems*, ed. Helen Peters (Oxford, 1980)

Donne, John, *Pseudo–Martyr*, ed. Francis J. Sypher (New York, 1974)

Donne, John, *Sermons*, ed. George R. Potter and Evelyn Simpson (Berkeley, 1953–1962) 10 vols.

Donnelly, John P. *et al.* eds., *A Bibliography of the Works of Peter Martyr Vermigli* (Kirksville, 1990)

Dowling, Maria, *Humanism in the Age of Henry VIII* (London, 1986)

Doyle, A. I., "More Light on Shirley", *Medium aevum*, 30 (1961), pp. 93–101

Drant, Thomas, *Impii cuiusdam epigrammatis* (London, 1565) STC 7167

Drayton, Michael, *Works*, ed. J. W. Hebel (Oxford, 1931–1941) 5 vols.

Drummond, William (of Hawthornden), *Poetical Works*, ed. L. E. Kastner (Manchester, 1913) 2 vols.

Du Bartas, Guillaume de Saluste, *Works*, ed. Urban T. Holmes (Chapel Hill, 1935) 2 vols.

Du Bartas, Guillaume de Saluste, *La Sepmaine*, transl. Joshua Sylvester as *Deuine weekes and workes* (London, 1605) STC 21649

Du Bellay, Joachim, *Oeuvres poetiques*, ed. Henri Chamard (Paris, 1961, 4th ed.) 6 vols.

Duncan, G.D., "Public Lectures and Professional Chairs", in T. H. Aston, ed., *History of the Univ. of Oxford* (Oxford, 1986) vol. 3, pp. 335–361

Durr, Robert A., *On the Mystical Poetry of Henry Vaughan* (Cambridge, Mass., 1962)

Dyer, George, *The Privileges of the University of Cambridge* (London, 1824) 2 vols.

Ebin, Lois A., *John Lydgate* (Boston, 1985)

Échecs amoureux, (c. 1370–1380) anon, OF imitation of *Roman de la Rose* in Dresden, Sächsische Landesbibliothek MS Oc. 66, and in Venice, Bibl. Naz. Marciana MS Fr. App. 23

Eisenbichler, Konrad and Olga Pugliese, eds., *Ficino and Renaissance Neoplatonism* (Ottawa, 1986) (Papers of 1984 Ficino Conference)

Edward VI, King of England, *Orationes*, London, BL, MS Addit. 4724

Elizabeth I, Queen of England, *Translations*, ed. Caroline Pemberton as *Englishings of Elizabeth* (London, 1899) (EETS: os113)

Ellrodt, Robert, *Neoplatonism in the Poetry of Spenser* (Geneva, 1960; repr. New York, 1975)

Elviden, Edmund, *The Closet of Counsells* (London, 1569) STC 7622

Elyot, Sir Thomas, *The bankette of sapience* (London, 1539) STC 7630

Elyot, Sir Thomas, *Bibliothecae Eliotae* (London, 1538) STC 7659 enlarged ed. by Thomas Cooper (London, 1548) STC 7661

Elyot, Sir Thomas, *The Boke named the Gouernovr*, ed. H. H. S. Croft (London, 1883) 2 vols. (repr. New York, 1967)

Elyot, Sir Thomas, *Of the Knowledge which maketh a wise man*, ed. Edward J. Howard (Oxford, Ohio, 1946)

Emden, Alfred B., *Biographical Register of the University of Cambridge to 1500* (Cambridge, 1963)

Emden, Alfred B., *Biographical Register of the University of Oxford to 1500* (Oxford, 1957–1959) 3 vols., supplements in *BLR*, 6 (1961), pp. 668–688; and 7 (1964), pp. 149–164

Emden, Alfred B., *Biographical Register of the University of Oxford 1501–1540* (Oxford, 1974)

Emery, F. V., "England circa 1600" in Henry C. Darby, ed., *A New Historical Geography of England before 1600* (Cambridge, 1976) pp. 248–301

England's Helicon, see Bodenham

Erasmus, Desiderius, *Opera*, gen. ed. J. H. Waszink (Amsterdam, 1969–)

Erasmus, Desiderius, *Opera*, transl. gen. ed. Peter G. Bietenholz (Toronto, 1974–)

Erasmus, Desiderius, *Apophthegmata*, transl. Nicholas Udall (London, 1542) STC 10443

Erasmus, Desiderius, *Epistolae*, ed. Percy S. Allen *et al.* (Oxford, 1906–1965) 12 vols.

Euclid, *Elements of Geometry*, transl. Sir Henry Billingsley (London, 1570) STC 10560 (Preface by John Dee)

Evans, Frank B., "Platonic Scholarship in Eighteenth Century England", *MP*, 41 (1943), pp. 103–110

Fairchild, A. H. R., "The Phoenix and Turtle..." *Englische Studien*, 33 (1904), pp. 337–384

Farrington, Benjamin, *The Philosophy of Francis Bacon* (Liverpool, 1964) (includes transl. *Temporis partus masculus, Cogitata et visa, Redargutio philosophorum*)

Faurelle, G., "Le platonisme d'Eusèbe" in his *Eusèbe de Césarée* (Paris, 1982) pp. 239–391

Fehrenbach, Robert J. and Elizabeth Leedham–Green, eds., *Private Libraries in Renaissance England* (Binghamton, 1992–1994) 3 vols. to date

Feingold, Mordechai, *The Mathematicians' Apprenticeship* (Cambridge, 1984)

Fell, John, see Albinus

Fenne, Thomas, *Fennes frutes* (London, 1590) STC 10763

Fenton, Geoffrey, see Guevara; Pasquier; Talpin

Fernando de Córdoba; *De laudibus Platonis* Rome, Vallicelliana MS 1.22, fols. 1–21

Festugière, A.–J., *La philosophie de l'amour de Marsile Ficin* (Paris, 1941; repr. Paris, 1980)

Ficino, Marsilio, *Opera* (Basle, 1576; repr., ed. P. O. Kristeller, Turin, 1959) 2 vols.

Ficino, Marsilio, (untitled Anthology of Minor Platonists) (Venice, 1497) BL (repr. Lyons, 1570) (begins with work of Jamblichus)

Ficino, Marsilio, *De amore*, (1469), ed. and transl. (Fr.) Raymond Marcel (Paris, 1956)

Ficino, Marsilio, *De amore*, transl. (Fr.) Gilles Corrozet in his *La diffinition d'amour* (Paris, 1542) BN

Ficino, Marsilio, *De amore*, transl. (Fr.) Jean de la Haye (Poitiers, 1546) BN

Ficino, Marsilio, *De amore*, transl. (Fr.) Guy Lefèvre de la Boderie as *Discours de l'honneste amour sur le banquet de Platon* (Paris, 1578) BN; 2nd ed. with Pico's *Commento* (Paris, 1588) BN

Ficino, Marsilio, *De amore*, transl. Sears Jayne (Dallas, 1985)

Ficino, Marsilio, *De religione christiana* (Florence, 1474) BL

Ficino, Marsilio, *De triplici vita* (Florence, 1489) BL (repr. Paris, 1492) BN (contains I. *De studiosorum sanitate tuenda;* II. *De vita longa;* III. *De coelitus comparanda*)

Ficino, Marsilio, *De triplici vita*, transl. Charles Boer (Dallas, 1980)

Ficino, Marsilio, *De voluptate* (1457), see Anthol. of Minor Platonists above

Ficino, Marsilio, *Epistolae* (Venice, 1495) BL (repr. Hildesheim, 1978)

Ficino, Marsilio, *Epistolae*, ed. Sebastiano Gentile (Florence, 1990–)

Ficino, Marsilio, *Epistolae*, transl. as *Letters*, London School of Economics (London, 1975–)

Ficino, Marsilio, *Theologia platonica* (Florence, 1482) BL

Ficino, Marsilio, *Theologia platonica*, ed. and transl. (Fr.) Raymond Marcel (Paris, 1964–1970) 3 vols.

Field, Arthur, "John Argyropoulos and the 'Secret Teachings ' of Plato" in James Hankins, ed., *Supplementum Festivum* (Binghamton, 1987) pp. 299–326 (Festschrift Paul O. Kristeller)

Field, Arthur, *The Origins of the Platonic Academy* (Princeton, c. 1988)

Fior di virtù historiale, see Mubashshir ibn Fatik

Firmicus Maternus, *Mathesis*, ed. W. Kroll *et al.* (Stuttgart, 1961) 2 vols. (Teubner)

Firpo, Luigi, "John Dee, scienziato, negromante et aventuriero", *Rinascimento*, 3 (1952), pp. 25–84

Fisher, John, *John Gower* (New York, 1964)

Fisher, John, "Platonism in Philosophy and Poetry", *DHI*, vol. 3, pp. 502–508

Fisher, John (of St. John's College, Cambridge), *English Works*, ed. John E. R. Mayor (London, 1876) (EETS:es 27)

Fiston, William, *The welspring of wittie conceites* (London, 1584) STC 5615 and 10925 (trans. out of Italian; original unidentified)

Fletcher, Jefferson B., "Précieuses at the court of Charles I", *JCL*, 1 (1903), pp. 120–153

Fletcher, John, *The faithfull shepheardess* (London, c. 1610) STC 11068

Fletcher, John, *The faithfull shepheardess*, ed. Florence A. Kirk (new York, 1980)

Flint, Valerie I. J., *Ideas in the Medieval West* (London, 1988) (reprints of essays, mainly on Honorius)

Flint, Valerie I. J., see also Honorius

Florio, John, *First fruites* (London, 1578) STC 11090, facs. ed. Arundell Del Re (Formosa, 1936)

Fogel, Ephrim G., "A Possible Addition to the Sidney Canon", *MLN*, 75 (1960), pp. 389–394

Fogel, French, *William Drummond* (New York, 1952)

Fontaine, Charles, *La Contr' amye de court* (Paris, 1541)

Fortescue, Thomas, see Mexia

Fox, Richard, *The Foundation Statutes...for Corpus Christi College, Oxford*, transl. anon. ed. G. R. M. Ward (Oxford, 1843)

Fraunce, Abraham, *Amintas dale*, ed. Gerald Snare (Northridge, 1975)

Fraunce, Abraham, *Insignium, armorum, emblematum...* (London, 1588) STC 11342

Fraunce, Abraham, *The Lawiers Logike* (London, 1588) STC 11343

Fraunce, Abraham, *Victoria*, ed. G. C. Moore–Smith (Louvain, 1906)

French, Peter, *John Dee* (London, 1972)

Frigillanus, Mattheus (pseudonym used in Paris, 1556–1562, for Marsilio Ficino, q.v.)

Fubini, Riccardo, "Tra umanesimo e concilii", *Studi medioevali*. 3ª ser. 7 (1966), pp. 323–353

Fulbecke, William, *A booke of christian ethicks* (London, 1587) STC 11409

Fullwood, William, *The enimie of idlenesse* (London, 1568) STC 11476

Fullwood, William, *The enimie of idlenesse*, ed. Paul Wolter (Potsdam, 1907)

Gaguin, Robert, *Epistolae et orationes* (Paris, 1498) BN

Gale, Theophilus, *The Court of the Gentiles* (Oxford, 1669–London, 1678) 4 vols. (Wing G136, 138, 141, 143)

Galen, *De placitis Hippocratis et Platonis* ed. and transl. Phillip de Lacy as *On the Doctrines of Hippocrates and Plato* (Berlin, 1984) (in *Corpus Medicorum Graecorum*, vol. 5)

Gandillac; Maurice de, "Platonisme et Aristotelisme chez Nicolas de Cues" in *Platon et Aristote à la Renaissance* (Paris, 1876) (XVIᵉ Colloque International de Tours) pp. 7–23

Garfagnini, Giancarlo, ed. *Marsilio Ficino e il ritorno de Platone* (Florence, 1986) 2 vols.

Garin, Eugenio, *L'età nuova* (Naples, 1969)

Garin, Eugenio, "Marsilio Ficino e il ritorno di Platone" in Giancarlo Garfagnini, ed., *Marsilio Ficino e il ritorno di Platone* (Florence, 1986) vol. 1, pp. 3–13

Garin, Eugenio, "Ricerche sulle traduzioni di Platone nella prima metà del secolo XV" in *Medioevo e Rinascimento* (Florence, 1955) vol. 1, pp. 339–374 (Festschrift Bruno Nardi, pp. 7–23)

Garrigues, Marie-Odile, "L'anonymat d'Honorius Augustodinensis", *Studia Monastica*, 25 (1938), pp. 31–71

Gascoigne, George, *The Complete Works*, ed. John W. Cunliffe (Cambridge, 1907–1910) 2 vols. *(Princely*

Pleasures, vol. 2, pp. 91–131)

Gascoigne, George, see also Nichols

Gaskell, Philip, "Books Bought by Whitgift's Pupils in the 1570's", *TCBS*, 7 (1979), pp. 284–293

Gatti, Hilary, *The Renaissance Drama of Knowledge* (London, 1989) (on Giordano Bruno in England)

Gee, John A., *Life and Works of Thomas Lupset* (New Haven, 1928)

Gellius, Aulus, *Noctes atticae*, ed. and transl. John C. Rolfe (Cambridge, Mass., 1967–1970) 3 vols. (Loeb)

Gemmae Platonis, see Liburnio

Gentile, Sebastiano, *Marsilio Ficino e il ritorno di Platone* (Florence, 1984) (Catalogue of Exhibition)

Gentile, Sebastiano, "Note sui manoscritti greci di Platone utilizzati da Marsilio Ficino" in *Studi in onore di Eugenio Garin* (Pisa, 1987) pp. 51–84

Gentili, Alberico, *Commentatio ad l. III C (odicis)* (Oxford, 1593) STC 11732 (Commentary on Justinian; see Binns, 1990)

Gentili, Alberico, *Lectionum et epistolarum* (London, 1583) STC 11739

George of Trebizond, *Comparationes phylosophorum Aristotelis et Platonis*, (1458) (Venice, 1523) HD (repr. Frankfurt, 1965)

George of Trebizond, *Comparationes phylosophorum Aristotelis et Platonis*, ed. John Monfasani in *Collectanea Trapezuntiana* (Binghamton, 1984)

Gerardus, Andreas, (Hyperius) *Compendium physices Aristotelicae* (London, 1583) STC 758

Gerardus, Andreas, *The regiment of the pouertie*, (sic) transl. Henry Tripp (London, 1572) STC 11759

Gibson, Strickland, see Oxford, University of, *Statuta*

Gifford, Humphrey, *Poems*, ed. Alexander B. Grosart (London, 1870) (Fuller Worthies Library, vol. 1, pp. 269–441)

Gill, Joseph, *Constance et Bâle-Florence* (Paris, 1965) *(Histoire des conciles oecumeniques*, vol. 9)

Giorgi, Domenico, *Vita Nicolai Quinti* (Rome, 1742)

Giorgio, Franceso, *De harmonia mundi* (Venice, 1525) BL

Giovio, Paolo, *Opera* (Rome, 1956–date) 9 vols.

Giovio, Paolo, *Descriptio Britanniae...* (Venice, 1548) BL (contains George Lily, *Virorum aliquot in Britannia)*

Giovio, Paolo, *Descriptio Britanniae*, ed. and transl. (Ital.) Renzo Meregazzi (Rome, 1972)

Giovio, Paolo, *Descriptio Britanniae*, (selections) transl. Florence Gragg (Boston, 1935)

Giovio, Paolo, *Dialogo dell' imprese militari e amorose*, (1555) ed. Maria L. Doglio (Rome, 1978)

Giovio, Paolo, *Dialogo dell' imprese militari e amorose*, transl. Samuel Daniel as *The Worthy tract of Paulus Jovius* (London, 1585) STC 11900

Giovio, Paolo, *Dialogo dell' imprese militari e amorose*, transl. Samuel Daniel, facs. ed. Stephen Orgel in *The Philosophy of Images* (New York, 1979)

Giraldi Cinthio, Giovanni Battista; *Tre dialoghi della civil vita* (Venice, 1554) BNF

Giraldi Cinthio, Giovanni Battista; *Tre dialoghi della civil vita*, transl. Gabriel Chappuys as *Dialogues philosophiques...touchant la vie civile* (Paris, 1583) BN

Giraldi Cinthio, Giovanni Battista; *Tre dialoghi della civil vita*, transl. Gabriel Chappuys, (selections) transl. Lodowick Bryskett as *A Discourse of Civill Life* (London, 1606) STC 3958

Giraldi Cinthio, Giovanni Battista; *Tre dialoghi della civil vita*, transl. Gabriel Chappuys, (selections) transl. Lodowick Bryskett, ed. Thomas E. Wright. Northridge, 1970

Glanvill, Joseph, *Lux orientalis* (London, 1682) Wing G814 (on pre-existence)

Glanvill, Joseph, *Philosophia pia* (London, 1671) Wing G817

Glanville, Bartholomaeus, see Bartholomaeus Anglicus

Glass, D. V. and D. E. C. Eversly, *Population in History* (London, 1945)

Gleason, John B., *John Colet* (Berkeley, 1989)

Goddu, A. A. and Richard H. Rouse, "Gerald of Wales and the *Florilegium Angelicum"*, *Speculum*, 52 (1977), pp. 488–521

Goffe, Thomas, *The careles shepherdess* (London, 1656) Wing G1005

Golding, Arthur, see Mornay; Ovid; Paleario; Seneca

Goldwell, Henry, ed., *A briefe declaration of the shews...* (London, 1581) STC 11990 (an ed. of Sidney's *Fortress of Perfect Beauty*)

Goldwell, Henry, see also Nichols; Sidney, Sir Philip

Googe, Barnabe, *Eglogs, epytaphes and sonettes*, ed. Judith M. Kennedy (Toronto, 1989)

Googe, Barnabe, see also Lopez de Mendoza; Manzolli

Gordan, Phyllis, *Two Renaissance Book-Hunters* (New York, 1974) (on Bracciolini and Niccoli)

Gorges, Arthur, *Poems*, ed. Helen E. Sandison (Oxford, 1953)

Gorsch, Robert, *Veiling the Truth* (Harvard Univ. diss., 1984, on Chapman)

Gosson, Stephen, *Dramatic Criticism*, ed. Arthur F. Kinney as *Markets of Bawdrie* (Salzburg, 1974)

Gossuin, de Metz, *Imago mundi*, transl. William Caxton as *The myrrour of the worlde* (Westminster, 1481) STC 24762 (STC attributes to Vincent of Beauvais, but Gossuin's work is an adaptation of *Imago mundi* of Honorius Augustodunensis, q.v.)

Gossuin, de Metz, *Imago mundi*, transl. William Caxton, ed. Oliver H. Prior (London, 1913; repr. Millwood, 1987) (EETS: es. 110)

Gossuin, de Metz, see Honorius

Gower, John, *Complete Works*, ed. G. C. Macaulay (Oxford, 1899–1902) 4 vols. (vol. 1= French; vols. 2–3 = English; vol. 4 = Latin)

Grafton, Anthony and Lisa Jardine, *From Humanism to the Humanities* (Cambridge, Mass., 1986)

Grattan, J. H. G. and Charles Singer, *Anglo–Saxon Magic and Medicine* (London, 1952)

Gray, George J. and William M. Palmer, *Abstracts from the Wills and Testamentary Documents...of Cambridge from 1504 to 1609* (London, 1915)

Gray, Howard, "Greek Visitors to England in 1455–1456" in *Anniversary Essays* (Boston, 1929) (Festschift Charles H. Haskins)

Greek Anthology, ed. and transl. W. R. Paton (Cambridge, Mass., 1916–1918) 5 vols. (Loeb)

Greek Anthology, (selections) ed. Janus Cornarius as *Selecta epigrammata graeca* (Basle, 1529) BL (xerox copy at Univ. of Wisconsin, Madison)

Greene, Robert, *Life and Complete Works*, ed. Alexander B. Grosart (London, 1881–1886) 15 vols. (repr. New York, 1964)

Greene, Robert (of Welby), see *Plato's Fourth Book*

Grennen, Joseph E., "Chaucer and Calcidius", *Viator*, 15 (1984), pp. 237–262

Greville, Fulke (First Lord Brooke), *Poems and Dramas*, ed. Geoffrey Bullough (New York, 1945) 2 vols., 2nd ed.

Grierson, Philip, "John Caius' Library", in John Venn, *Biographical History of Gonville and Caius College* (Cambridge, 1897–1978) 7 vols., vol. 7, pp. 509–525

Griffiths, Gordon *et al*, eds., *The Humanism of Leonardo Bruni* (Binghamton, 1987)

Grynaeus, Simon, see Plato, *Works*

Guasti, C., "Inventario della Libreria Urbinate", *Giornale storico degli archivi Toscani*, 6 (1982) and 7 (1863) (Greek MSS in vol. 7, pp. 130–154

Guazzo, Stefano, *La civil conversatione* (Brescia, 1575) BL

Guazzo, Stefano, *La civil conversatione*, transl. George Pettie as *The Civile Conversation* (London, 1581) STC 12422 (Books I–III only)

Guazzo, Stefano, *La civil conversatione*, transl. Bartholomew Yonge (London, 1586) STC 12423 (Book IV)

Guazzo, Stefano, *La civil conversatione*, ed. Sir Edward Sullivan (London, 1925) 2 vols.

Guevara, Antonio de, *Epistolas familiares* (Valladolid, 1539–1541) (2 parts)

Guevara, Antonio de, *Epistolas familiares*, Part I (1539), transl. Edward Hellowes as *The Familiar Epistles* (London, 1575) STC 12432

Guevara, Antonio de, *Epistolas familiares*, Part II (1541), transl. Geoffrey Fenton as *Golden Epistles* (London, 1575) STC 10794 and 12433

Guevara, Antonio de, *Libro aureo del emperador Marco Aurelio*, (Seville, 1528)

Guevara, Antonio de, *Libro aureo del emperador Marco Aurelio*, transl. John Bourchier as *The golden boke of Marcus Aurelius* (London, 1535) STC 12436

Guevara, Antonio de, *Le relox de principes*, (Valladolid, 1529)

Guevara, Antonio de, *Le relox de principes*, transl. (Fr.) René Berthault (Paris, 1540) BN

Guevara, Antonio de, *Le relox de principes*, transl. Thomas North as *The Diall of Princes...* (London, 1557) STC 12427

Guevara, Antonio de, *Menosprecio de Corte y Alabanza de Aldea* (Valladolid, 1539)

Guevara, Antonio de, *Menosprecio de Corte y Alabanza de Aldea*, transl. Sir Francis Briant as *A Looking glasse for the Court, A dispraise of the life of the courtier* (London, 1548) STC 12431 (repr. by Thomas Tynne, 1575) STC 12448

Guffey, George R., *Traherne and the Seventeenth Century English Platonists* (London, 1969) (a bibliography; sections on Cudworth, Culverwel, H. More, J. Norris, G. Rust, John Smith, P. Sterry, T. Traherne, B. Whichcote, and J. Worthington)

Guicciardini, Lodovico, *Detti e fatti* (Venice, 1565) BL

Guicciardini, Lodovico, *Detti e fatti*, transl. James Sanford as *The Garden of Pleasure* (London, 1573) STC 12464

Guicciardini, Lodovico, *L'historia d'Italia* (Florence, 1561) BL

Guillaume de Lorris and Jean de Meun, *Le roman de la rose*, ed. Felix Lecoy (Paris, 1965–1970) 3 vols.

Guillaume de Lorris and Jean de Meun, *Le roman de la rose*, transl. Charles Dahlberg (Princeton, 1971)

Guillaume de Lorris and Jean de Meun, *Le roman de la rose*, transl. Geoffrey Chaucer, see Chaucer, *Works*

Guilpin, Everard, *Skialetheia*, ed. D. Allen Carroll (Chapel Hill, 1974)

Guilpin, Everard, *The Whipper of the Satyre*, ed. Arnold Davenport in *The Whipper Pamphlets* (Liverpool, 1951)

Habington, William, *Poems*, ed. Kenneth Allott (Liverpool, 1948)

Habington, William, *Castara* (London, 1634) STC 12583

Haddon, Walter, *Poetry*, ed. Charles J. Lees (Hague, 1967)

Haddon, Walter, *Lucubrationes* (London, 1567) STC 12596

Haddon, Walter, *Vita et obitus duorum fratrum* (London, 1551) STC 25816 and 12594a

Hall, Joseph, *Poems*, ed. Arnold Davenport (Liverpool, 1949)

Hamilton, Gertrude K., *Three Worlds of Light...* (Univ. of Rochester diss., 1974) (On Ficino, Thomas Vaughan, and Henry Vaughan)

Hankins, James, "Cosimo de' Medici and the 'Platonic Academy'", JWCI 53 (1990), 144–162

Hankins, James, *Latin Translations of Plato in the Renaissance* (Columbia diss., 1984)

Hankins, James, *Plato in the Italian Renaissance* (Leiden, 1990) 2 vols.

Hankins, John E., *The Life and Works of George Turberville* (Laurence, 1940)

Hankins, John E., *Source and Meaning in Spenser's Allegory* (Oxford, 1971)

Hankins, John E., see also Turberville

Hannay, Margaret, *Philip's Phoenix: Mary Sidney, Countess of Pembroke* (New York, 1990)

Harding, Thomas, *An answere to maister Juelles challenge* (Louvain, 1564) STC 12758

Harington, Sir John, see Ariosto

Harrison, John S., *Platonism in English Poetry of the Sixteenth and Seventeenth Centuries* (New York, 1903; repr. Westport, 1980)

Hartfelder, Karl, *Philipp Melanchthon als Praeceptor Germaniae* (Berlin, 1889; repr. Nieuwkoop, 1972)

Harvey, Gabriel, *Works*, ed. Alexander B. Grosart (London, 1884–1885) 3 vols.

Harvey, Gabriel, *Letter–Book*, ed. Edward J. L. Scott (Westminster, 1884)

Harvey, Gabriel, *Marginalia*, ed. G. C. Moore-Smith (Stratford, 1913)

Harvey, Gabriel, *Pierces supererogation* (London, 1593) STC 12903 (Scolar repr. Menston, 1970)

Harvey, Gabriel, *Three proper and wittie familiar letters* (London, 1580) STC 23095

Hawenreuther, Johann Ludwig, *Compendium librorum physicorum Aristotelis* (Cambridge, 1594) STC 12938

Hawes, Stephen, *Minor Poems*, ed. Florence W. Gluck and Alice B. Morgan (London, 1974) (EETS: os 271)

Hawes, Stephen, *The Pastime of Pleasure*, ed. William B. Mead (London, 1928) (EETS:os 173)

Heninger, S. K., "Sidney and Serranus' Plato", ELR, 13 (1983), pp. 146–161

Heninger, S. K., *Touches of Sweet Harmony* (San Marino, 1974) (On Pythagoras)

Henry, John and Sarah Hutton, eds., *New Perspectives on Renaissance Thought* (London, 1990) (memorial volume for Charles B. Schmitt)

Heresbach, Conrad, *De laudibus graecarum literarum oratio* (Strasbourg, 1551) BL (Appendix contains correspondence of Ascham and Sturm under title *Epistolae duae de nobilitate anglicana*)

Hermes Trismegistus, *Corpus Hermeticum*, ed. A. D. Nock and transl. (Fr.) A. J. Festugière (Paris, 1944–1973) 5 vols. *(Asclepius*, i.e. Latin transl. of *Logos teleos* by Apuleius, is in vol. 2)

Hermes Trismegistus, (Gk. *Corpus Hermeticum* and Latin *Asclepius)*, transl. Brian P. Copenhaver (Cambridge, 1992)

Hermes Trismegistus, *Pimander*, transl. (Lat.) Marsilio Ficino as *De potestate et sapientia dei* (Treviso, 1471) BL

Héroet, Antoine, *Oeuvres poétiques*, ed. Ferdinand Gohin (Paris, 1943)

Heywood, Thomas, *Plays*, ed. R. H. Shepherd (London, 1875) 6 vols. (repr. New York, 1964)

Heywood, Thomas, *Troia Britannica* (London, 1609) STC 13366

Higden, Ranulf, *Polychronicon* (London, 1865–1886) 9 vols.: vols. 1–2, ed. Churchill Babington with transl. of John Trevisa; vols. 3–9, ed. J. R. Lumby (repr. New York, 1964)

Higden, Ranulf, *Polychronicon*, transl. John   Trevisa, ed. William Caxton (Westminster, 1482) STC 13438

Historia Alexandri magni, see *Wars of Alexander*

Hoby, Edward, see Coignet

Hoby, Sir Thomas, see Castiglione

Hodge, C. E., *The Abbey of St. Albans under John of Whethamstede* (Univ. of Manchester thesis, 1933)

Hoeltgen, Karl–Josef, *Aspects of the Emblem* (Kassel, 1986)

Hogrefe, Pearl, "Elyot and the Boke called 'Cortigiano in Italian'", *MP* 27 (1930), pp. 303–309

Hollingsworth, T. H., *Historical Demography* (Ithaca, 1967)

Homer, *Works*, transl. George Chapman (1589–1624), ed. Allardyce Nicoll (New York, 1956) 2 vols.

Homer, *Works*, transl. George Chapman, published individually as follows: *Ilias* (London, 1591) STC 13629; *Achilles Shield* (London, 1598) STC 13635; *Seaven bookes of the Iliades* (London, 1589) STC 13623 (Books 1–2, 7–11); *The Iliades of Homer* (London, 1611) STC 13634; *Homer's Odysses* (London, 1614) STC 13636; *The Whole Works of Homer* (London, 1616) STC 13624; *The Creame of all Homers Worcke* (London, 1624) STC 13628

Homilies, see Church of England

Honorius Augustodunensis, *Imago mundi*, ed. Valerie I. J. Flint, *AHDLM* 49 (1983), 7–153 (=PL 172:115–186)

Honorius Augustodunensis, *Imago mundi*, transl. (Anglo–Norman, c. 1210) as *La petite philosophie* by Pierra D'Abernun of Fetcham, ed. William Tretheway (Oxford, 1939) (ANTS, 1)

Honorius Augustodunensis, *Imago mundi*, transl. (Fr.) Gossuin de Metz as *L'image du monde*, ed. Oliver H. Prior (Paris, 1913)

Honorius Augustodunensis, *Imago mundi*, transl. Gossuin de Metz and transl. William Caxton as *Mirrour of the World* (Westminster, 1481) STC 24762

Honorius Augustodunensis, *Imago mundi*, transl. Gossuin de Metz, transl. William Caxton, ed. Oliver H. Prior (London, 1912; repr. London, 1966) (EETS: es 110)

Hopf, Constantin, *Martin Bucer and the English Reformation* (Oxford, 1946)

Horatius Flaccus, Quintus, *Poemata omnia* (London, 1574) STC 13784

Horatius Flaccus, Quintus, *Ars poetica*, transl. Thomas Drant (London, 1567) STC 13797

Horatius Flaccus, Quintus, *Odes and Epodes*, ed. and transl. C. E. Bennett (London, 1978) (Loeb)

Horatius Flaccus, Quintus, *Satires*, transl. Thomas Drant (London, 1566) STC 13805

Horatius Flaccus, Quintus, *Satires, Epistles, and Ars Poetica*, ed. and transl. H. R. Fairclough (London, 1978) (Loeb)

Hoskins, John, "Absence", ed. H. J. C. Grierson in John Donne, *Poems* (Oxford, 1912) vol. 1, pp. 428–429

Houppelande, Guillaume, *De immortalitate anime* (Paris, 1489) BN

Houppelande, Guillaume, *De immortalitate anime*, transl. as *The soule is imortall* (London, 1611) STC 14297.a.3

Howell, Thomas, *Poems*, ed. Alexander B. Grosart (Manchester, 1879)

Howell, Thomas, see also Ovid

Hrabanus Maurus, *De universo*, PL 111:9–614

Hudson, Hoyt H., *The Epigram in the English Renaissance* (Princeton, 1947; repr. New York, 1966)

Humphrey, Lawrence, *Interpretatio linguarum* (Basle, 1559) BL

Humphrey, Lawrence, *Optimates sive de nobilitate* (Basle, 1560)

Humphrey, Lawrence, *Optimates sive de nobilitate*, transl. Humphrey as *The Nobles* (London, 1563) STC 13964

Hunt, Richard W., "The Library of the Abbey of St. Albans" in Malcolm B. Parkes and Andrew G. Watson, eds., *Medieval Scribes, Manuscripts, and Libraries* (London, 1978) pp. 251–277 (Festschrift Neil R. Ker)

Hunt, Richard W., et al., eds., *Duke Humfrey and English Humanism in the Fifteenth Century* (Oxford, 1970) (Exhibition Catalogue)

Hunter, G. K., *John Lyly* (London, 1962)

Huppe, Bernard D., "Allegory of Love in Lyly's Court Comedies", *ELH* 14 (1947), pp. 93–113

Hurnard, N. D., *Studies in Intellectual Life in England* (Univ. of Oxford diss., 1936)

Huting, Serge, *Henry More* (Hildesheim, 1966)

Hutton, James, *The Greek Anthology in Italy to the Year 1800* (Ithaca, 1935)

Hutton, James, *The Greek Anthology in France* (Ithaca, 1946; repr. New York, 1967)

Hutton, Richard, see Morel

Hutton, Sarah, "Thomas Jackson, Oxford Platonist...", *JHI* 39 (1979) pp. 635–652

Hutton, Sarah, see also Baldwin, A. ; Henry

Isidore of Seville, *Etymologiae*, ed. W. M. Lindsay (Oxford, 1911) 2 vols. *(PL= 82)*

Isidore of Seville, *Etymologiae*, transl. (selections only) Ernest Brehant in his *An Encyclopedist of the Dark Ages* (New York, 1912)

Ivanoff, N., "La beauté dans la philosophie de Marsilio Ficino et de Léon Hébreu", *Humanisme et Renaissance* 3 (1936), pp. 12–21

Izard, Thomas C., *George Whetstone* (New York, 1942)

Jackson, Thomas, *Works* (Oxford, 1844) 12 vols.

Jackson, Thomas, *Commentaries upon the Apostles Creed* (Oxford and London, 1613–1657) 12 vols., STC 14308–14319; Wing J89, J92

Jacquot, Jean, "L'élément Platonicien dans *L'Histoire du monde* de Sir Walter Ralegh" In *Mélanges d'histoire littéraire de la renaissance offerts à Henri Chamard* (Paris, 1951) pp. 347–353

James, Montague R., "Catalogue of the Library of Leicester Abbey", *TLAS* 19 (1936–1937), pp. 111–161 and 377–440; and 21 (1940–1941), pp. 1–88

James, Montague, *A Catalogue of the Manuscripts...of King's College, Cambridge* (Cambridge, 1895)

James, Montague, *A Descriptive Catalogue of the Manuscripts in...Corpus Christi College, Cambridge* (Cambridge, 1909–1912) 2 vols.

James, Montague, *A Descriptive Catalogue of the Manuscripts...of Gonville and Caius College* (Cambridge, 1907–1908) 2 vols.

James, Montague, *The Western Manuscripts in the Library of Trinity College, Cambridge* (Cambridge, 1900–1904) 4 vols.

James, Montague, "Greek Manuscripts in England before the Renaissance", *Library*, 4th ser. 7 (1927), pp. 337–353

Jardine, Lisa, "The Place of Dialectic Teaching in Sixteenth Century Cambridge", *SRen* 21 (1974), pp. 31–62

Jardine, Lisa, see also Grafton

Jayne, Sears, *John Colet and Marsilio Ficino* (London, 1963; repr. Greenwood, 1980)

Jayne, Sears, "Marsilio Ficino and Platonism of the English Renaissance", *CL* 4 (1952), pp. 214–238

Jayne, Sears, *Plato in Early Medieval England* (1991, unpublished) 2 vols., Copies at Harvard and Warburg Institute

Jayne, Sears, *Plato in Tudor England* (1993), unpublished) 6 vols., Copies at Harvard and Warburg Institute

Jayne, Sears, *Plato Monographs* (1994, unpublished) copy in Brown Univ. Archives (contains monographs on Roger Bacon and Roger Ascham)

Jayne, Sears, *Plato Studies* (1994, unpublished) copy in Brown Univ. Archives (contains essays on

Stephen Hawes, Sir Philip Sidney, John Donne after 1603, George Chapman after 1603, and Sir Walter Ralegh)

Jayne, Sears, *Shakespeare's Phoenix and Jonson* (1991, unpublished) copies at Bodleian and Huntington

Jayne, Sears, "The Subject of Milton's Ludlow *Mask*" in John S. Diekhoff, ed., *A Maske at Ludlow* (Cleveland, 1968) pp. 165–187

Jeaneau, Edouard, ed., *Glosae super Platonem* (Paris, 1965)

Jenkins, Harold, *Edward Benlowes* (London, 1952)

Jerome, Saint, *Adversus Jovinianum*, PL 23: 221–352

Jerome, Saint, *Adversus Jovinianum*, transl. W. H. Fremantle *et al.* in *Principal Works* (New York, 1892; repr. Grand Rapids, 1979)

Jerome, Saint, *Epistolae*, ed. Isidore Hilberg (Leipzig, 1910–1918) 3 vols (CSEL, 54–56=PL 22:325–1224)

Jewel, John, *Works*, ed. John Ayre (Cambridge, 1845–1850) 4 vols. (Parker Society) (repr. New York, 1968)

Jewel, John, *A Defence of the Apologie of the Churche of England...* (London, 1567) STC 14600

Jewel, John, *Apologia ecclesiae anglicanae* (London, 1562) STC 14581

Jewel, John, *Apologia ecclesiae anglicanae*, transl. anon. (London, 1562) STC 14590

Jewel, John, *Apologia ecclesiae anglicanae*, transl. anon., repr. ed. John Booty (Ithaca, 1963)

Jewel, John, *Apologia ecclesiae anglicanae*, transl. Lady Ann Bacon (London, 1564) STC 14591

Jewel, John, *A replie vnto M. Hardinges answeare* (London, 1565) STC 14606

John of Salisbury, *Policraticus*, ed. Clement C. J. Webb (Oxford, 1909–1911) 2 vols. (repr. Frankfort, 1965)

John of Wales, *Summa de regimine vitae humanae* (Venice, 1496) HD (includes *Breviloquium* and *Compendiloquium)*

Jonson, Ben, *Works*, ed. C. H. Herford and Percy S. Simpson (Oxford, 1925–1952) 11 vols.

Jonson, Ben, *Complete Masques*, ed. Stephen Orgel (New Haven, 1969)

Jonson, Ben, see also *Loues Martyr*

Judd, Arnold, *The Life of Thomas Bekynton* (Chichester, 1961)

Junius, Adriaan, *Nomenclator omnium rerum propria nomina* (Augsburg, 1555) NNBW.

Junius, Adriaan, *Nomenclator omnium rerum propria nomina*, transl. John Higgins (London, 1585) STC 14860

Justinian I, Emperor of the East, *Corpus Juris Civilis*, ed. Paul Krueger *et al.* (Berlin, 1954) 3 vols.

Kearney, Hugh, *Scholars and Gentlemen* (London, 1970)

Kendall, Timothy, *Flowers of epigrammes* (London, 1577) STC 14927 (repr. London, 1874) (Spenser Society, vol. 15)

Kepers, John, see Romei

Ker, Neil R., *Books, Collectors, and Libraries*, ed. Andrew G. Watson (London, 1985) (posthumous collection of essays 1937–1981)

Ker, Neil R., "Oxford College Libraries before 1500" in Jozef Ijsewijn *et al.* eds., *The Universities in the Late Middle Ages* (Louvain, 1978) pp. 293–311 repr. in Ker's *Books, Collectors*, pp. 301–320

Ker, Neil R., *Oxford College Libraries in 1556* (Oxford, 1956) (Catalogue of a Bodleian Exhibition)

Ker, Neil R., "Oxford College Libraries in the 16th Century", *BLR* 6 (1959), pp. 459–515, repr. In Ker's *Books, Collectors*, pp. 379–436

Ker, Neil R., *Pastedowns in Oxford Bindings* (Oxford, 1954) *Oxford Bibliographical Society Publications*, n.s. 5 (1951–1952)

Ker, Neil R., "The Provision of Books" in T. H. Aston, ed., *History of the University of Oxford* (Oxford, 1986) vol. 3, pp. 441–519

Killigrew, Thomas, *Comedies and Tragedies* (London, 1664) BL

King, Gregory, *Natural...conclusions upon (the population)...of England* (1696), ed. George E. Barnett (Baltimore, 1936)

Kinney, Arthur F., see Gosson; Reynolds

Klibansky, Raymond, *The Continuity of the Platonic Tradition* (Munich, 1981, 2nd ed.)

Kretzmann, Norman *et al.*, eds., *Cambridge History of Later Medieval Philosophy 1100–1600* (Cambridge, 1982)

Kristeller, Paul O., "The First Printed Edition of Plato's Works" in *Science and History* (Wroclaw, 1978) pp. 25–35 (Festschrift Edward Rosen)

Kristeller, Paul O., *Marsilio Ficino and his Work after 500 Years* (Florence, 1987)

Kristeller, Paul O., "Marsilio Ficino as a Beginning Student of Plato", *Scriptorium* 20 (1966), pp. 41–54

Kristeller, Paul O., *Studies in Renaissance Thought and Letters* (Rome, 1985) 2 vols.

Kristeller, Paul O., *Supplementum Ficinianum* (Florence, 1937) 2 vols.

Kyd, Thomas, see Tasso

Kynaston, Sir Francis, *Corona Minervae* (London, 1635) STC 15100

Lactantius, Lucius C. F., *Divinarum institutionum*, ed. Samuel Brandt (Prague, 1890) (CSEL 19.1 and 2)

Laertius, Diogenes, see Diogenes

Lamb, John, ed., *A Collection of Letters, Statutes, and other Documents* (London, 1838) (on Corpus Christi College, Cambridge)

Lambin, Denys, *De philosophia cum arte dicendi conjugenda* (Paris, 1568) BN

Landi, Ortensio, *I Paradossi* (Venice, 1543) BL

Landi, Ortensio, *I Paradossi*, transl. (Fr.) Charles Estienne (Paris, 1553) HD

Landi, Ortensio, *I Paradossi*, transl. Anthony Munday as *The defence of contraries* (London, 1593) STC 6467 (facs repr. New York, 1969)

Langbaine, Gerard, see Albinus

Languet, Hubert, *Epistolae*, ed. D. Dalrymple (Edinburgh, 1776) BL

La Place, Pierre de, *Commentaires de l'estat de la religion...* (Paris, 1565) BL

La Place, Pierre de, *Commentaires de l'estat de la religion...*, transl. Thomas Tymme, *Fyrst parte...* (London, 1573) STC 22241, *Three parts* (London, 1574) STC 22241.5, *Fourth part* (London, 1576) STC 22243

La Place, Pierre de, *Commentaires de l'estat de la religion...*, transl. Aegremont Ratcliffe (i.e. Edward Aggas) as *Politique Discourses* (London, 1578) STC 15230.5

Laslett, Peter, *The World We Have Lost* (New York, 1971, 2nd ed.)

Lathrop, Henry B., "Janus Cornarius *Selecta Epigrammata Graeca* and the Early English Epigrammatists", *MLN* 43 (1928), pp. 223–229

Lathrop, Henry B., *Translations from the Classics into English...1477–1620* (New York, 1967) (Univ. Wisconsin Studies in Lang. and Lit., 35)

Leedham–Green, Elisabeth, "A Catalogue of Caius College Library in 1569" *TCBS* 8 (1981), pp. 29–41

Leedham–Green, Elisabeth, ed., *Books in Cambridge Inventories* (Cambridge, 1986) 2 vols.

Leedham–Green, Elisabeth, see also Fehrenbach

Lefèvre d'Étaples, Jacques, *Hecatonomiae* in his ed. Aristotle, *Politics and Economics*, transl. (Lat.) Leonardo Bruni (Paris, 1506) fols. 145^v–182^r

Lefèvre d'Étaples, Jacques, *Hecatonomiae* ed. Jean Boisset and Robert Combès (Paris, 1979)

Lefranc, Pierre, *Sir Walter Ralegh Écrivain* (Paris, 1968)

Le Grand, E., *Bibliothèque héllénique* (Paris, 1885–1906) 4 vols. (Works in Greek by Greeks, 15th and 16th centuries)

Lehmberg, Sanford, *Sir Thomas Elyot* (Austin, 1960)

Leishman, J. B., see *Parnassus Plays*

Leland, John, *Commentarii de scriptoribus Britannicis* (Oxford, 1709) 2 vols. HD

Leland, John, *De rebus britannicis collectanea*, ed. Thomas Hearne (London, 1770–1774) 4 vols. (lists of books in vol. 4)

Leo Hebreus, *Dialoghi d'amore*, transl. F. Friedeberg–Seeley and Jean H. Barnes as *The Philosophy of Love* (London, 1937)

Leo Hebreus, *Dialoghi d'amore*, transl. (Fr.) Pontus de Tyard (Lyons, 1551) BN

Leo Hebreus, *Dialoghi d'amore*, transl. Pontus de Tyard, ed. T. A. Perry (Chapel Hill, 1974)

Le Roy, Louis, *De la vicissitude ou variété des choses en l'Univers* (1575), transl. Robert Ashley as *Of the interchangeable course or variety of things...*(London, 1594) STC 15488

Levi, Anthony H., "The Neoplatonic Calculus" in his *Humanism in France* (Manchester, 1970) pp. 229–248

Liburnio, Niccolò, *Sentenze et aurei detti* (Venice, 1545) Univ. Michigan

Liburnio, Niccolò, *Sentenze et aurei detti* ed. and transl. (Fr.) Gilles Corrozet (Paris, 1546) HD

Liburnio, Niccolò, *Sentenze et aurei detti*, transl. (Lat.) as *Divini Platonis gemmae* (Paris, 1566) BN (also called *Dicta notabilia, Gemmae Platonis*, and *Platonis gnomologia*)

Lichtenstein, Aharon, *Henry More* (Cambridge, Mass., 1962)

Liddell, J. R., "The Library of Corpus Christi College, Oxford in the 16th century", *Library* 4th ser. 18 (1938), pp. 385–416

Lily, George, *Virorum aliquot in Britannia* in Paolo Giovio, *Descriptio Britanniae...* (Venice, 1548) BL

Lily, William, *Epigrammata* (Basle, 1518) HD (with Thomas More)

Linche, Richard, see Cartari

Ling, Nicholas, *Politeuphuia: Wits Commonwealth* (London, 1597) STC 15685

Llwyd, Humphrey, *Commentarioli Britannicae descriptionis fragmentum* (1572), transl. Thomas Twyne as *The Breuiary of Britayne* (London, 1573) STC 16636

Lodge, Thomas, *Complete Works*, ed. Edmund Gosse (London, 1883; repr. New York, 1963 and 1966

Logan, F. Donald, "The Origins of the So-called Regius Professorships" in Derek Baker, ed., *Renaissance and Renewal in Christian History, Studies in Church History* 14 (1977), pp. 271–278

Lok, Henry, *Poems*, ed. Alexander B. Grosart (London, 1811)

London Stationers Company, *Transcript of Register 1554–1640*, ed. Edward Arber (London, 1875–1894) 5 vols.

Long, Percy W., "The Purport of Lyly's Endimion", *PMLA* 24 (1909), pp. 164–184

Lopez de Mendoza, Inigo, *Los proverbios* (1494), transl. Barnabe Googe as *The Prouerbes of Sir James Lopez de Mendoza* (London, 1579) STC 16809

Lorens d'Orleans (Frère Laurent), *Somme le roi* (Paris, c.1488) BL

Lorens d'Orleans (Frère Laurent), transl. anon. as *Book of Vices and Virtues*, ed. W. Nelson Francis (London, 1942) (EETS: os 217)

Lorens d'Orleans, (Frère Laurent), transl. Dan Michel of Northgate as *Ayenbite of Inwyt*, text ed. Richard Morris (London, 1866) (EETS: os 23); introd. by Pamela Gradon (Oxford, 1979) (EETS: os 278)

Lorens d'Orleans (Frère Laurent), transl. William Caxton as *The boke named the Royal* (Westminster, 1487) STC 21429

Loues Martyr (1601), ed. Alexander B. Grosart (London, 1878) *New Shakespeare Society Misc.* ser. 8, no. 2, contains poems attributed to Chapman, Chester, Donne, Jonson, Marston, Salusbury, and Shakespeare)

Lucian of Samosata, *Dialogues*, ed. and transl. A. M. Harmon *et al.* (London, 1913–1980) 8 vols. (Loeb; *Halcyon* is in vol. 8, pp. 303–317)

Lucian of Samosata, *Dialogues*, (Gk.) ed. John Lair (Cambridge, 1521) STC 16896

Lucian of Samosata, *Dialogues*, selections transl. (Lat.) D. Erasmus (London, 1528) STC 16891 (repr. London, 1531) STC 16892

Lucian of Samosata, *Dialogues*, selections transl. (Lat.) D. Erasmus and Thomas More (Paris, 1506; repr. Louvain, 1512) Van der Haeghen

Lucian of Samosata, *Dialogues*, selections transl. (Lat.) Thomas More, ed. Craig R. Thompson (New Haven, 1974) (in Yale ed. of *Works* of More, vol. 3, Part 1)

Lucian of Samosata, *Cynicus*, transl. Thomas Elyot as *A dialogue between Lucian and Diogenes* (London, c. 1532) STC 16894

Lucian of Samosata, *Menippus*, transl. (Lat.) Thomas More as *Necromantia* (London, c. 1530) STC 16895

Luiso, Franceso P., *Studi su l'Epistolario di Leonardo Bruni* (Rome, 1980)

Luke, Mary, *The Nine Days Queen* (New York, 1986) (on Lady Jane Grey)

Lupset, Thomas, *Works*, ed. John A. Gee (New Haven, 1931)

Lycosthenes, Conrad, *Apophthegmatum* (London, 1579) STC 17003.3, see also Parinchef

Lycosthenes, Conrad, *Prodigiorum ac ostensorum chronica* (Basle, 1557) BL. transl. Stephen Bateman as *The doome warning all men to the Iudgemente* (London, 1581) STC 1582

Lydgate, John, *Poems*, ed. J. Norton–Smith (Oxford, 1966)

Lydgate, John, *The Minor Poems*, ed. Henry N. MacCracken (London, 1911–1934) 2 vols. (EETS: es

107, os 192)

Lydgate, John, *The assemble of goddes* (Westminster, 1498) STC 17005

Lydgate, John, *The assemble of goddes*, ed. Oscar L. Triggs (London, 1895) (EETS: es 69)

Lydgate, John, *Reson and Sensuallyte*, ed. Ernst Sieper (London, 1901–1903) 2 vols. (EETS: es 84,89)

Lydgate, John, see also Boccaccio; *Court of Sapience*; Guillaume de Guilleville; Pseudo–Aristotle, *Secreta secretorum*

Lyly, John, *The Complete Works*, ed. R. W. Bond (Oxford, 1902) 3 vols.

Lyte, H. C. M., *A History of the University of Oxford* (Oxford, 1886)

MacCaffrey, Wallace, *Queen Elizabeth and the Making of Policy 1572–1588* (Princeton, 1981)

Machiavelli, Niccolo, *Il principe* (London, 1584) STC 17167

Mackinnon, Flora L., *The Philosophy of John Norris of Bemerton* (Baltimore, 1910)

Maclean, Hugh, "Greville's Poetic", *SP* 61 (1964), pp. 170–191

Maclean, Ian, "Philosophical Books in European Markets, 1570–1630" in Henry (1990) pp. 253–263

Maclure, Millar, *George Chapman* (Toronto, 1966)

Macrobius, *Commentariorum in Somnium Scipionis*, ed. and transl. (Ital.) Luigi Scarpa (Padua, 1981)

Macrobius, *Commentariorum in Somnium Scipionis*, transl. William H. Stahl (New York, 1952; repr. New York, 1990)

Macrobius, *Saturnalia*, ed. James Willis (Leipzig, 1963) (Teubner)

Macrobius, *Saturnalia*, transl. Percival V. Davies (New York, 1969)

Macronius, Martin, *Sententiae Platonis* (Basle, 1596) (appended to his ed. of *Opera* of Galen)

Madan, Falconer, "The Daily Ledger of John Dorne, 1520", *OHS Collectanea* I (Oxford, 1885) pp. 71–177 and Append. in *OHS Collectanea* II (Oxford, 1890) pp. 453–480

Major, John (of Haddington), *A History of Greater Britain...* (Paris, 1521) BL

Malden, H. E., *Trinity Hall, Cambridge* (Cambridge, 1902)

Malynes, Gerard de, *Saint George for England* (London, 1601) STC 17226a

Mamertus, Claudianus, see Claudianus

Mandel, E. F., "Recent Research in European Historical Demography", *AHR* 75 (1970), pp. 1065–1073

Manzolli, Pietro Angelo (Palingenius), *Zodiacus vitae* (1531), transl. anon. (London, c. 1569) STC 19138.5

Manzolli, Pietro Angelo (Palingenius), *Zodiacus vitae*, transl. Barnabe Googe, Books 1–3 (London, 1560) STC 19148, Books 1–6 (London, 1561) STC 19149, Book 1–12 (London, c.1569) STC 19138.5

Marbecke, John, *A Book of Notes and Commonplaces* (London, 1581) STC 17299

Marcel, Raymond, *Marsile Ficin* (Paris, 1958)

Marcel, Raymond, see also Ficino

Marlowe, Christopher, *The Complete Works*, ed. Fredson Bowers (Cambridge, 1973)

Marsilio of Padua, *Defensor pacis*, ed. C. W. Previté–Orton (Cambridge, 1928)

Marston, John, *Plays*, ed. H. Harvey Wood (London, 1934–1930) 3 vols.

Marston, John, *Poems*, ed. Arnold Davenport (Liverpool, 1961)

Marston, John, see also *Loues Martyr*

Martin, C., "Impeding the Progress: Sidney's 'The Lady of May'" *ISJR* 60 (1986), pp. 395–405

Marx, Jacob, *Verzeichnis der Handschriften–Samlung des Hospitals zu Cues* (Trier, 1905) (manuscripts of Nicolaus Cusanus)

Masai, François, *Pléthon et le platonisme de Mistra* (Paris, 1956)

Masai, R. and F., "L'oeuvre de Georges Gemiste Pléthon", Académie Royale de Belgique, *Bulletin de la classe des lettres* ser. 5, 40 (1954) pp. 536–555

Mason, Robert, *Reasons Monarchie* (London, 1602) STC 17621

Massa, David, "Giordano Bruno's Ideas in Seventeenth Century England", *JHI* 38 (1977), pp. 227–242

Mauch, Katherine, "Angel Imagery and Neoplatonic Love in Donne's 'Air and Angels'", *SCN* 35 (1977), pp. 106–111

Mayer, Thomas F., *Thomas Starkey* (Cambridge, 1989)

Mayor, John E., *Early Statutes of the College of St. John, Cambridge* (1859)

168　Bibliography

Mazzatinti, G., *Inventario dei manoscritti italiani delle biblioteche di Francia* (Rome, 1886–1888) 3 vols.

McCabe, Richard, "Conflicts of Platonic Love and Sensual Desire in *Astrophil and Stella*" in John Scattergood, ed., *Literature and Learning in Medieval and Renaissance England* (Dublin, 1984) pp. 103–126 (Festschrift Fitzroy Pyle)

McConica, James K., *English Humanists and Reformation Politics* (Oxford, 1965)

McConica, James K., ed., *The History of the University of Oxford*, vol. 3 (Oxford, 1986) (and author of chapters pp. 1–68, 151–156, 645–732; gen. ed., T. H. Aston)

McKitterick, David, "The Sixteenth Century Catalogues of St. John's College Library" *TCBS* 7 (1978), pp. 135–155

McLelland, Joseph C., ed., *Peter Martyr Vermigli* (Waterloo, 1977)

McNulty, Robert, "Bruno at Oxford", *RN* 13 (1960), pp. 300–305

Medcalf, Stephen, "Shakespeare on beauty, truth, and transcendence" in A. Baldwin, pp. 117–125

Melanchthon, Philipp, *Opera*, ed. Carolus G. Bretschneider *et al.* (Halle, 1834–1860) 28 vols. (repr. New York, 1963)

Malczer, William, "Neoplatonism and Petrarchism...", *Neohelicon* 3 (1975), pp. 9–27

Melczer, William, "Platonisme et Aristotelisme dans la pensée de Léon l'Hébreu in *Platon et Aristote* (1976), pp. 293–306

Mercati, Giovanni, *Ultimi contributi alla storia degli umanisti* (Città del Vaticana, 1939) vol. 1, *Traversariana*

Mercati, Giovanni, "Un lamento di Giovanni Eugenico per la disfatta di Comito nel 1446" in Mercati's *Opere minori* (Città del Vaticana, 1937) vol. 4, pp. 25–28

Meres, Francis, *Palladis Tamia* (1598), facs. ed. Don C. Allen (New York, 1938)

Merrill, L. R., *Nicholas Grimald* (New Haven, 1928)

Merrill, Robert V. and Robert J. Clements, *Platonism in French Renaissance Poetry* (New York, 1957)

Mexia, Pedro, *Silva de varia lección*(1543), transl. Thomas Fortescue as *The Foreste* (London, 1571) STC 17849

Meyer, Robert J., "Pleasure Reconciled to Virtue", *SEL* 21 (1981), pp. 193–208 (on Lyly's *Gallathea*)

Meyland, Edouard, "L'évolution de la notion de l'amour platonique", *BHR* 5 (1938), pp. 418–442

Michel, Alain, "Les théories de la beauté littéraire, de Marsile Ficin à Torquato Tasso" in *Acta Conventus Neo–Latini Sanctandreani*, ed. I. D. McFarlane (Binghamton, 1986) pp. 159–171

Michel, Alain, see also Harvey

Mignault, Claude, see Alciati

Milton, John, *Works*, ed. Frank A. Patterson *et al.* (New York, 1931–1938) 18 vols. (the Columbia Milton)

Minnis, Alastair, "Aspects of the Medieval French and English Traditions of the *De consolatione philosophiae*" in Margaret T. Gibson, ed., *Boethius* (Oxford, 1981) pp. 312–361

Mitchell, Ruth J., "English Students at Bologna in the 15th Century", *EHR* 51 (1936), pp. 270–287

Mitchell, Ruth J., "English Students at Ferrara in the 15th Century", *Italian Studies* 1 (1937), 74–82

Mitchell, Ruth J., "English Students at Padua 1460–1475", *TRHS* 4th Ser., 19 (1936), pp. 101–117

Mitchell, Ruth J., "English Students in Early Renaissance Italy", *Italian Studies* 7 (1952), pp. 62–81

Mitchell, Ruth J., *John Free* (London, 1955)

Mitchell, Ruth J., *John Tiptoft* (London, 1938)

Mohler, Ludwig, *Kardinal Bessarion als Theologe, Humanist, und Staatsmann* (Paderborn, 1923–1942) 3 vols. (includes eds. of *In calumniatorem Platonis* of Bessarion and *Reductorium* of Niccolò Perotti)

Monfasani, John, "Bessarion Latinus", *Rinascimento* 21 (1981), pp. 165–209

Monfasani, John, *George of Trebizond* (Leiden, 1976)

Monfasani, John, ed. *Collectanea Trapezuntia* (Binghamton, 1984)

Montagu, Walter, *The shepheards paradise* (London, 1659) STC 18040.5 and Wing M2475

Montemayor, Jorge, *Diana*, transl. Bartholomew Yonge (London, 1598) STC 18044, ed. Judith Kennedy (Oxford, 1968)

Moore–Smith, G. C., "Life and Works of Abraham Fraunce" in his ed. Fraunce's *Victoria* (Louvain, 1906) pp. xiv–xl (W. Bang, *Materialen zur Kunde des alteren Englischen Dramas*, vol. 14)

Morcillo, Sebastian Fox, *De natura philsophia seu de Platonis et Aristotelis consensione* (Paris, 1554) BL (repr. Hildesheim, 1977)

More, Henry, *Opera* (London, 1675–1679) 3 vols. Wing M2633

More, Sir Thomas, *The workes...in the Englysh tonge* (London, 1557) STC 18076, facs ed. W. E. Campbell *et al.* (London, 1931) 2 vols.

More, Sir Thomas, *Epigrammata* (Basle, 1518) HD (with William Lily)

More, Sir Thomas, *The Latin Epigrams*, ed. Leicester Bradner and Charles A. Lynch (Chicago, 1953)

More, Sir Thomas, *Translations of Lucian*, ed. Craig R. Thompson (New Haven, 1974) (Yales ed. vol 3, Part 1)

More, Sir Thomas, *Utopia*, ed. Edward Surtz (New Haven, 1964) (Yale ed.)

Morel, Guillaume, *Verborum latinorum...*, ed. Richard Hutton (London, 1583) STC 18101

Mornay, Philippe de, *De la vérité de la religion chrestienne* (1581), transl. Philip Sidney and Arthur Golding as *The Trewnesse of the Christian Religion* (London, 1587) STC 18149, facs. ed. Francis J. Sypher (New York, 1976)

Mornay, Philippe de, *Discours de la vie et du mort*, (1576), transl. Edward Aggas as *The Defense of death* (London, 1576) STC 18136

Mornay, Philippe de, *Discours de la vie et du mort*, (1576), transl. Mary Sidney, Countess of Pembroke as *A discourse of life and death* (London, 1592) STC 18138 ed.

Mornay, Philippe de, *Discours de la vie et du mort*, Countess of Pembroke, transl. Mary Sidney, ed. Diane Bornstein (Detroit, 1983)

Mornay, Philippe de, *Discours de la vie et du mort,* transl. Mary Sidney, Countess of Pembroke, repr. in her *Six excellent treatises of life and death* (London, 1607) STC 18155 (includes her tr. of *Axiochus*)

Mornay, Philippe de, *Discours de la vie et du mort*, transl. Mary Sidney, Countess of Pembroke, ed. Mario Richter (Milan, 1964)

Morris, John, "Repressive Practices" and "Thomas Thomas" (a 2–part study of Thomas Thomas), *TCBS* 4 (1968), pp. 276–290, 339–362

Mubashshir ibn Fatik, Abu-al-Wafa-Al-, *Muhtar-al-Hikam*, (1049), transl. (Span., c.1257) as *Bocados de Oro*, ed. Mechtild Crombach (Bonn, 1971)

Mubashshir ibn Fatik, *Muhtar-al-Hikam*, transl. (Lat., c.1290) Giovanni da Proceda as *Placita philosophorum moralium*, ed. Salvatore de Renzi in *Collectio Salernitana* (Naples, 1854) vol. 3.

Mubashshir ibn Fatik, *Muhtar-al-Hikam*, transl. (Lat., c.1290) Giovanni da Proceda as *Liber philosophorum moralium*, ed. Ezio Franceschini, in *Atti del Reale Istituto Veneto di Scienze, Lettere, ed Arti* 91.1 (1931–1932)

Mubashshir ibn Fatik, *Muhtar-al-Hikam*, transl. (Fr., c.1390) Guillaume de Tignonville as *Dits moraulx*, ed. Robert Eder in *Romanische Forschungen* 33 (1915)

Mubashshir ibn Fatik, *Muhtar-al-Hikam*, transl. (1450) Stephen Scrope as *Dicts or Sayings of the Philosophers*, ed. Margaret E. Schofield (Philadelphia, 1936)

Mubashshir ibn Fatik, *Muhtar-al-Hikam*, (transl. (1450) Stephen Scrope with revisions by William of Worcester, ed. Curt F. Bühler, (London, 1941) (EETS:os 211)

Mubashshir ibn Fatik, *Muhtar-al-Hikam*, transl. (c.1460) anon. as *The Booke of Morall Seyenges of Phylosophres*, ed. Curt F. Bühler (London, 1941) (EETS:os 211)

Mubashshir ibn Fatik, *Muhtar-al-Hikam*, transl. (c.1470) George Ashby as *Dicta et opiniones diversorum philosophorum*, ed. Mary Bateson (London, 1899) (EETS: es 76)

Mubashshir ibn Fatik, *Muhtar-al-Hikam*, transl. (c.1475) Anthony, Earl Rivers as *Dictes or sayengis of the philosophres*, ed. William Caxton (London, 1477) STC 626, repr. William Blades (London, 1877; also repr. Detroit, 1901)

Mubashshir ibn Fatik, *Muhtar-al-Hikam*, transl. (Ital.) as *Fior di virtù historiale* (Florence, 1491) BL

Mubashshir ibn Fatik, *Muhtar-al-Hikam*, as *Fior di virtù historiale*, transl. Nicholas Fersing, ed. Lessing J. Rosenwald (Washington, 1953)

Mubashshir ibn Fatik, *Muhtar-al-Hikam*, transl. John Larke as *The boke of wysdome* (London, 1532) STC 3357 (repr. London, 1565) STC 3358

Mulcaster, Richard, *Positions,* (1581), ed. William W. Barker (Univ. of Toronto diss, 1982)

Mullett, Charles F., "Hugh Plat" in Charles Prouty ed., *Studies in Honor of A. H. R. Fairchild* (Columbia, 1946) pp. 91–118

Mulligan, Winifred J., *John Whethamstede* (Duke Univ. diss., 1974)

Mullinger, James, *The University of Cambridge...to 1535* (Cambridge, 1873–1911) 3 vols.

Munby, A. N. L., "Notes on King's College Library in the Fifteenth Century", *TCBS* 1 (1951), pp. 280–286

Munday, Anthony, *A second and third blast of retrait from plaies and theaters* (London, 1580) STC 21677 (see Salvianus)

Munday, Anthony, *A second and third blast of retrait from plaies and theaters*, ed. William C. Hazlitt in *The English Drama and Stage* (London, 1869) pp. 97–155

Munday, Anthony, ed. *Bel–vedere* (London, 1600) STC 3189

Munday, Anthony, see also Landi

Mütz, Eugene, *La Bibliothèque du Vatican sous...Nicholas V...* (Le Puy, c.1887)

Mynors, Roger A. B., *Catalogue of the Manuscripts of Balliol College Oxford* (Oxford, 1963)

Nani–Mirabelli, Domenico, *Polyanthea* (Saon, 1503) BL

Nashe, Thomas, *Works,* ed. Ronald B. McKerrow, rev. F. P. Wilson (London, 1958) 5 vols.

Nelson, John C., "Platonism in the Renaissance" in *DHI*, vol. 3, pp. 508–515

Newman, W. L., "The Correspondence of Humphrey, Duke of Gloucester and Pier Candido Decembrio", *EHR* 20 (1905), pp. 484–498

Nichols, John, *The Progresses of Queen Elizabeth* (London, 1788–1821) 4 vols. (2nd ed., London, 1823) in 3 vols. (repr. New York, 1969) (Note: Hartwell speech during 1564 visit to Cambridge is in 1788 ed. only, vol. 1, pp. 12–14; ed. of 1823 includes: Sidney, *Lady of May*, vol. 2, pp. 94–103; Sidney, *Fortress* pageant, vol. 2, pp. 310–329; Gascoigne, *Princely Pleasures*, vol. 1, pp. 485–623)

Nolhac, Pierre de, *Pétrarque et l'humanisme* (Paris, 1954) 2 vols., 2nd ed.

Norris, John, *The theory and regulation of love* (Oxford, 1688) Wing N1272

Northbrooke, John, *A treatise against Dicing, Dancing, Plays, and Interludes*, (1577), ed. J. P. Collier (London, 1843)

Novati, Francesco, "Uberto Decembrio e Coluccio Salutati", *Archivio storico lombardo* ser. 4, 9 (1908), pp. 193–216

Oates, J. C. T. and H. L. Pink, "Three 16th Century Catalogues of the University Library", *TCBS* 1 (1952), pp. 310–340

Oliver, Revilo P,, "Plato and Salutati", *TAPA,* 71 (1940), pp. 315–334

Oliver, Revilo P., "Salutati's Criticism of Petrarch", *Italica* 16 (1939), pp. 49–57

O'Malley, Charles, D., *English Medical Humanists* (Laurence, 1965)

O'Malley, Charles D., *Jacopo Aconcio* (Rome, 1955)

O'Malley, Charles D., "John Caius", *DSB* vol. 3, pp. 12–13

Omont, Henri, "Les manuscrits grecs de Guarino de Vérone" *Revue des bibliothèques* 2 (1892), pp. 79–81

Ong, Walter, *Ramus and Talon Inventory* (Cambridge, Mass., 1958)

Orgel, Stephen, see Daniel; Giovio

Osborn, James M., *Young Philip Sidney 1572–1577* (New Haven, 1972)

O'Sullivan, William, "John Manyngham, an Early Oxford Humanist", *BLR* 7 (1962), pp. 28–39

Ovidius Naso, Publius, *Opera*, ed. R. Ehwald (Leipzig, 1910)

Ovidius Naso, Publius, *Works*, transl. H. T. Riley (London, 1851–1852) 3 vols.

Ovidius Naso, Publius, *Metamorphoses* (Cambridge, 1584) STC 18951

Ovidius Naso, Publius, *Metamorphoses*, ed. and transl. Frank J. Miller (London, 1984) 2 vols. (Loeb)

Ovidius Naso, Publius, *Metamorphoses*, transl. Arthur Golding (London, 1567) STC 18956

Ovidius Naso, Publius, *Metamorphoses* (Lyons, 1518; repr. New York, 1976) (includes moralizations by Pierre Bersuire)

Ovidius Naso, Publius, *The Fable of Narcissus*, transl. Thomas Howell (London, 1560) STC 18970 (includes verse Moralization)

Ovidius Naso, Publius, *The Fable of Narcissus,* transl. Thomas Howell, repr. in ed. by W. E. Buckley of Thomas Edwards, *Cephalus and Procris. Narcissus* (London, 1882) pp. 129–171

Oxford, University of, *Register 1575–1622*, ed. Andrew G. Clark (Oxford, 1887–1889) 4 vols.

Oxford, University of, *Statuta antiqua*, ed. Strickland Gibson (Oxford, 1931)

Oxford, University of, *Statutes of the Colleges of Oxford*, ed. E. A. Bond (London, 1853) 3 vols.

Oxford, University of, Vice–chancellor's court, *Inventories*, original in University Archives, called "Register A"; there is also a transcription by Walter Mitchell in the Archives

Oxford, University of, Vice–chancellor's court, *Inventories*, Booklists are being edited by Robert Fehrenbach *et al.* under title *Private Libraries of Renaissance England* (Binghamton, 1992–1994) 3 vols. to date

Page, William, see *Victoria History of Hertfordshire*

Painter, George D., *William Caxton* (London, 1976)

Paleario, Aonio (i.e. Antonio dalla Paglia), *Del beneficio di Gesu Cristo crocifisso*, (1534), transl. Edward Courtenay (1548), ed. C. Babington (Cambridge, 1855; repr. Boston, 1860)

Paleario, Aonio, *Del beneficio di Gesu Cristo crocifisso*, transl. Arthur Golding (London, 1573) STC 19114 (repr. London, 1874)

Palfreyman, Thomas, *The treatise of heauenlie philosophie* (London, 1578) STC 19138, see also Baldwin W.

Palingenius, see Manzolli

Palladis Tamia, see Meres

Panizza, Diego, *Alberico Gentili...* (Padua, 1981)

Pantzer, Katherine F., ed., *A Short–title Catalogue of Books Printed in England...1475–1640* (London, 1986–1991) 3 vols., 2nd ed.

Paradin, Claude, *Devises héroiques*, (1557), transl. P.S. as *The heroicall deuises* (London, 1591) STC 19183

Paradise, Nathaniel, *Thomas Lodge* (New Haven, 1971)

Paredi, Angelo, *La biblioteca del Pizolpasso* (Milan, 1961)

Parinchef, John, *An extracte of examples, apothegmes and histories...*(sic) (London, 1572) STC 19196 (includes selections from Lycosthenes' *Apophthegmata)*

Parker, Samuel, *A free and impartial censvre of the Platonick philosophie* (Oxford, 1666) Wing P463

Parkhurst, John, *Ludicra* (London, 1573) STC 19299

Parks, George, "The Decline and Fall of the English Admiration of Italy". *HLQ* 31 (1968), pp. 341–357

Parks, George, *The English Traveller to Italy* (Rome, 1954)

Parks, George, "The Genesis of Tudor Interest in Italian", *PMLA* (1963), pp. 529–535

Parnassus Plays, ed. J. B. Leishman (London, 1949)

Parry, Robert, *Sinetes passions vppon his fortunes* (London, 1597) STC 19338

Partee, Morris H., "Anti–Platonism in Sidney's Defense", *English Miscellany* 22 (1971), pp. 7–29

Partee, Morris H., "Sir Philip Sidney and the Renaissance Knowledge of Plato", *English Studies* (Amsterdam) 51 (1970), pp. 411–424

Pasquier, Etienne, *Le monophile*, (1554), transl. Geoffrey Fenton as *Monophylo* (London, 1572) STC 10797

Paston Letters, ed. James Gairdner (Edinburgh, 1910) 4 vols.

Pastor, Ludwig, *The History of the Popes* (St. Louis, 1910) 4 vols.

Patrizi, Francesco, da Cherso, *L'amorosa filosofia*, ed. John C. Nelson (Florence, 1963)

Patrizi, Francesco, da Cherso, "Capita...in quibus Plato concors...catholicae fidei ostenditur" in his *Nova de universis philosophia* (Ferrara, 1591) BNF

Patrizi, Francesco, da Cherso, *Della poetica* (Ferrara, 1586) BL

Patrizi, Francesco, da Cherso, *Della poetica*, ed. Danielo A. Barbagli (Florence, 1969–1971) 3 vols.

Patrizi, Francesco, da Cherso, *De regno et regis institutione* (Paris, 1519) BN

Patrizi, Francesco, da Cherso, *Discussionum peripateticarum* (Venice, 1571) BL (repr. Basle, 1581) BL

Patrizi, Francesco, da Cherso, *Lettere ed opuscoli*, ed. Cesare Vasoli (Rome, 1989) (includes Patrizi's essay on order of Plato's dialogues)

Patrizi, Francesco, da Cherso, *Magia philosophica* (Hamburg, 1593) HD (an anthology containing *Asclepius* of Apuleius, and Latin translations of *Chaldaean Oracles* of Zoroaster, *Corpus Hermeticum* of Hermes Trismegistus, and *Secrets of the Egyptians*, by Jamblichus)

Patrizi, Francesco, da Cherso, *Nova de universis philosophia* (Ferrara, 1591) BNF (includes as an appendix a reprint of *Magia philosophica*, with *Theology of Aristotle* added)

Patrouch, John F., *Reginald Pecock* (New York, 1970)

Paulet, William, *The lord marques idlenes* (London, 1586) STC 19485

Peacham, Henry, the Elder, *The Garden of Eloquence* (London, 1583) 2nd ed. STC 19489 repr. ed. William G. Crane (Gainsville, 1954)

Pearsall, Derek, *John Lydgate* (London, 1970)

Pearson, Lu Emily, *Elizabethan Love Conventions* (Berkeley, 1933; repr. New York, 1966)

Pélétier du Man, Jacques, *Oeuvres poétiques*, ed. Léon Séché (Paris, 1904)

Pemberton, Caroline, see Elizabeth I, Queen of England

Pembroke, Countess of, see Sidney, Mary

Perry, Theodore A., *Erotic Spirituality* (University, Alabama, 1980)

Perry, Theodore A., see also Leo Hebreus

Pertusi, Agostino, *Leonzio Pilato fra Petrarca e Boccaccio* (Venice, 1964)

Peter Martyr, see Vermigli

Petrarca, *Opera*, ed. various (Florence, 1926–1943) 7 vols.

Petrarca, *De ignorantia sui ipsiusque aliorum*, ed. L. M. Capelli (Paris, 1906)

Petrarca, *De ignorantia sui ipsiusque aliorum*, transl. Hans Nachod in Ernst Cassirer *et al.* eds., *The Renaissance Philosophy of Man* (Chicago, 1948) pp. 47–133

Petrarca, *Lettere*, ed. G. Fracassetti (Florence, 1892) 5 vols.

Pettie, George, *A petite pallace of Pettie his pleasure* (London, 1576) STC 19819, see also Guazzo

Pettigrove, James, see Cassirer

Pflaum, Heinz, "Sortes, Plato, Cicero", *Speculum* 6 (1931), pp. 499–533

Philippson, Johann, *Summa doctrinae platonis de republica et legibus* in Claude Seyssel, *De republica Galliae* (Strasbourg, 1548) fols. 73^r–111^r, HD (Ascham copy in London, BL 645.a.7)

Piccolomini, Enea, "Delle condizioni e delle vicende della libreria Medicea privata, dal 1494–1508", *Archivio storico italiano* ser. 3, vol. 19 (1874), pp. 101–129, 254–281, vol. 20 (1874) pp. 51–94, vol. 21 (1875), pp. 102–112, 282–296

Pickett, Penny, "Sidney's Use of *Phaedrus* in 'Lady of May'", *SEL* 16 (1976), pp. 33–50

Pico della Mirandola, Giovanni, *Opera* (Basle, 1557_ facs ed. Cesare Vasoli (Hildesheim, 1969)

Pico della Mirandola, Giovanni, (selections) *De hominis dignitate, Heptaplus, De ente et uno, e scritti vari*, ed. Eugenio Garin (Florence, 1942) (includes *Commento*)

Pico della Mirandola, Giovanni, *Commento sopra un canzone di Girolamo Benivieni*, transl. (Fr.) Gabriel Chappuys (Paris, 1588) BN

Pico della Mirandola, Giovanni, *Commento sopra un canzone di Girolamo Benivieni*, transl. Sears Jayne (New York, 1984)

Pilkington, James, "Homily against Gluttony and Drunkenness" in *Certain Sermons* (2nd *Book of Homilies*, ed. G. E. Corrie (Cambridge, 1850) pp. 298–310

Pintaudi, Rosario, ed., *Lessico Greco–Latino* (Rome, 1977) (Greek phrasebook used by Ficino)

Pinto, Vivian de Sola, *Peter Sterry...* (Cambridge, 1934)

Pintor, Fortunato, "Per la storia della libreria Medicae nel Rinascimento", *IMU* 3 (1960), pp. 189–210

1. Complete Works

Plato, (Gk.) ed. Aldo Manuzio (Venice, 1513) BL

Plato, (Gk. and Lat.) ed. Henri Estienne, with transl. Jean de Serres (Geneva, 1578–1579) 3 vols. ("Stephanus" ed.) BL

Plato, (Lat.) transl. Marsilio Ficino (Florence, 1484) HD

Plato, (Lat.) transl. Marsilio Ficino, ed. Simon Grynaeus (Basle, 1532) Yale

Plato, (Lat.) transl. Janus Cornarius (Basle, 1561) HD (with Ficino's commentaries added)

Plato, (Engl.) transl. Benjamin Jowett, rev. by Allan and Dale (Oxford, 1953) 4 vols., 4th ed. (includes Index by Evelyn Abbott)

2. Selections

Plato, (Gk.) ed. Johann Sturm (Strasbourg, 1538) BL (includes *Alcibiades II, Menexenus*)

Plato, (Gk.) ed. Johann Sturm (Strasbourg, 1541) BL (includes *Gorgias, Apology, Crito*)

Plato, (Gk. and Lat.) ed. John North (Cambridge, 1573) BL (includes *Apology, Crito, Phaedo, Laws X,*

Alcibiades II, and 5 others, Latin transl. is Ficino's)

Plato, (Lat.) transl. Janus Cornarius (Basle, 1549) (Includes *Alcibiades I and II, Hipparchus, Amatores)*

Plato, (Engl.) transl. unknown (London, 1675) BL

3. Individual works

Plato, *Meno,* ed. and transl. W. R. M. Lamb (London, 1924) (Loeb)

Plato, *Meno,* transl. (Lat.) Henricus Aristippus (1155), ed. Victor Kordeuter (London, 1940)

Plato, *Phaedo*, ed. and transl. Harold N. Fowler (London, 1914)

Plato, *Phaedo*, transl. (Lat.) Henricus Aristippus (1156), ed. Lorenzo Minio–Paluello (London, 1940)

Plato, *Republic,* ed. and transl. Paul Shorey (London, 1930) 2 vols. (Loeb)

Plato, *Timaeus,* ed. and transl. R. G. Bury (London, 1966) (Loeb)

Plato, *Timaeus,* transl. (Lat.) Calcidius, ed. Jan H. Waszink (London, 1975, 2nd ed.)

Plato, see also Xenocrates (for *Axiochus)*

Platoes Cap Cast at the Year 1604 (London, 1604) STC 19975

Platon et Aristote à la Renaissance (Paris, 1976) (XVIᵉ Colloque International de Tours)

Plato's Calf (Vacca Platonis), in Oxford Bodl., MS Digby 71, fols. 36ʳ–56ʳ

Plato's Circle (Platonis sphaera, ed. Frederick Warren in *Leofric Missal* (Oxford, 1883) pp. 44–45

Plato's Fourth Book (Platonis quartorum, Lat. tr. of Arabic original), ed. Lazarus Zetzner in *Theatrum Chemicum* (Strasbourg, 1616–1661), vol. 4 (also called *Four Books of Plato, Plato's Stars, Plato's Suns)*

Plato's Fourth Book, transl. (Books II–IV only) by Robert Greene of Welby as *Three Books of Plato* (1528–1529), Cambridge University Library MS Ff.IV.13, fols. 191ʳ–273ʳ

Platt, Sir Hugh, *The floures of philosophie* (London, 1572) STC 19990.5, ed. Richard J. Panofsky (Delmar, 1982)

Platt, Sir Hugh, *Manuale sententias aliquot diuinas et morales complectens* (London, 1594) STC 19992

Pletho, Giorgios Gemisthus, *De differentiis Platonis et Aristotelis,* (1439), *PG* 160: cols. 889–934

Pletho, Giorgios Gemisthus, *De differentiis Platonis et Aristotelis,* ed. B. Lazarde., *Byzantion* 43 (1974), pp. 312–343

Pletho, Giorgios Gemisthus, *De differentiis Platonis et Aristotelis,* transl. (Lat.) Bernardino Donato (Venice, 1540) BL

Pletho, Giorgios Gemisthus, *De differentiis Platonis et Aristotelis,* transl. (Lat.) Georgios Chariandros (Basle, 1574) BL

Pliny the Elder, *Naturalis historia,* ed. and transl. Horace Rackham *et al.* (Cambridge, Mass., 1938–1963) 10 vols. (Loeb)

Plomer, Henry, *Wynkyn de Worde and his Contemporaries* (London, 1925)

Plomer, Henry and Thomas P. Cross, *Life and Correspondence of Lodowick Bryskett* (Chicago, 1923)

Plutarch, *Moralia* ed. and transl. Frank C. Babbitt *et al.* (London, 1949–1969) 15 vols. (Loeb)

Plutarch, *Moralia,* transl. Philemon Holland (London, 1603) STC 20063

Plutarch, *Moralia,* selections transl. Thomas Blundeville (London, 1561) STC 20063.5

Plutarch, *Moralia,* individual essays transl. as follows: 1530, Thomas Elyot STC 20056.7; 1531, Thomas Elyot STC 22052; 1528, Thomas Wyatt. STC 20058.5; 1571, Edward Grant. STC 20057.5; 1589, John Clapham. STC 20059; 1543, John Hales. STC 20062

Plutarch, *Vitae parallelae,* transl. Thomas North (London, 1579) STC 20065

Poetical Rhapsody, see Davison

Politeuphia, see Ling

Politique Discourses, see La Place

Politique Discourses vpon trueth and lying, see Coignet

Porter, H. C., *Reformation and Reaction in Tudor Cambridge* (Cambridge, 1958)

Posie of Gilliflowers, see Gifford

Prescott, Anne L., *French Poets and the English Renaissance* (New Haven, 1978)

Prescott, Anne L., "The Influence of Du Bartas in England" *SRen* 15 (1968), pp. 144–173

Primaudaye, Pierre de la, *Academie françoise,* (1581), transl. Thomas Bowes (London, 1586) STC 15233

Primaudaye, Pierre de la, *Academie françoise, The Second Part,* transl. Thomas Bowes (London, 1589)

STC 15238

Primaudaye, Pierre de la, *Academie françois, The Third volume...*, transl. Richard Dolman (London, 1601) STC 15240

Problemata Aristotelis ac philosophorum medicorumque complurium (London, 1583) STC 761

Pseudo–Aristotle, *Secreta secretorum*, ed. Charles B. Schmitt and W. F. Ryan (London, 1982)

Pseudo–Aristotle, *Secreta secretorum, Nine English Versions*, ed. M. A. Manzalaoui (Oxford, 1977) (EETS: os 276)

Pseudo–Aristotle, *Secreta secretorum, Three Prose Versions*, ed. Robert S. Steele (London, 1898) (EETS:es 74)

Pseudo–Aristotle, *Secreta secretorum, Eastern Arabic original*, (c.1220), transl. Ismail Ali, ed. A. S. Fulton in Roger Bacon, *Opera hactenus inedita* (OHI) ed. Robert S. Steele *et al*. (Oxford, 1920) Fasc.5

Pseudo–Aristotle, *Secreta secretorum*, transl. (Lat.) Philip of Tripoli as *Secreta Secretorum vel De regimine principum* (c.1243), ed. Roger Bacon (c.1257), ed. Robert S. Steele in *Opera* of Bacon (Oxford, 1920) OHI, Fasc. 5

Pseudo–Aristotle, *Secreta secretorum*, transl. Anglo–Norman, c.1265) Pierre d'Abernun as *Le secre de secrez*, ed. Oliver A. Beckerlegge (Oxford, 1944) (ANTS 5), also ed. Robert S. Steele in *Opera* of Roger Bacon (Oxford, 1920) OHI, Fasc. 5

Pseudo–Aristotle, *Secreta secretorum*, transl. (ME, c.1400) anon., ed. Robert S. Steele in *Three Prose Versions...* (London, 1898) (EETS:es74)

Pseudo–Aristotle, *Secreta secretorum*, transl. (ME, c.1412) John Hoccleve as *Regiment of Princes*, ed. Frederick J. Furnivall (London, 1897) (EETS:es 72)

Pseudo–Aristotle, *Secreta secretorum*, transl. (ME, 1422) James Yonge, ed. Robert S. Steele in *Three Prose Versions...*(London, 1898) (EETS:es 74)

Pseudo–Aristotle, *Secreta secretorum*, transl. (ME, c.1440) John Lydgate and Benedict Burgh as *Secrees of Old Philisoffres* (sic), ed. Robert S. Steele (London, 1894) (EETS:es 66) London, 1511, STC 17017 ed., repr., Dewitt T. Starnes (Gainesville, 1957)

Pseudo–Aristotle, *Secreta secretorum*, transl. (ME, c.1450) John Shirley as *The Governance of Kynges and of Prynces*, ed. M. A. Manzalaoui in *Nine English Versions* (London, 1977) (EETS:os 276; #6 in Manzalaoui's series)

Pseudo–Dionysius, *Works*, (Gk.) PG 3:119–1122

Pseudo–Dionysius, *Works*, transl. (Lat.) George Pachymere (1300) (Paris, 1561–1562) 3 vols. BL

Pseudo–Dionysius, *Works*, transl. (Lat.) various authors, collected as *Dionysiaca*, ed. Philippe Chevalier, *et al*. (Paris, 1937–1947) 2 vols.

Pseudo–Dionysius, *Works*, transl. Colm Luidhéid (New York, 1987)

Pseudo–Dionysius, *The Divine Names* and the *Mystical Theology*, transl. (Lat.) Marsilio Ficino (Florence, 1497)

Pseudo–Dionysius, *The Divine Names* and the *Mystical Theology*, transl. John D. Jones (Milwaukee, 1980)

Pseudo–Plutarch, *De placitis philosophorum*, ed. Jurgen Mau in Plutarch's *Moralia* (Leipzig, 1971) (Teubner)

Pseudo–Pythagoras, *A brefe and pleasant worke and science of Pictagoras* (London, 1560) STC 20524, see also Singer, 1928

Purcell, J. M., "Sidney's *Astrophil and Stella* and Greville's *Caelica*", *PMLA* 50 (1935), pp. 413–422

Purnell, Frederick, *Jacopo Mazzini and his Comparison of Plato and Aristotle* (Columbia Univ. diss., 1971)

Purnell, Frederick, "The Theme of Philosophic Concord and the Source of Ficino's Platonism" in Garfagnini, 1986, vol. 2, pp. 397–415

Purvis, John S., *Tudor Parish Documents of the Diocese of York* (Cambridge, 1948)

Puttenham, George, *The Arte of English Poesie*, (1589), ed. Gladys Willcock and Alice Walker (Cambridge, 1936)

Rae, Wesley, *Thomas Lodge* (New York, 1987)

Rainolds, John, *Oratio in laudem artis poeticae*, ed. William Ringler and transl. Walter Allen (Princton, 1940) (actual author Henry Dethick, q.v.)

Rainolds, John, *Th'ouerthrow of stage–playes* (Middelburg, 1599) STC 20616

Ralegh, Sir Walter, *Works*, ed. William Oldys and Thomas Birch (Oxford, 1829) 8 vols. *(History of the World* is in vols. 2–7)

Ralegh, Sir Walter, *Poems*, ed. Agnes C. Latham (London, 1951)

Ramus, Petrus, *Dialecticae institutiones*, (1543), transl. Roland McIlwaine (London, 1574) (ong inv. #253; facs. ed. (Menston, 1969)

Randolph, Thomas, *Poetic and Dramatic Works*, ed. W. C. Hazlitt (London, 1875) 2 vols.

Randolph, Thomas, *Poems*, ed. G. Thorn–Drury (London, 1929)

Rankins, William, *Seauen satyres* (London, 1598) STC 20700

Ratcliffe, Aegremont, see Aggas

Ravisius Textor, see Tixier

Ray, John, *A Handbook of Proverbs* (London, 1847)

Read, Conyers, *Lord Burghley and Queen Elizabeth* (New York, 1961)

Rebholz, Ronald, *Life of Fulke Greville* (Oxford, 1971)

Rees, Joan, *Fulke Greville, Lord Brooke* (London, 1971)

Res publica litterarum, 4 (1981) (entire volume devoted to papers on Niccolò Perotti)

Resta, Gianvito, "Antonio Cassarino", *DBI* vol. 21, pp. 442–446

Resta, Gianvito, "Antonio Cassarino e le sui traduzioni di Plutarcho et Platone", *IMU* 2 (1959), pp. 207–283

Reyher, Paul, *Les Masques Anglais* (Paris, 1909)

Reynolds, Henry, *Mythomystes* (London, 1632) STC 20939 (includes "The Tale of Narcissus" paraphrased from G. Anquillara's transl. of Ovid)

Reynolds, Henry, *Mythomystes*, facs. ed. Arthur F. Kinney (Menston, 1972) (Scholar)

Reynolds, Henry, *Mythomystes*, modern ed. lacking "Tale of Narcissus" in J. E. Spingarn, *Critical Essays of the Seventeenth Century* (Oxford, 1908) vol. 1, pp. 141–179 (repr. ed. Edward W. Tayler in *Literary Criticism of Seventeenth Century England* (New York, 1967) pp. 225–258

Ricchieri, Ludovico (Coelius Rhodiginus), *Antiquarum lectionum*, (1509) (Venice, 1516) BL (repr. Basle, 1559) HD

Ricci, Piero, "La prima cattedra di Greco in Firenze", *Rinascimento* 3 (1952), pp. 159–165

Ricci, Piero, see also Boccaccio; Petrarca

Rich, E. F., "The Population of Elizabethan England", *EHR* 2nd ser. 2 (1950), pp. 247–265

Ringler, William, "The Sense of Lodge's Reply to Gosson", *RES* 15 (1939), pp. 164–171

Ringler, William, *Stephen Gosson* (Princeton, 1942)

Ringler, William, see also Dethick; Rainolds; Sidney; Sir Philip

Rivers, Earl, see Mubashshir ibn Fatik

Rivers, Isabel, *Classical and Christian Ideas in English Renaissance Poetry* (London, 1979)

Robb, Nesca, *Neoplatonism of the Italian Renaissance* (London, 1935)

Roberts, Julian and Andrew G. Watson, eds., *John Dee's Library Catalogue* (London, 1990)

Robson, Simon, *The choise of change* (London, 1585) STC 21131.5

Roe, John, "Italian Neoplatonism and the Poetry of Sidney, Shakespeare, Chapman, and Donne" in A. Baldwin, pp. 100–116

Rogers, Thomas, M.A., *A Philosophical Discourse* (London, 1576) STC 21239

Roman de la rose, see Guillaume de Lorris

Romei, Annibale, *Discorsi*, (1586), transl. (part) John Kepers as *The courtiers academie* (London, 1598) STC 21311

Ronsard, Pierre, *Oeuvres complètes*, ed. Gustave Cohen (Paris, 1938) 2 vols.

Rud, Thomas, *Codicum manuscriptorum Ecclesiae Cathedralis Dunelmensis* (Durham, 1825)

Ruska, Julius, "Chaucer und das Buch *Senior*" *Anglia* (Halle), 61 (1937), 136–137.

Russell, J.V., *British Medieval Population* (Albuquerque, 1948)

Rust, George, *A Discourse of the use of reason in matters of religion*, transl. (from Latin) N. Hallywell (London, 1683) Wing R2361

Rutter, Joseph, *The Shepheards Holy–Day* (London, 1635) BL

Sabbadini, Remigio, *Guariniana* (Turin, 1964)

Sabbadini, Remigio, *Le scoperte dei codici latini e greci ne' secoli XIV e XV* (Florence, 1905) rev. ed.

Eugenio Garin (Florence, 1967)

Salusbury, Sir John, *Poems*, ed. Carleton Brown (London, 1913) (EETS:es 11)

Salusbury, Sir John, see also *Loues Martyr*

Saluste du Bartas, see Du Bartas

Salutati, Coluccio, *De fato et fortuna*, ed. Concetta Bianca (Florence, 1985)

Salutati, Coluccio, *De laboribus Herculis*, ed. B. L. Ullman (Zurich, 1951) 2 vols.

Salutati, Coluccio, *Epistolario*, ed. Francesco Novati (Rome, 1891–1911) 4 vols. (repr. Rome, 1965)

Salvianus of Marseille, *Oeuvres*, ed. George Loganique (Paris, 1971)

Salvianus of Marseille, *De gubernatione dei* (Oxford, 1629) STC 21674

Salvianus of Marseille, *De gubernatione dei*, transl. Anthony Munday as *A second and third blast of retrait from plaies and theaters* (London, 1580) STC 21677

Sammut, Alfredo, *Unfredo duca di Gloucester e gli umanisti italiani* (Padua, 1980)

Samuel, Irene, "The Influence of Plato on Sir Philip Sidney's Defense of Poesy". *MLQ* 1 (1940), pp. 383–391

Samuel, Irene, *Plato and Milton* (Ithaca, 1947)

Sansovino, Francesco, *Concetti politici* (1578), transl. Robert Hitchcock as *The Quintesence of wit* (London, 1590) STC 21744

Saunders, J. W., *The Profession of English Letters* (London, 1967, 2nd ed.)

Saveson, J. E., "The Library of John Smith, the Cambridge Platonist", *N & Q* 203 (1958), pp. 215–216

Saveson, J. E., *...John Smith, the Cambridge Platonist* (Cambridge diss., 1955)

Sayle, Charles E., "The Library of Thomas Lorkyn", *Annals of Medical History* 3 (1921), pp. 310–323

Scève, Maurice, *Oeuvres complètes*, ed. Pascal Quignard (Paris, 1974)

Schenk, Wilhem, *Reginald Pole* (London, 1956)

Schio, Giovanni da, *Sulla vita e sugli scritti di Anthonio Loschi* (Padua, 1858)

Schirmer, Walter F., *Antike, Renaissance, und Puritanismus* (Munich, 1933, 2nd ed.)

Schirmer, Walter F., *John Lydgate* (Tubingen, 1952)

Schmidt–Albert–Marie, *La poésie scientifique en France au XVIe siècle* (Lausanne, 1970)

Schmidt–Albert–Marie, "Traductions français de Platon, 1536–1550" in his *Études sur le XVIe siècle* (Paris, 1967) pp. 17–44

Schmitt, Charles B., *Aristotle and the Renaissance* (Cambridge, Mass, 1983)

Schmitt, Charles B., "L'introduction de la philosophie platonicienne dans l'enseignement des universités de la Renaissance" in *Platon et Aristote à la Renaissance* (Paris, 1976) (XVIe Colloque International de Tours), pp. 93–104, repr. in *Studies*

Schmitt, Charles B., *John Case And Aristoteleanism in Renaissance England* (Kingston, 1983)

Schmitt, Charles B., "Perennial Philosophy: from Agostino Steuco to Leibniz", *JHI* 27 (1966), pp. 505–532, repr. in *Studies*

Schmitt, Charles, B., *Studies in Renaissance Philosophy and Science* (London, 1981) (reprint of published articles)

Schoeck, Richard, "The Libraries of Common Lawyers in England", *Manuscripta* 6 (1962), pp. 155–167

Schoell, Frank, *Études sur l'humanisme continental en Angleterre* (Paris, 1926)

Schofield, Margaret E., see Mubashshir ibn Fatik

Schrinner, Walter, *Castiglione und die englische Renaissance* (Berlin, 1939)

Schroeder, Kurt, *Platonismus in der englischen Renaissance vor und bei Thomas Elyot* (Berlin, 1920) (includes ed. of Elyot's *Of the knowledge*, 1533)

Scolaker, Anthony, *Diaphantus* (London, 1604) STC 21853

Scribonius, Gulielmus Adolphus, *Rerum physicarum juxta leges...* (London, 1581) STC 221095 (repr. London, 1583) STC 22110

Scrope, Stephen, see Mubashshir ibn Fatik

Seager, Francis, *The scoole of vertue* (London, c. 1550) STC 22134.5

Secretum secretorum, see Pseudo–Aristotle

Seneca, Lucius A., *Works*, transl. Thomas Lodge (London, 1614) STC 22213

Seneca, Lucius A., *De beneficiis*, transl. Arthur Golding (London, 1578) STC 22215

Seneca, Lucius A., *De remediis utriusque fortunae*, transl. Robert Whittinton (London, 1547) STC 22216

Seneca, Lucius A., *Epistulae morales*, ed. and transl. Richard M. Gummere (1917–1925) 3 vols. (Loeb)

Sensabaugh, George F., "Love Ethics in Platonic Court Drama 1625–1642", *HLQ* 1 (1938), pp. 277–304

Sensabaugh, George F., "The Milieu of Comus", *SP* 41 (1944), pp. 238–249

Sensabaugh, "Platonic Love and the Puriton Revolution", *SP* 37 (1940), pp. 457–481

Seyssel, Claude de, *La monarchie de France*, (1519), transl. (part) Johann Philippson as *De republica Galliae et regum officiis* (Strasbourg, 1548) BL (appended to this work is Philippson's *Summa doctrina Platonis de republica et legibus*

Shakespeare, William, *Works*, ed. G. B. Evans *et al.* (Boston, 1974)

Sicherl, M., "Neuendeckte Hanschriften von Marsilio Ficino und Johannes Reuchlin", *Scriptorium* 16 (1962), pp. 50–61

Sicherman, Carol M., "Thomas Traherne and Cambridge Platonism", *PLMA* 81 (1966), pp. 521–534

Sicherman, Carol M., "Thomas Traherne and Hermes Trismegistus", *RN* 19 (1966), pp. 118–131

Sicherman, Carol M., "Thomas Traherne's Commonplace Book", *PBSA* 58 (1964), pp. 458–465

Sicherman, Carol M., "Traherne's Ficino Notebook", *PBSA* 63 (1964), pp. 73–81

Sidney, Mary, Countess of Pembroke, *Poems*, ed. G. F. Walker (Salzburg, 1977)

Sidney, Mary, Countess of Pembroke, see also Mornay; Xenocrates

Sidney, Sir Philip, *Poems*, ed. William Ringler (Oxford, 1962)

Sidney, Sir Philip, *Prose Works*, ed. Albert Feuillerat (Cambridge, 1968–1970) 4 vols.

Sidney, Sir Philip, *Miscellaneous Prose*, ed. Katherine Duncan–Jones and Jan Van Dorsten (Oxford, 1973)

Sidney, Sir Philip, *An apologie for poetrie*, ed. Geoffrey Shepherd (London, 1965)

Sidney, Sir Philip, *Arcadia*, (Old), ed. Katherine Duncan–Jones (Oxford, 1985)

Sidney, Sir Philip, *Arcadia*, (New), ed. Victor Skretkowicz (Oxford, 1987)

Sidney, Sir Philip, *Correspondence with Languet*, see Languet

Sidney, Sir Philip, *Fortress of Perfect Beauty*, ed. Henry Goldwell as *A Briefe declaration of the shews...* (London, 1581) STC 11990

Sidney, Sir Philip, *Fortress of Perfect Beauty*, ed. John Nichols in *Progresses...of Queen Elizabeth* (London, 1823) vol. 2, pp. 310–329

Sidney, Sir Philip, *Fortress of Perfect Beauty*, ed. Jean Wilson as *Four Foster Children of Desire* in *Entertainments for Elizabeth I* (Woodbridge, 1980) pp. 61–85

Sidney, Sir Philip, *The Lady of May*, ed Katherine Duncan–Jones and Jan Van Dorsten in *Miscellaneous Prose* (Oxford, 1973) pp. 13–32

Sidney, Sir Philip, *The Lady of May*, see also Nichols

Sidney, Sir Philip, *Poems*, ed. P. J. Croft (Oxford, 1984)

Sieper, Ernst, *Les Échecs amoureux* (Weimar, 1898)

Sinfield, Alan, "Sidney, du Plessir–Mornay, and the Pagans", *PQ* 58 (1979), pp. 26–39

Singer, Charles, *From Magic to Science* (London, 1928) (includes essay on *Circle of Plato* and *Circle of Pythagoras*, pp. 133–167)

Skeat, Walter W., ed., see *Wars of Alexander*

Skretkowicz, Victor, "Devices and their Narrative Function in Sidney's Arcadia", *Emblematica* 1 (1986), pp. 267–291

Skretkowicz, Victor, "Sir Philip Sidney and the Elizabethan Literary Device", *Emblematica* 3 (1988), pp. 171–179

Skretkowicz, Victor, see also Sidney, Sir Philip

Sleidanus, see Philippson

Smith, G. Gregory, *Elizabethan Critical Essays* (Oxford, 1904) 2 vols. (repr. Oxford, 1967)

Smith, Henry, *Sermons* (London, 1592) STC 22718

Smith, Henry, *Gods arrowe against atheists* (London, 1593) STC 22666

Smith, Henry, *Twelve Sermons* (London, 1632) STC 22782

Smith, John, Fellow of Queens' College, Cambridge, *Select discourses* (Cambridge, 1660) Wing S4117

Smith, Sir Thomas, *De republica Anglorum* (1565) (London, 1583) STC 22857 (repr. Menston, 1970)

Snare, Gerald, *The Mystification of George Chapman* (Durham, 1989)

Solé–Leris, A., "The Theory of Love in the two Dianas: a Contrast", *BHS* 36 (1959), pp. 65–79

Sottili, Agostino, "Ambrogio Traversari, Francesco Pizolpasso, Giovanni Aurispa...", *Romanische*

Forschungen 78 (1966), pp. 42–63

Southern, A. C., *Elizabethan Recusant Prose* (London, 1950)

Souverain, Mattieu, *Le Platonisme dévoilé* (1700), transl. anon. as *Platonisme unveil'd* (London, 1700) BL

Spenser, Edmund, *Works*, ed. Edwin Greenlaw *et al.* (Baltimore, 1932–1949) 10 vols. (Variorum edition)

Spenser, Edmund, *Poetical Works*, ed. R. E. Neil Dodge (Boston, 1936)

Spenser, Edmund, see also Xenocrates

Stanley, Thomas, *The History of Philosophy* (London, 1655–1660) 3 vols. (Wing S5237–5238A)

Starkey, Thomas, *A Dialogue between Pole and Lupset*, ed. Kathleen M. Burton (London, 1948)

Stationers Register, see London

Staton, Walter, "Thomas Watson and Abraham Fraunce", *PMLA* 76 (1961), pp. 150–152

Statuta antiqua universitatis, see Oxford

Statutes of the Colleges of Oxford, see Oxford

Staudenbauer, Craig A., ". . . Recent Views of the Cambridge Platonists", *JHI* 35 (1974), pp. 157–169

Stein, Heinrich von, *Sieben Bücher zur Geschichte des Platonismus* (Göttingen, 1862–1875) 3 vols. (repr. Frankfort, 1965)

Stephanus Plato, see Plato, *Works*

Stern, Virginia, *Gabriel Harvey, His Life, Marginalia, and Library* (Oxford, 1979)

Sterry, Peter, *A Discourse of the Freedom of the Will* (London, 1675)

Steuco, Agostino, *De perenni philosophia* (Lyons, 1540) LC

Stinger, Charles L., *Humanism in the Church Fathers* (Albany, 1977) (on Traversari)

Stinger, Charles, L., *The Renaissance in Rome* (Bloomington, 1985)

Stob, Ralph, *Platonism in English Educators and Theologians of the Sixteenth Century* (Univ. of Chicago diss, 1930)

Stone, Lawrence, "The Educational Revolution in England 1560–1640", *Past and Present* 28 (1964), pp. 41–80

Stonor Letters and Papers 1290–1483, ed. Charles L. Kingford, Camden Series, 3rd ser. 29, 30 (1919), 2 vols.

Stonor Letters and Papers 1290–1483, ed. Charles L. Kingford, Suppl. 1314–1482, Camden Series, 3rd ser. 34 (1924)

Strype, John, *Life of Sir John Cheke* (Oxford, 1821; repr. New York, 1974)

Strype, John, *Life of Sir Thomas Smith* (Oxford, 1920; repr. New York, 1974)

Stubbes, Philip, *The anatomie of abuses*, ed. Frederick J. Furnivall (London, 1877; repr. New York, 1965)

Sturm, Johann, *Ad Werteros fratres, Nobilitas literata* (Strasbourg, 1549) BL

Sturm, Johann, *Ad Werteros fratres, Nobilitas literata*, transl. Thomas Browne of Lincoln's Inn as *A ritch storehouse...for Nobilitye and Gentlemen* (London, 1570) STC 23408

Sturm, Johann, ed., *Epistolae duae de nobilitate anglicana* appended to Conrad Heresbach, *De laudibus graecarum literarum oratio* (Strasbourg, 1551) BL

Sturm, Johann, see also Plato, Selections

Suckling, Sir John, *Works*, ed. Thomas Clayton and L. A. Beaurline (Oxford, 1971)

Swift, Carolyn L., "The Allegory of Wisdom in Lyly's *Endimion*", *Comparative Drama* 10 (1976), pp. 235–257

Sylvester, Joshua, see Du Bartas

Takada, Yasunari, "Chaucer's Use of Neoplatonic Traditions" in A. Baldwin, pp. 45–51

Talon, Omar, see Ramus

Talpin, Jean, *La policie chrestienne*, (1568), transl. Geoffrey Fenton as *A forme of christian pollicie* (London, 1574) STC 10793a

Tasso, Torquato, *Il padre di famiglia* (1580), ed. Cesare Guasti in Tasso, *I Dialoghi* (Florence, 1838–1859), 3 vols., vol. 1, pp. 341–398; also ed. Fazio Raimondi (Florence, 1958) 3 vols.

Tasso, Torquato, *Il padre di famiglia*, transl. Thomas Kyd as *The Householder's Philosophy* (London, 1588) STC 23702.5 (repr. Amsterdam, 1975)

Tasso, Torquato, *Il padre di famiglia*, transl. Kyd, ed. F. S. Boase in his ed. of *Works* of Kyd (Oxford, 1967, 2nd ed.) pp. 231–284

Taylor, A. E., "Spenser's Knowledge of Plato", *MLR* 19 (1924), pp. 208–210

Taylor, John, *The Universal Chronicle of Ranulf Higden* (Oxford, 1966)

Thompson, Craig R., see More, Thomas

Thompson, W. D. J. Cargill, "Notes on King's College Library 1500–1570", *TCBS* 2 (1954), pp. 38–54

Thomson, Ian, "Manuel Chrysoloras and the Early Italian Renaissance", *Greek, Roman and Byzantine Studies*, 7 (1966), pp. 63–82

Thorndike, Lynn, *History of Magic and Experimental Science* (New York, 1923–1958) 8 vols.

Tigerstedt, Eugene N., *The Decline and Fall of the Neoplatonic Interpretation of Plato* (Helsinki, 1974)

Tignonville, Guillaume de, see Mubashshir ibn Fatik

Tilley, Arthur, "Greek Studies in England in the Early Sixteenth Century, *EHR* 53 (1938), pp. 221–239, 438–456

Tixier, Jean (i.e., Joannes Ravisius Textor), *Officina* (Paris, 1520) BL (repr. Basle, 1552) HD

Tomeo, Niccolò Leonico, *Dialogi* (Venice, 1525) BN

Townshend, Aurelian, *Poems and masques*, ed. Cedric C. Brown (Reading, 1983) *(Tempe restor'd, 1631, pp. 93–108)*

Trapp, Joseph B., "An English Late Medieval Cleric and Italian Thought" in *Medieval English Religious and Ethical Literature* (Cambridge, 1986) pp. 233–250 (Festschrift G. H. Russell); repr. in Trapp's *Essays on the Renaissance and the Classical Tradition* (London, 1990)

Traversari, Ambrogio, *Latinae epistolae*, ed. Laurenzio Mehus (Florence, 1759) 2 vols. (repr. Bologna, 1968)

Traversari, Ambrogio, see also Pseudo–Dionysius

Trinkaus, Charles, *The Poet as Philosopher* (New Haven, 1979) (on Petraca)

Tripp, Henry, see Gerardus

Tung, Mason, "From Impresa to Emblem", *Emblematica* 3 (1988), pp. 79–100

Turberville, George, *Poems*, ed. John E. Hankins (Yale univ. diss., 1929)

Turler, Jerome, *De peregrinatione*, (1574), transl. anon. as *The Traveiler* (London, 1575) STC 24336

Turler, Jerome, *De peregrinatione*, 1575 ed. repr. D. E. Baughan (Gainesville, 1951)

Turnèbe, Adrien, *Opera* (Paris, 1552) 3 vols. (Commentary on *Phaedo* is in vol. 3, pp. 49–53

Twyne, Thomas, see Llwyd

Tyard, Pontus de, *Oeuvres poétiques complètes*, ed. John C. Lapp (Paris, 1966)

Tyard, Pontus de, *Les Erreurs amoureuses*, ed. John McClelland (Geneva, 1967)

Tyard, Pontus de, see also Leo Hebreus

Udall, Nicholas, see Erasmus *Apophthegmata*

Ullman, Berthold L., *The Humanism of Coluccio Salutati* (Padua, 1963)

Ullman, Berthold L., "Manuscripts of Duke Humphrey of Gloucester", *EHR* 52 (1937) pp. 670–672, repr. in his *Studies*, pp. 345–356

Ullman, Berthold L., *Studies in the Italian Renaissance* (Rome, 1973, 2nd ed.)

Valerius Maximus, *Factorum et dictorum*, ed. Karl Kempf (Stuttgart, 1966) (Teubner)

Van der Haeghen, Ferdinand, *Bibliotheca Erasmiana Repertorium* (Nieuwkoop, 1972)

Vansteenberghe, Edmond, *Nicholas de Cues* (Paris, 1920; repr. Frankfort, 1963)

Vatican Library, *Codices Vaticani Latini* (Vatican, 1902–)

Vaughan, William, *The Golden Grove* (London, 1600) STC 24610

Velcurio, Joannes, *Commentariorum libri iii in universam Aristotelis physicen* (London, 1588) STC 24632

Vergil, Polydore, *De rerum inventoribus* (1557), transl. (part) Thomas Langley (London, 1546) STC 24654, repr. William A. Hammon (New York, 1868)

Vermigli, Pietro, (Peter Martyr), *Life, Early Letters, and Eucharistic Writings*, ed. J. C. McLelland and G. E. Duffield (Appleford, 1989)

Vermigli, Pietro, *Commentary on Judges* (Zurich, 1565, 2nd ed.) HD

Vermigli, Pietro, *Loci communes*, ed. R. Massoni (London, 1576) STC 24667 (repr. London, 1583) STC 24668

Vermigli, Pietro, *Loci communes*, transl. and enlarged by Anthonie Marten (London, 1583) STC 24669

Verro, Sebastiano, *Physicorum libri X* (London, 1581) STC 24688

Vickers, K. H., *Humphrey, Duke of Gloucester* (London, 1907)

Victoria History of...Hertfordshire, ed. William Page (Westminster, 1903–1914) 4 vols. (repr. Folkestone, 1971)

Victorinus, Marius, *Explanationes in Ciceronis rhetoricam*, ed. Karl Halm in *Rhetores latini minores* (Leipzig, 1863) pp. 152–304

Vincent of Beauvais, *Speculum naturale* (Venice, 1494) BL

Vincent of Beauvais, *Speculum doctrinale* (Cologne, 1494) BL

Vincent of Beauvais, *Speculum historiale* (Venice, 1494) BL

Vittorini, Demenico, "Salutati's Letters to the Archbishop of Canterbury", *MLJ* 36 (1952), pp. 373–377

Vives, Juan Luis, *Opera*, ed. Gregoria Majansio (Valencia, 1782–1790) 8 vols. (repr. London, 1964)

Vives, Juan Luis, *Introductio ad sapientiam*, transl. Richard Morison (London, 1539) STC 24846.5 repr. of 1540 ed., Marian L. Tobriner (New York, 1968)

Waddington, Raymond B., *The Mind's Empire* (Baltimore, 1974)

Wales, National Library of, *Handlist of Manuscripts* (Aberystwyth, 1940–)

Walser, Ernst, *Poggius Florentinus* (Leipzig, 1914)

Ward, G. R. M., see Fox

Ward, Seth, *Vindiciae academiarum* (Oxford, 1654) Wing W832, facs. repr. in Allen G. Debus, *Science and Education in the Seventeenth Century* (London, 1970) pp. 193–259

Waring, Robert, *Amoris effigies* (London, 1657) Wing W860

Warner, George F. and Julian P. Gilson, eds. *Catalogue of Manuscripts in the Old Royal and King's Collections* (in the British Library_ (London, 1921) 4 vols.

Warren Frederick E., ed., *The Leofric Missal* (Oxford, 1883)

Wars of Alexander, (c. 1450), ed. Walter Skeat (London, 1886) (EETS: es 47)

Waswo, Richard A., *The Fatal Mirror* (Charlottesville, 1977) (on Greville)

Watson, Thomas, *Poems*, ed. Edward Arber (London, 1870)

Webbe, William, *A Discourse of English Poetrie* (London, 1586) STC 25172, ed. Edward Arber (London, 1871; repr. New York, 1966)

Webster, John, Chaplain, *Academiarum examen* (London, 1564) BL, repr. in Allen G. Debus, *Science and Education in the Seventeenth Century* (London, 1970) pp. 67–192

Weever, John, *Epigrammes* (1599) ed. R. B. McKerrow (London, 1911)

Weever, John, *Poems*, ed. Arnold Davenport (Liverpool, 1948)

Weiss, Roberto, "Cornelio Vitelli in France and England", *JWCI* 2 (1939), pp. 219–226

Weiss, Roberto, "England and the Decree of the Council of Vienne...", *BHR* 14 (1952), pp. 1–21, repr. in his *Medieval and Humanist Greek* , pp. 68–79

Weiss, Roberto, "Gli inizi dello studio del greco a Firenze", in *Medieval and Humanist Greek* (Padua, 1977) pp. 227–254

Weiss, Roberto, "Gli studi greci di Coluccio Salutati" in *Miscellanea...Roberto Cessi* (Rome, 1958) vol. 1, pp. 349–356

Weiss, Roberto, *Humanism in England during the Fifteenth Century* (Oxford, 1967)

Weiss, Roberto, "Il debito degli umanistici inglesi verso l'Italia", *Lettere italiane* 7 (1958), pp. 298–313

Weiss, Roberto, "Jacopo Angeli da Scarperia" in *Medioevo e Rinascimento* (Florence, 1955) vol. 2, pp. 801–827 (Festschrift Bruno Nardi)

Weiss, Roberto, "John Tiptoft, Earl of Worcester and Ludovico Carbone", *Rinascimento* 8 (1957), pp. 209–212

Weiss, Roberto, "Leonardo Bruni Aretino and Early English Humanism", *MLR* 36 (1941), pp. 443–448

Weiss, Roberto, "The Library of John Tiptoft, Earl of Worcester", *BQR* 8 (1936), pp.157–164

Weiss, Roberto, "Piero del Monte, John Wethamstede, and the library of St. Albans Abbey", *EHR* 60 (1945), pp. 399–406

West, Richard, *The Court of Conscience* (London, 1607) STC 25263

Whethamstede, John, *De historiis historigraphicis* (London) BL MS Cotton Nero C VI (includes *Granarium*)

Whethamstede, John, *Registra...monasterii S. Albani*, ed. Henry T. Riley (London, 1872–1873) 2 vols.

(Rolls)

Whetstone, George, *An heptameron of civill discourses* (London, 1582) STC 25337, ed. Diana Shklanka (New York, 1977)

Whetstone, George, *The...historye of Promos and Cassandra* (London, 1578) STC 25347, facs. ed. anon. (London, 1910)

Whichcote, Benjamin, *Theophoroumena dogmata* (London, 1685) Wing W1643

Willett, Andrew, *De animae natura* (Cambridge, 1585) STC 25674

Williams, Franklin B., *Index of Dedications and Commendatory Verses in English books before 1641* (London, 1962)

Willoby, Henry, *Willobie his Auisa* (London, 1594) STC 25755 ed. G. B. Harrison (London, 1926)

Wills, Richard, *Oratio de poetica*, ed. as *De re poetica* by A. D. S. Fowler (Oxford, 1958)

Wills, Richard, *Poematum liber* (London, 1573) STC 25671

Wilson, Frank P. *The Plague in Shakespere's London* (Oxford, 1927; repr. London, 1963)

Wilson, Jean, ed., *Entertainments for Elizabeth I* (Woodbridge, 1980)

Wilson, Thomas, *The Arte of rhetorique* (London, 1553) STC 25799 ed. Thomas J. Derrick (New York, 1982)

Wilson, Thomas, *De vita et obitu fratrum Suffolciensum* (London, 1551) STC 25817

Witt, Ronald G., *Hercules at the Crossroads* (Durham, 1983)

Woolton, John, *The castell of Christians* (London, 1577) STC 25977

Woolton, John, *A new anatomie of the whole man* (London, 1576) STC 25977

Woolton, John, *A treatise of the immortalitie of the soule* (London, 1576) STC 25979

Wright, Thomas, *The passions of the minde* (London, 1601) STC 26039

Wright, Thomas, *The passions of the minde*, repr. of 1604 ed. Thomas D. Sloan (Urbana, 1971)

Wrigley, E. A., *An Introduction to English Historical Demography* (New York, 1966)

Xenocrates, *Axiochus*, (sometimes called *Socrates de contempnenda morte*), ed. and transl. E. H. Blakeney (London, 1937)

Xenocrates, *Axiochus*, transl. George Burges in Plato, *Works* (London, 1854) vol. 6, pp. 241–314 (Bohn)

Xenocrates, *Axiochus*, transl. (Lat.) Rudolph Agricola (Daventry, C. 1477) BL

Xenocrates, *Axiochus*, ed. and transl. Herman Rayan (Wesdalius) (Cologne, 1568, repr. by F. M. Padelford with Spenser's English transl.)

Xenocrates, *Axiochus*, transl. Edmund Spenser (London, 1592) STC 19974.6, ed. Frederick M. Padelford in Variorum ed. Spenser, *Works* (Baltimore, 1934) vol. 9, pp. 19–38, 269–277, 487–496

Xenocrates, *Axiochus*, transl. Mary Sidney, Countess of Pembroke in *Six excellent treatises...* (London, 1607) STC 18155

Young, John *et al.* eds., *A Catalogue of the Manuscripts in the Library of the Hunterian Museum* (Glasgow, 1908)

Zaccaria, Vittorio, "L'epistolario di P. C. Decembrio" *Rinascimento* 3 (1952)

Zaccaria, Vittorio, "Pier Candido Decembrio e Leonardo Bruni", *Studi medievali* 8 (1967), pp. 504–527

Zaccaria, Vittorio, "Pier Candido Decembrio traduttore della *Reppublica* di Platone", *IMU* 2 (1959), pp. 179–206

Zaccaria, Vittorio, "Sulle opere di Pier Candido Decembrio", *Rinascimento* 7 (1956), pp. 14–74

Zambelli, Paolo, "Il problema della magia naturale nel rinascimento", *Rivista critica di storia della filosofia* 28 (1973), pp. 271–296

Zambelli, Paolo, "Platone, Ficino e la magia" in K. Eisenbichler *et al.* eds., *Ficino and Renaissance Neoplatonism* (Toronto, 1986) pp. 121–142

Zetzner, Lazarus, *Theatrum chemicum* (Strasbourg, 1613–1661) 6 vols.

INDEX

ARCHIVES INTERNATIONALES D'HISTOIRE DES IDÉES

*

INTERNATIONAL ARCHIVES OF THE HISTORY OF IDEAS

ARCHIVES INTERNATIONALES D'HISTOIRE DES IDÉES

*

INTERNATIONAL ARCHIVES OF THE HISTORY OF IDEAS

43. P. Dibon: *Inventaire de la correspondance (1595-1650) d'André Rivet (1572-1651).* 1971   ISBN 90-247-5112-8

44. K.A. Kottman: *Law and Apocalypse.* The Moral Thought of Luis de Leon (1527?- 1591). 1972   ISBN 90-247-1183-5

45. F.G. Nauen: *Revolution, Idealism and Human Freedom.* Schelling, Hölderlin and Hegel, and the Crisis of Early German Idealism. 1971   ISBN 90-247-5117-9

46. H. Jensen: *Motivation and the Moral Sense in Francis Hutcheson's* [1694-1746] *Ethical Theory.* 1971   ISBN 90-247-1187-8

47. A. Rosenberg: *[Simon] Tyssot de Patot and His Work (1655–1738).* 1972   ISBN 90-247-1199-1

48. C. Walton: *De la recherche du bien.* A study of [Nicolas de] Malebranche's [1638- 1715] Science of Ethics. 1972   ISBN 90-247-1205-X

49. P.J.S. Whitmore (ed.): *A 17th-Century Exposure of Superstition.* Select Text of Claude Pithoys (1587-1676). 1972   ISBN 90-247-1298-X

50. A. Sauvy: *Livres saisis à Paris entre 1678 et 1701.* D'après une étude préliminaire de Motoko Ninomiya. 1972   ISBN 90-247-1347-1

51. W.R. Redmond: *Bibliography of the Philosophy in the Iberian Colonies of America.* 1972   ISBN 90-247-1190-8

52. C.B. Schmitt: *Cicero Scepticus.* A Study of the Influence of the *Academica* in the Renaissance. 1972   ISBN 90-247-1299-8

53. J. Hoyles: *The Edges of Augustanism.* The Aesthetics of Spirituality in Thomas Ken, John Byrom and William Law. 1972   ISBN 90-247-1317-X

54. J. Bruggeman and A.J. van de Ven (éds.): *Inventaire* des pièces d'Archives françaises se rapportant à l'Abbaye de Port-Royal des Champs et son cercle et à la Résistance contre la Bulle *Unigenitus* et à l'Appel. 1972   ISBN 90-247-5122-5

55. J.W. Montgomery: *Cross and Crucible.* Johann Valentin Andreae (1586–1654), Phoenix of the Theologians. Volume I: Andreae's Life, World-View, and Relations with Rosicrucianism and Alchemy; Volume II: The *Chymische Hochzeit* with Notes and Commentary. 1973   Set ISBN 90-247-5054-7

56. O. Lutaud: *Des révolutions d'Angleterre à la Révolution française.* Le tyrannicide & *Killing No Murder* (Cromwell, *Athalie*, Bonaparte). 1973   ISBN 90-247-1509-1

57. F. Duchesneau: *L'Empirisme de Locke.* 1973   ISBN 90-247-1349-8

58. R. Simon (éd.): *Henry de Boulainviller - Œuvres Philosophiques, Tome I.* 1973   ISBN 90-247-1332-3

For Œvres Philosophiques, Tome II *see below under Volume 70.*

59. E.E. Harris: *Salvation from Despair.* A Reappraisal of Spinoza's Philosophy. 1973   ISBN 90-247-5158-6

60. J.-F. Battail: *L'Avocat philosophe Géraud de Cordemoy (1626-1684).* 1973   ISBN 90-247-1542-3

61. T. Liu: *Discord in Zion.* The Puritan Divines and the Puritan Revolution (1640-1660). 1973   ISBN 90-247-5156-X

62. A. Strugnell: *Diderot's Politics.* A Study of the Evolution of Diderot's Political Thought after the *Encyclopédie.* 1973   ISBN 90-247-1540-7

ARCHIVES INTERNATIONALES D'HISTOIRE DES IDÉES
*
INTERNATIONAL ARCHIVES OF THE HISTORY OF IDEAS

63. G. Defaux: *Pantagruel et les Sophistes*. Contribution à l'histoire de l'humanisme chrétien au 16ᵉ siècle. 1973   ISBN 90-247-1566-0
64. G. Planty-Bonjour: *Hegel et la pensée philosophique en Russie (1830-1917)*. 1974
                                                                    ISBN 90-247-1576-8
65. R.J. Brook: *[George] Berkeley's Philosophy of Science*. 1973   ISBN 90-247-1555-5
66. T.E. Jessop: *A Bibliography of George Berkeley*. With: *Inventory of Berkeley's Manuscript Remains* by A.A. Luce. 2nd revised and enlarged ed. 1973
                                                                    ISBN 90-247-1577-6
67. E.I. Perry: *From Theology to History*. French Religious Controversy and the Revocation of the Edict of Nantes. 1973   ISBN 90-247-1578-4
68. P. Dibbon, H. Bots et E. Bots-Estourgie: *Inventaire de la correspondance (1631–1671) de Johannes Fredericus Gronovius* [1611–1671]. 1974
                                                                    ISBN 90-247-1600-4
69. A.B. Collins: *The Secular is Sacred*. Platonism and Thomism in Marsilio Ficino's *Platonic Theology*. 1974   ISBN 90-247-1588-1
70. R. Simon (éd.): *Henry de Boulainviller*. Œuvres Philosophiques, Tome II. 1975
                                                                    ISBN 90-247-1633-0
    For Œvres Philosophiques, Tome I *see under Volume 58.*
71. J.A.G. Tans et H. Schmitz du Moulin: *Pasquier Quesnel devant la Congrégation de l'Index*. Correspondance avec Francesco Barberini et mémoires sur la mise à l'Index de son édition des Œuvres de Saint Léon, publiés avec introduction et annotations. 1974   ISBN 90-247-1661-6
72. J.W. Carven: *Napoleon and the Lazarists (1804–1809)*. 1974   ISBN 90-247-1667-5
73. G. Symcox: *The Crisis of French Sea Power (1688–1697)*. From the *Guerre d'Escadre* to the *Guerre de Course*. 1974   ISBN 90-247-1645-4
74. R. MacGillivray: *Restoration Historians and the English Civil War*. 1974
                                                                    ISBN 90-247-1678-0
75. A. Soman (ed.): *The Massacre of St. Bartholomew*. Reappraisals and Documents. 1974   ISBN 90-247-1652-7
76. R.E. Wanner: *Claude Fleury (1640-1723) as an Educational Historiographer and Thinker*. With an Introduction by W.W. Brickman. 1975   ISBN 90-247-1684-5
77. R.T. Carroll: *The Common-Sense Philosophy of Religion of Bishop Edward Stillingfleet (1635-1699)*. 1975   ISBN 90-247-1647-0
78. J. Macary: *Masque et lumières au 18ᵉ [siècle]*. André-François Deslandes, Citoyen et philosophe (1689-1757). 1975   ISBN 90-247-1698-5
79. S.M. Mason: *Montesquieu's Idea of Justice*. 1975   ISBN 90-247-1670-5
80. D.J.H. van Elden: *Esprits fins et esprits géométriques dans les portraits de Saint-Simon*. Contributions à l'étude du vocabulaire et du style. 1975   ISBN 90-247-1726-4
81. I. Primer (ed.): *Mandeville Studies*. New Explorations in the Art and Thought of Dr Bernard Mandeville (1670-1733). 1975   ISBN 90-247-1686-1
82. C.G. Noreña: *Studies in Spanish Renaissance Thought*. 1975   ISBN 90-247-1727-2
83. G. Wilson: *A Medievalist in the 18th Century*. Le Grand d'Aussy and the Fabliaux ou Contes. 1975   ISBN 90-247-1782-5
84. J.-R. Armogathe: *Theologia Cartesiana*. L'explication physique de l'Eucharistie chez Descartes et Dom Robert Desgabets. 1977   ISBN 90-247-1869-4

85. Bérault Stuart, Seigneur d'Aubigny: *Traité sur l'art de la guerre*. Introduction et édition par Élie de Comminges. 1976   ISBN 90-247-1871-6

86. S.L. Kaplan: *Bread, Politics and Political Economy in the Reign of Louis XV*. 2 vols., 1976   Set ISBN 90-247-1873-2

87. M. Lienhard (ed.): *The Origins and Characteristics of Anabaptism / Les débuts et les caractéristiques de l'Anabaptisme*. With an Extensive Bibliography / Avec une bibliographie détaillée. 1977   ISBN 90-247-1896-1

88. R. Descartes: *Règles utiles et claires pour la direction de l'esprit en la recherche de la vérité*. Traduction selon le lexique cartésien, et annotation conceptuelle par J.-L. Marion. Avec des notes mathématiques de P. Costabel. 1977   ISBN 90-247-1907-0

89. K. Hardesty: *The 'Supplément' to the 'Encyclopédie'*. [Diderot et d'Alembert]. 1977   ISBN 90-247-1965-8

90. H.B. White: *Antiquity Forgot*. Essays on Shakespeare, [Francis] Bacon, and Rembrandt. 1978   ISBN 90-247-1971-2

91. P.B.M. Blaas: *Continuity and Anachronism*. Parliamentary and Constitutional Development in Whig Historiography and in the Anti-Whig Reaction between 1890 and 1930. 1978   ISBN 90-247-2063-X

92. S.L. Kaplan (ed.): *La Bagarre*. Ferdinando Galiani's (1728-1787) 'Lost' Parody. With an Introduction by the Editor. 1979   ISBN 90-247-2125-3

93. E. McNiven Hine: *A Critical Study of [Étienne Bonnot de] Condillac's* [1714-1780] *'Traité des Systèmes'*. 1979   ISBN 90-247-2120-2

94. M.R.G. Spiller: *Concerning Natural Experimental Philosphy*. Meric Casaubon [1599-1671] and the Royal Society. 1980   ISBN 90-247-2414-7

95. F. Duchesneau: *La physiologie des Lumières*. Empirisme, modèles et théories. 1982   ISBN 90-247-2500-3

96. M. Heyd: *Between Orthodoxy and the Enlightenment*. Jean-Robert Chouet [1642-1731] and the Introduction of Cartesian Science in the Academy of Geneva. 1982   ISBN 90-247-2508-9

97. James O'Higgins: *Yves de Vallone* [1666/7-1705]: *The Making of an Esprit Fort*. 1982   ISBN 90-247-2520-8

98. M.L. Kuntz: *Guillaume Postel* [1510-1581]. Prophet of the Restitution of All Things. His Life and Thought. 1981   ISBN 90-247-2523-2

99. A. Rosenberg: *Nicolas Gueudeville and His Work (1652-172?)*. 1982   ISBN 90-247-2533-X

100. S.L. Jaki: *Uneasy Genius: The Life and Work of Pierre Duhem* [1861-1916]. 1984   ISBN 90-247-2897-5; Pb (1987) 90-247-3532-7

101. Anne Conway [1631-1679]: *The Principles of the Most Ancient Modern Philosophy*. Edited and with an Introduction by P. Loptson. 1982   ISBN 90-247-2671-9

102. E.C. Patterson: *[Mrs.] Mary [Fairfax Greig] Sommerville* [1780-1872] *and the Cultivation of Science (1815-1840)*. 1983   ISBN 90-247-2823-1

103. C.J. Berry: *Hume, Hegel and Human Nature*. 1982   ISBN 90-247-2682-4

104. C.J. Betts: *Early Deism in France*. From the so-called 'déistes' of Lyon (1564) to Voltaire's 'Lettres philosophiques' (1734). 1984   ISBN 90-247-2923-8

ARCHIVES INTERNATIONALES D'HISTOIRE DES IDÉES

*

INTERNATIONAL ARCHIVES OF THE HISTORY OF IDEAS

105. R. Gascoigne: *Religion, Rationality and Community.* Sacred and Secular in the Thought of Hegel and His Critics. 1985   ISBN 90-247-2992-0

106. S. Tweyman: *Scepticism and Belief in Hume's 'Dialogues Concerning Natural Religion'.* 1986   ISBN 90-247-3090-2

107. G. Cerny: *Theology, Politics and Letters at the Crossroads of European Civilization.* Jacques Basnage [1653-1723] and the Baylean Huguenot Refugees in the Dutch Republic. 1987   ISBN 90-247-3150-X

108. Spinoza's *Algebraic Calculation of the Rainbow & Calculation of Changes.* Edited and Translated from Dutch, with an Introduction, Explanatory Notes and an Appendix by M.J. Petry. 1985   ISBN 90-247-3149-6

109. R.G. McRae: *Philosophy and the Absolute.* The Modes of Hegel's Speculation. 1985
          ISBN 90-247-3151-8

110. J.D. North and J.J. Roche (eds.): *The Light of Nature.* Essays in the History and Philosophy of Science presented to A.C. Crombie. 1985   ISBN 90-247-3165-8

111. C. Walton and P.J. Johnson (eds.): *[Thomas] Hobbes's 'Science of Natural Justice'.* 1987   ISBN 90-247-3226-3

112. B.W. Head: *Ideology and Social Science.* Destutt de Tracy and French Liberalism. 1985   ISBN 90-247-3228-X

113. A.Th. Peperzak: *Philosophy and Politics.* A Commentary on the Preface to Hegel's *Philosophy of Right.* 1987   ISBN Hb 90-247-3337-5; Pb ISBN 90-247-3338-3

114. S. Pines and Y. Yovel (eds.): *Maimonides* [1135-1204] *and Philosophy.* Papers Presented at the 6th Jerusalem Philosophical Encounter (May 1985). 1986
          ISBN 90-247-3439-8

115. T.J. Saxby: *The Quest for the New Jerusalem, Jean de Labadie* [1610-1674] *and the Labadists (1610-1744).* 1987   ISBN 90-247-3485-1

116. C.E. Harline: *Pamphlets, Printing, and Political Culture in the Early Dutch Republic.* 1987   ISBN 90-247-3511-4

117. R.A. Watson and J.E. Force (eds.): *The Sceptical Mode in Modern Philosophy.* Essays in Honor of Richard H. Popkin. 1988   ISBN 90-247-3584-X

118. R.T. Bienvenu and M. Feingold (eds.): *In the Presence of the Past.* Essays in Honor of Frank Manuel. 1991   ISBN 0-7923-1008-X

119. J. van den Berg and E.G.E. van der Wall (eds.): *Jewish-Christian Relations in the 17th Century.* Studies and Documents. 1988   ISBN 90-247-3617-X

120. N. Waszek: *The Scottish Enlightenment and Hegel's Account of 'Civil Society'.* 1988
          ISBN 90-247-3596-3

121. J. Walker (ed.): *Thought and Faith in the Philosophy of Hegel.* 1991
          ISBN 0-7923-1234-1

122. Henry More [1614-1687]: *The Immortality of the Soul.* Edited with Introduction and Notes by A. Jacob. 1987   ISBN 90-247-3512-2

123. P.B. Scheurer and G. Debrock (eds.): *Newton's Scientific and Philosophical Legacy.* 1988   ISBN 90-247-3723-0

124. D.R. Kelley and R.H. Popkin (eds.): *The Shapes of Knowledge from the Renaissance to the Enlightenment.* 1991   ISBN 0-7923-1259-7

ARCHIVES INTERNATIONALES D'HISTOIRE DES IDÉES

*

INTERNATIONAL ARCHIVES OF THE HISTORY OF IDEAS

KLUWER ACADEMIC PUBLISHERS – DORDRECHT / BOSTON / LONDON